Problems from Philosophy

Problems from Philosophy

SECOND EDITION

JAMES RACHELS

Second Edition by

STUART RACHELS

McGraw-Hill
Higher Education

Boston   Burr Ridge, IL   Dubuque, IA   New York
San Francisco   St. Louis   Bangkok   Bogotá   Caracas   Kuala Lumpur
Lisbon   London   Madrid   Mexico City   Milan   Montreal   New Delhi
Santiago   Seoul   Singapore   Sydney   Taipei   Toronto

The **McGraw-Hill** Companies

Mc Graw Hill McGraw-Hill Higher Education

PROBLEMS FROM PHILOSOPHY

Published by McGraw-Hill, an imprint of The McGraw-Hill Companies, Inc., 1221 Avenue of the Americas, New York, NY 10020. Copyright © 2009, 2005. All rights reserved. No part of this publication may be reproduced or distributed in any form or by any means, or stored in a database or retrieval system, without the prior written consent of The McGraw-Hill Companies, Inc., including, but not limited to, in any network or other electronic storage or transmission, or broadcast for distance learning.

This book is printed on acid-free paper.

1 2 3 4 5 6 7 8 9 0 DOC/DOC 0 9 8

ISBN: 978-0-07-338660-7
MHID: 0-07-338660-X

Editor in Chief: *Mike Ryan*
Editorial Director: *Beth Mejia*
Sponsoring Editor: *Mark Georgiev*
Marketing Manager: *Pamela Cooper*
Manuscript Editor: *Thomas L. Briggs*
Production Editor: *David Blatty*
Design Manager: *Allister Fein*
Production Supervisor: *Tandra Jorgensen*
Composition: *11/12 Baskerville by Macmillan Publishing Solutions*
Printing: *45# New Era Matte, R. R. Donnelley*

Cover art: Rodchenko, Alexander, "Abstract Composition," 1920. Oil on canvas. Rodchenko Archive, Moscow, Russia. Art © Estate of Alexander Rodchenko/RAO, Moscow/VAGA, New York. Photo: © Scala/Art Resource, NY.

Library of Congress Cataloging-in-Publication Data

Rachels, James, 1941–2003.
  Problems from philosophy.—2nd ed. / James Rachels, Stuart Rachels.
    p. cm.
  Includes bibliographical references and index.
  ISBN-13: 978-0-07-338660-7 (alk. paper)
  ISBN-10: 0-07-338660-X (alk. paper)
  1. Philosophy. I. Rachels, Stuart, 1969- II. Title.
B72.R26 2009
100—dc22   2008002252

The Internet addresses listed in the text were accurate at the time of publication. The inclusion of a Web site does not indicate an endorsement by the authors or McGraw-Hill, and McGraw-Hill does not guarantee the accuracy of the information presented at these sites.

www.mhhe.com

About the Authors

JAMES RACHELS (1941–2003) wrote *The End of Life: Euthanasia and Morality* (1986), *Created from Animals: The Moral Implications of Darwinism* (1990), *Can Ethics Provide Answers? And Other Essays in Moral Philosophy* (1997), *The Elements of Moral Philosophy* (editions 1–4), and *The Legacy of Socrates: Essays in Moral Philosophy* (2007). James Rachels' official website is www.JamesRachels.org.

STUART RACHELS is Associate Professor of Philosophy at the University of Alabama. A former United States Chess Champion and a Life Master at bridge, he wrote the fifth edition of *The Elements of Moral Philosophy* (2007). Also, he edited the fourth edition of *The Right Thing to Do* (2007) and the second edition of *The Truth about the World* (2008), which is the companion anthology to this book.

Contents

Preface

This book is an introduction to some of the main problems of philosophy—the existence of God, the nature of the mind, human freedom, the limits of knowledge, and the truth about ethics. The chapters may be read independently of one another, but when read in order, they tell a more or less continuous story. We begin with some reflections on the life of Socrates and then go on to the existence of God, which is the most basic philosophical question, because our answer to it affects everything else. This leads naturally to a discussion of death and the soul, and then to more modern ideas about the nature of persons. The later chapters are about whether we can have objective knowledge in either science or ethics.

It is a weakness of contemporary culture that such issues are often taken to be mere matters of opinion. After all, it is said, no one can prove whether God exists or whether life has a meaning. But these are topics for rational investigation. Even if the questions are so complex that we cannot expect agreement, we should ask what is most reasonable to believe, rather than grab at whatever ideas seem attractive. Like every responsible human inquiry, philosophy is first and last an exercise in reason. We should embrace the ideas that are supported by the best arguments.

Some philosophers believe that philosophy is a "pure" subject that can be pursued in isolation from the sciences. I do not share that belief. Problems from philosophy are best approached by using every available resource. W. V. Quine once remarked that "The universe is not the university." The division of human inquiry into discrete disciplines may be useful in organizing academic departments, but it is of little interest when trying to figure out what the world is like. In this book you will find references to biology, psychology, history, and even the discoveries of the Amazing Randi. They are all part of a single project—the human attempt to understand the world and our place in it.

About the Second Edition

Instructors who taught the first edition of this book need not reread whole chapters, except for chapter 5, "The Problem of Personal Identity," and chapter 10, "Our Knowledge of the World around Us." Those chapters have been reorganized and reworked.

Otherwise, the book has been revised only in small ways. Most of the changes are too trivial to mention, but a few things should be noted:

- In chapter 2, "God and the Origin of the Universe," the Not-by-Chance Argument has been reformulated and is now called the Best-Explanation Argument. Also, I have slightly reworded the Same-Evidence Argument.
- In chapter 3, "The Problem of Evil," I've added a third objection to the subsection "A Complete Account?" This objection asks why God doesn't intervene to prevent acts of extreme cruelty.
- In chapter 4, "Do We Survive Death?" I have revised the critique of Socrates' argument for the simplicity of the soul.
- In chapter 6, "Body and Mind," Descartes' Conceivability Argument for Dualism has been added to section 6.1, and a materialist response to it now appears at the end of the subsection on the Mind–Brain Identity Theory. Also, I have added a brief subsection on "Radical Emergence."
- In chapter 7, "Could a Machine Think?" I have added a subsection called "The Tipping Point Objection" in response to the Piecemeal-Replacement Argument. Also, the chapter's conclusion is now gone, its content merged with the chapter's final subsection.

- In chapter 9, "The Debate over Free Will," I've given another reason why the indeterminacy of quantum mechanics doesn't establish human freedom. Also, the discussion of "The Argument That We Cannot Predict Our Own Decisions" has been shortened, and "The Argument from Accountability" is no longer claimed to be transcendental. Most significantly, in section 9.4, "Ethics and Free Will," James Rachels claimed in the first edition that the failure of free will would not undermine our ordinary beliefs about human value and responsibility. With apologies, I now claim the opposite at the end of the chapter.
- In chapter 12, "Why Should We Be Moral?" I point out some complications for the idea that we should be moral in order to avoid hellfire.

Problems from Philosophy was James Rachels' last book. It seems fitting that a great philosopher would spend his final days trying to communicate the most basic things in his subject to the next generation. In revising this wonderful book, I received help from Torin Alter, David Chalmers, Janice Daurio, Kevin Dybvig, Heather Elliott, Mike Huemer, Carlo Maley, Justin McBrayer, Nathan Nobis, Carol Rachels, David Rachels, Kerry Ressler, Lynn Stephens, Barbara Stock, and Mark Walton. I thank them. I also thank James Rachels, not just for the obvious reasons, but because I made some revisions based on his personal notes.

Readers who would like to know more about James Rachels can visit www.JamesRachels.org.

—Stuart Rachels

Problems from Philosophy

CHAPTER 1

The Legacy of Socrates

But my dear Crito, why should we pay so much attention to what "most people" think?

—SOCRATES, IN PLATO'S *CRITO* (CA. 390 B.C.)

1.1. Why Was Socrates Condemned?

In the British Museum there is a statue of Socrates that could have been carved as early as 330 B.C., 69 years after his death. He is pictured as short and muscular, with a balding head, a beard, and a broad, flat nose—details consistent with what Plato tells us of his appearance. Socrates wrote nothing, and so we depend on Plato, his pupil, for almost everything we know about him. In Plato's dialogues we see Socrates in the public places of Athens, discussing the great questions of truth and justice with the city's young men. But we also see him being charged with corrupting those young men, and we watch as he is put on trial and sentenced to death. Why this happened is something of a mystery. The Athenians were democrats, proud of their intellectual accomplishments and freedoms. Why would they put a philosopher to death for his teachings?

According to Plato, Socrates was charged with "corrupting the youth" and "impiety toward the gods." The first charge is vague, and no details are given. Socrates does say that his young followers have annoyed their neighbors by demonstrating their ignorance through the Socratic method of question-and-answer. The second charge also seems trumped-up. Socrates was not antireligious, and at his trial he protested that he does believe in the supernatural. But apparently he did hold unorthodox views. Merely holding such views would not have gotten Socrates arrested, but "pushing them on the streets of

1

Athens," as one scholar put it, could easily have provoked the charges. Still, Plato's account leaves us wondering whether this is the whole story.

So why was Socrates condemned? It may help to remember that, although he has been revered by subsequent generations, Socrates was not a popular figure in his own time. He himself suggested that the charges were brought because people didn't like him. The Oracle at Delphi had said he was the wisest of men, and Socrates accepted the accolade, but with a peculiar qualification. He said he was wise because he realized how ignorant he was. This sounds agreeably modest. The problem was that Socrates took it as his "divine mission" to show others that they were also ignorant. A typical Socratic conversation would have him demonstrating to his listeners, to their evident annoyance, that their opinions were all wrong. No doubt people wanted to see him taken down a notch. Despite his gentle approach, Socrates must have been an irritating neighbor.

Politics may also have played a part. The Athenians were proud of their democratic institutions, but Socrates did not share their pride. He was, according to Plato, democracy's severest critic. He complained that democracy elevates men to positions of authority not as a result of their wisdom or their fitness to govern, but as a result of their ability to sway the masses with empty rhetoric. In a democracy, it is not truth that matters; it is public relations. There were already specialists in this endeavor in Athens. The most influential teachers of the day were the Sophists, who taught the art of persuasion and were openly skeptical about "truth." Had they lived 2400 years later, they would have been media consultants, radio personalities, and talk show hosts.

If the Athenian democracy had been secure, Socrates' hostility could have been taken in stride, much as Western democracies today tolerate criticism. But their democracy was not stable; it had suffered a series of traumatic disruptions. The latest had occurred only five years before Socrates' trial, when a group known as the Thirty Tyrants—led by Critias, a former pupil of Socrates—had staged a bloody coup. At his trial, which took place after the democracy was restored, Socrates pointedly denounced the Thirty Tyrants, calling them "wicked." Nevertheless, it is easy to imagine that the leaders of Athens might have breathed easier with Socrates gone.

Trying to figure out why something happened 2400 years ago is a frustrating business, made even harder because the people involved had different motives. Who knows why the 500-plus jurors voted as they did? Plato does not help; he gives us Socrates' speech, but not the accusers'. At any rate, Socrates was tried, convicted, and sentenced to death. The penalty seems excessive, but to some extent Socrates brought it on himself. After he had been found guilty, he was permitted under the rules of the court to propose his own punishment. Instead of suggesting something realistic, he proposed that he be given a lifetime pension for his services to the state—the "services" being the same activities of which he had just been convicted. Only as an afterthought did he offer to pay a small fine. Little wonder that the jurors accepted the alternative proposal of his accusers.

The sentence was not really all that harsh, however, because no one expected Socrates actually to die. Exile was an unofficial alternative. While he was awaiting execution, his friends planned for his escape. Several cities were willing to take him, and emissaries had come with money. Plato lets us understand that no one would have prevented Socrates from going. His enemies wanted him to leave, and his friends were ready to bid him goodbye.

But Socrates did not leave. Instead, he began to consider the reasons for and against escaping. He had always maintained that our conduct should be guided by reason: In any situation, he said, we ought to do what there are the best reasons for doing. Here, then, was the ultimate test of his commitment to that idea. While the chariot waited, he told Crito that if the best arguments were for going, he would go; but if the best arguments were for staying, he would stay. Then, after looking at the matter from all sides, Socrates concluded that he could not justify disobeying the court's order. So he stayed, drank the hemlock—the poison prescribed by the court—and died. Perhaps he had some inkling that this would secure his place in history. He warned the Athenians that it would be their reputation, not his, that would be tarnished by his death.

1.2. Why Did Socrates Believe He Had to Die?

Socrates was not "the first philosopher"—that title is traditionally reserved for Thales, who lived a century earlier. (Why Thales? Because Aristotle listed him first.) Nevertheless, historians customarily refer to Thales and the others who came before Socrates as "pre-Socratics," as though they inhabited some kind of philosophical prehistory and Socrates marked the real beginning.

It was not so much his doctrines as his method that set Socrates apart. He relied on argument, insisting that truth is discovered only through the use of reason. His legacy is, more than anything else, his unwavering conviction that even the most abstract questions are amenable to rational analysis. What is justice? Is the soul immortal? Can it ever be right to harm someone? Is it possible to know what is right and yet not do it? He believed that such questions are not merely matters of opinion. They have real answers that we can discover if we think hard enough. This was another thing that annoyed Socrates' accusers, who, in Plato's account, distrusted reason and preferred to rely on popular opinion, custom, and religious authority.

Socrates believed that there were arguments compelling him to remain in Athens and face death. Could this possibly be right? What arguments could be that powerful? The pivotal issue, he told Crito, was whether he was obliged to obey the laws of Athens. The laws had commanded him. Must he not obey? Their discussion was the first philosophical inquiry into the nature of legal obligation.

The Argument about Destroying the State. Socrates offered three arguments for why he should accept his fate. The first was that if he disobeyed the law, he would be destroying the state. He explains that the state cannot exist if people do not obey its laws:

> Suppose that while we were preparing to run away from here (or however one should describe it) the Laws and Constitution of Athens were to come and confront us and ask this question: "Now, Socrates, what are you proposing to do? Can you deny that by this act which you are contemplating you intend, so far as you have the power, to destroy, us, the Laws, and the whole state as well? Do you imagine that a city can continue to exist and not be turned upside down, if the legal judgements which are pronounced in it have no force but are nullified and destroyed by private persons?"

So, the argument says, in disobeying the law we destroy the state. Socrates adds that it would be especially ungrateful for someone who has benefited so much from "the Laws and Constitution" to offer injury in return.

It is startling that Socrates was willing to stake his life on such thoughts. Is this argument sound? One obvious problem is that Socrates' act of disobedience would not have had the harmful effects he describes. If he had gone into exile, Athens would not have been "turned upside down." Rather, the city would have gone on pretty much as before. Of course, chaos would ensue if people habitually disregarded the law. But if people disobey only once in a while, in extreme circumstances, the state will be unharmed.

Nonetheless, one might feel that the argument makes a legitimate point. The considerations adduced by Socrates do prove something, even if they do not prove as much as he thought. They show that we have an extensive, *but not unlimited,* obligation to obey the law. We might therefore recast the argument in this modified but more defensible form:

(1) If we do not in general obey the law (allowing only rare exceptions), the state cannot exist.

(2) It would be disastrous if the state did not exist, because we would all be much worse off without it.

(3) Therefore, we should in general obey the law (allowing only rare exceptions).

Although Socrates' original reasoning is weak, it suggests this modified argument that is much better. However, it does not follow from this argument that Socrates must stay and drink the hemlock. After all, this could be the "rare exception" that calls for disobedience.

The Analogy between the State and One's Parents. Socrates' second argument involves comparing our relation to the state with our relation to our parents. Our parents made our lives possible—they brought us into being, raised us, and educated us. We are therefore obligated to respect and obey them. The state also makes our lives possible, by providing a social environment that nurtures and sustains us. So we have a similar obligation to respect and obey the state. Again, Socrates imagines that "the Laws and Constitution of Athens" are speaking:

> "Then since you have been born and brought up and educated, can you deny, in the first place, that you were our child and servant, both you and your ancestors? . . . Are you so wise as to have forgotten that compared with your

mother and father and all the rest of your ancestors your country is something far more precious, more venerable, more sacred, and held in greater honour both among gods and among all reasonable men? Do you not realize that you are even more bound to respect and placate the anger of your country than your father's anger?"

And so Socrates concludes that he must abide by the court's verdict to drink the hemlock.

This is an example of argument by analogy. Such arguments are sometimes sound and sometimes not. Is this one sound? The problem is that our obligation to obey the law cannot be like our obligation to obey our parents because, as adults, we are *not* obligated to obey our parents. We must obey our parents when we are young because we lack judgment. As we mature, however, we learn to think for ourselves, and our relation to them changes. Although we may continue to owe our parents gratitude and respect, we no longer owe them obedience. An adult who still "obeys his parents" as if he were 12 years old is a sad case. So this argument is weak.

So far, then, we have found no good reason why Socrates had to drink the hemlock. Neither the Argument about Destroying the State nor the Analogy between the State and One's Parents compels that conclusion. There is, however, one other line of reasoning to consider.

The Argument from the Social Contract. Socrates' third argument is the most important. As he muses about the law, he brings up the idea of a social contract—an idea that would be developed by Thomas Hobbes (1588–1679) and Jean-Jacques Rousseau (1712–1778).

The key idea of the social contract is that society rests on an implicit bargain that we make with one another. Social living is a cooperative arrangement in which each of us gains enormous benefits, and in return we agree to support the institutions and practices that make those benefits possible.

What, exactly, are the benefits of social living? If we work together to maintain a stable social order, we can have industry, education, arts, business, agriculture, medicine, and much more. We can live in peace, have friends, and go to football games and concerts. The benefits are endless. But these good things cannot exist if people do not cooperate in upholding the system that produces them. Otherwise, everything will fall apart, and, as Hobbes put it, life will be "solitary, poor, nasty, brutish, and short."

In appealing to the social contract, Socrates again assumes the viewpoint of the laws:

> "[A]ny Athenian, on attaining to manhood and seeing for himself the political organization of the state and us its Laws, is permitted, if he is not satisfied with us, to take his property and go away wherever he likes. . . . On the other hand, if any one of you stands his ground when he can see how we administer justice and the rest of our public organization, we hold that by so doing he has in fact undertaken to do anything that we tell him. . . .
>
> "It is a fact, then," [the Laws and Constitution] would say, "that you are breaking covenants and undertakings made with us, although you made them under no compulsion or misunderstanding, and were not compelled to decide in a limited time; you had seventy years in which you could have left the country, if you were not satisfied with us or felt that the agreements were unfair. . . . And now, after all this, are you not going to stand by your agreement?"

So Socrates concludes that he must stand by his agreement, even if it means his own death.

Is this argument sound? The social contract is the most influential nonreligious account of legal obligation ever devised. Nonetheless, critics have lodged a number of complaints against it. The principal charge is that the "contract" is fictitious. Few of us enter into the social arrangement by means of an agreement. Immigrants, who pledge to uphold the law when they are granted citizenship, are the exception. The rest of us are simply born into the system. Since we never asked to be part of it, we might wonder about the nature of the "agreement" on which Socrates puts so much emphasis.

What can be said in reply? If the idea of a social contract is to be defended, we will need the idea of an *implicit* promise— a promise that is not uttered but is nevertheless implied in our conduct. Socrates' argument invokes this sort of implicit promise. We undertake the obligations of citizenship, he says, not by issuing a pledge, but by willingly accepting its benefits and otherwise making use of the social system for our own ends.

But there is another problem. We need to ask, as we did with the Argument about Destroying the State, just how extensive an obligation this argument supports. Does the appeal to a social contract support the conclusion that we must *always* obey the law, or only that we should in general obey it? It is pertinent to note that contracts are never 100 percent binding—there are always circumstances under which contractors would be released from their obligations. For example, if you and I have an agreement, and you do not keep your part of the bargain, I am released from the obligation to keep mine. No sensible person believes that the duty to fulfill one's contracts holds in every circumstance.

But once this is conceded, the question of Socrates' fate is reopened. We may grant that we have a general obligation to obey the social rules based on our mutual agreement to establish the rules and abide by them. But suppose that an innocent person has been condemned to death, and while awaiting execution, he has a chance to escape. If he takes the opportunity, has he acted wrongly? Did Dr. Richard Kimble act wrongly in *The Fugitive,* when he fled after the train crash? If Socrates had fled, would he have been making the same mistake? It is hard to see how escaping could be condemned on contractual grounds. If the state's effort to kill you does not release you from your agreement, what does? After all, the state is supposed to *protect* you from unjust threats.

So none of these arguments proves that Socrates had to drink the hemlock. But this leaves us with an awkward question: How could he have made such a disastrous mistake? How could he have failed to see that these were inconclusive arguments? Part of the answer may be that these issues were new and unfamiliar when Socrates discussed them. The nature of legal obligation may be an old topic for us, but 2400 years ago Socrates was feeling his way through it for the first time. Another part of the answer may be that Socrates' arguments—especially his first and third arguments—are not really so bad. They reveal a lot about why we should obey the law. Socrates' mistake was failing to distinguish (a) the idea that we should normally obey the law from (b) the idea that we must always obey the law. His arguments support the former, but he mistakenly thought they supported the latter.

There is a reason why he failed to make this distinction, or at least why he did not take it seriously. Socrates' conception of his relation to Athens and its laws was profoundly different from how most of us feel about "the government." Like other Greeks, he felt powerfully bound to his city; he could not imagine himself apart from it. The idea of violating his relationship to Athens must have been unthinkable to him. In the *Crito* we are told that in all his 70 years, Socrates never stepped outside the city, except for some military campaigns. He was an Athenian in the profound way that St. Paul was a Christian.

And as for death, Socrates had no fear of it. He believed that after the death of his body, his soul would go to another world, where his questions would at last be answered. Many people say they believe in paradise but are reluctant to go there. Socrates was not one of them. As Alcibiades said in the *Symposium:* "He is absolutely unique; there is no one like him, and I don't believe there ever was."

CHAPTER 2

*G*od and the Origin of the Universe

If God ceased from his co-operation, everything that he has created would at once vanish into nothing; for before things were created, before God provided his co-operation, they were nothing.
—RENÉ DESCARTES, *LETTER* (1641)

2.1. Is It Reasonable to Believe in God?

Most Americans believe in God. In fact, according to a recent Gallup Poll, 56 percent of Americans say that religion plays a "very important" part in their lives. In 2005 the Pew Research Center conducted a poll in 17 countries and found the United States to be much more religious than other Western, developed nations. In Great Britain only 18 percent say that religion is very important to them. In France the figure is 14 percent; in Spain, 21 percent; and in Canada and Germany, 27 percent. However, people in India, Pakistan, and Indonesia are even more religious than people in the United States. After a similar study in 2002, analysts concluded that American attitudes "are closer to people in developing nations than to the publics of developed nations."

Meanwhile, the Gallup International Millennium Survey asked people in 60 countries whether they believed in God at all. Only 45 percent said they believed in a "personal" God, while another 30 percent said they believed in "some sort of spirit or life force." The Gallup Poll found that religious belief is strongest in the elderly and the uneducated and that the rate of belief is highest in West Africa, where Islam dominates. There, 99 percent believe in a personal God. In the United States,

10

the figure is 86 percent, while Europeans, the survey concludes, "are the most agnostic."

Religion used to play a more important part in people's lives. What accounts for the decline? No doubt the explanation is complicated, and no one knows the whole story. One factor, at least in the "developed countries," may be the prestige of science and the increasing prevalence of the scientific worldview. Another may be the diminished importance of family life and social traditions generally. But whatever the cause, it seems clear that even in the United States religious people and institutions are in a different position today than they were only a short time ago. They enjoy a strong social and political position, to be sure, but rather than defining the social outlook, religion is now one among many forces competing for attention. When political leaders invoke their religious beliefs to justify public policy, many people get nervous.

But we want to know more than what people believe—we want to know whether religious beliefs are *true*. What is the most reasonable way of understanding what the world is like? Is there any good reason to believe it was created by an all-powerful deity? Of course, such belief may be said to be a matter of faith, to which reason is irrelevant. The pronouncements of Scripture or the Church may be thought to have an authority that does not require confirmation by rational argument. It is tempting to let the matter rest there—some choose to believe, others do not, and that's all there is to it. But before reaching that conclusion, we should first ask what evidence is available. Can good reasons be given to support belief in God? We should not say that religious belief is "merely" a matter of faith until we are sure that rational arguments cannot be found.

2.2. The Argument from Design

The problem is that God cannot be detected by any ordinary means of investigation. He cannot be seen or heard or touched, and scientific instruments are useless. Some people say they can sense his presence, but others cannot. This suggests that belief in God is only a matter of inner conviction. Nonetheless, religious thinkers have offered numerous arguments in defense of belief in God. Of these, the most impressive is the Argument from Design.

The basic idea of the argument is that we can infer God's existence from the nature of the world around us—the world is full of wonders that we can best explain with the supposition that an intelligent designer created them. As we shall see, this thought can be elaborated in various ways.

The Wonders of Nature. The world is full of amazing things that we take for granted. Consider, for example, the human eye. It is made of parts that work together in intricate, complicated ways. The eye has an opening through which light enters, while a mechanism makes the opening larger or smaller depending on the amount of light available. The light then passes through a lens that focuses it on a sensitive surface, which in turn translates the patterns into signals that can be transmitted to the brain through the optic nerve. If any detail is changed, the whole process stops working. Imagine that there was no hole in the front of the eyeball, or no lens, or no nerve connecting it to the brain—then everything else would be pointless.

Countless other examples could be given. The plants and animals that populate the earth are all composed of parts that work together beautifully. They support one another by providing each other with food and other needs. Together they form a delicate but viable ecosystem. The earth itself, moreover, is exquisitely fitted to support the life on it, being just the right distance from the sun and having just the right temperature, water, and atmosphere. Considering all this, we might well wonder whether it could all have come about by chance. It looks like the work of an intelligent designer.

This line of thought has occurred to many people, but it was William Paley (1743–1805), an Anglican clergyman and teacher at Cambridge University, who developed it most memorably. Paley wrote two books, *A View of the Evidence of Christianity* (1794) and *Natural Theology: or, Evidences of the Existence and Attributes of the Deity* (1802), in which he argued that the existence of God can be inferred from the facts of creation.

The eye was one of Paley's favorite examples. He argued that we have "precisely the same proof" that the eye was produced by an intelligent creator as that objects such as telescopes are produced by intelligence. After all, "They are made upon the same principles; both being adjusted to the laws by which the transmission and reflection of rays of light are regulated."

It is the details, however, that make the argument compelling. As Paley observed, there are many *more* indications that the eye was consciously designed and set in place than that telescopes were. Forget for a moment its ingenious internal construction, and consider only how it is situated in the head: For protection the eye is lodged in a deep, bony socket, within which it is protected by fat. There are lids to further protect it. Glands are constantly producing a wash to keep the eye moist, without which, once again, the whole contraption would be worthless.

But, one might ask, so what? Having observed these remarkable facts, the argument can continue in two ways.

The Best-Explanation Argument. First, we may note that the wonders of nature require some sort of *explanation*. How, exactly, did the various parts of the eye come to exist? One possibility is that it all happened by chance—the lens, the optic nerve, the eyelid, and all the rest just happened to spring into being simultaneously. How lucky for us! But that is hard to believe. Yet, if chance is eliminated, what remains? Intelligent design seems to be the obvious alternative. The eye and the other wonders of nature could have been made by God. Thus we have the Best-Explanation Argument:

(1) Either the wonders of nature occurred randomly, by chance, or they are the products of intelligent design.

(2) Intelligent design explains the existence of these things much better than blind chance does.

(3) Therefore, the wonders of nature are best explained as the products of intelligent design.

The Same-Evidence Argument. A different form of the argument appeals to the idea that *we have the same evidence* that the universe was designed by an intelligent creator as we have that other things, such as cars and computers, were designed. To make this point, Paley introduced one of the most famous analogies in the history of science, that of the watchmaker.

Suppose we find a watch lying on the ground. If we inspect it, we will conclude that it was designed by an intelligent being. After all, it is made of many small parts that work together to serve a purpose. The evidence that it was designed for timekeeping is overwhelming. In Paley's words, "[I]ts several parts are framed and put together for a purpose . . . they are so formed and adjusted as to produce motion, and that motion so regulated as to point out the hour of the day. . . . [T]he inference we think is inevitable [is] that the watch must have had a maker." Thus, from the existence of the watch, we are entitled to infer the existence of a watchmaker. But do we not have exactly the same sort of evidence that the universe was made by an intelligent designer? The universe also consists of "parts framed and put together for a purpose"—namely, the purpose of housing intelligent life. And do we not have the same sort of evidence that some things in the universe—such as the eye, with its parts magnificently aligned for vision—were made by an intelligent designer? The Same-Evidence Argument, then, goes like this:

(1) We conclude that watches were made by intelligent designers because they have parts that work together to serve a purpose.

(2) We have the same evidence that the universe, and some of the natural objects in it, were made by an intelligent designer: they are also composed of parts that work together to serve a purpose.

(3) Therefore, we are entitled to conclude that the universe was made by an intelligent designer.

Hume's Objections. These are impressive arguments, but are they sound? It would be nice if they were, because they would provide rational support for an ancient and satisfying way of understanding the universe. Unfortunately, these arguments are open to some crippling objections.

First, we may notice that the Argument from Design, in all its forms, tries to infer *what causes something* from information about the thing itself. In other words, we are to infer a *cause* from its *effects:* From observations about phenomena, the argument infers the causes of those phenomena. This is a common type of inference. But this type of inference seems justified only when we have a certain sort of background information.

For example, suppose we are presented with an AIDS patient and asked what caused her disease. We could reply, with confidence, that she must have the human immunodeficiency virus (HIV), and this is the cause. But why are we entitled to make this inference? It is because of our past experience. In the past we have seen plenty of cases in which HIV and AIDS were linked. Physicians have treated many patients with AIDS, and in each case the virus was present. Moreover, studies have identified the mechanism that connects HIV and AIDS, and other possible causes have been ruled out. We call upon this background knowledge when we are confronted with a new case of the disease. We know what generally causes AIDS, and we apply this knowledge to new cases.

Can we infer, in the same way, that an act of divine creation caused the universe? The problem is that we lack the sort of background knowledge that would license this inference. If we had observed God creating universes many times in the past and had never seen a universe not created by him, then we would be entitled to infer that he must have made our universe. But, in fact, we have no idea what causes universes to come into existence. We are familiar with only one universe; we did not observe its cause; and that's all we know.

The case of the watch is entirely different. When we examine the watch lying on the ground, we have lots of relevant background information. We have seen watches before, and we know they are made by watchmakers. We can visit the factories and workshops where they are produced; we know the names of the companies that make them and that they can be bought in stores. That is why we can say with such confidence that a particular watch must have been made by a watchmaker. This means that the Same-Evidence Argument is fatally flawed. Where causes are concerned, we have vastly more evidence about watches than about universes. Moreover, these observations also cast doubt on the Best-Explanation Argument. Because we have so little experience with the creation of universes, and so little experience with the origin of natural objects, it seems too ambitious to assume that there are just two possibilities: random chance and intelligent design.

But suppose we set these points aside, and we do try to infer how the world came to exist. If we were serious about this, what would we conclude? What conjecture would seem most reasonable? The idea that the world was made by a single all-powerful, all-good deity would not be very plausible. After all, the world is not perfect. As impressive as the human body is, it is weak and vulnerable to disease. Some people have leprosy or muscular dystrophy. If our eyes were perfect, so many of us would not need glasses—and some of us, of course, are blind. Taking this into account, it might be more reasonable to conjecture that the world was made by a somewhat inept or malicious world-maker, or that we were made by an apprentice world-maker who had not yet mastered the craft. Again, we might notice that the world contains elements that work against one another—humans struggle to survive in an environment that is often hostile to them. This might lead us to speculate that the world was designed by a committee of world-makers working at odds with one another. Of course, no one believes such things. But the point is that these conjectures would be at least as reasonable as the idea that the world was made by a perfect God, *if* we were seriously trying to infer the nature of the Creator from the nature of the Creation.

All these points were made by David Hume (1711–1776), the greatest of the English-speaking philosophers, in his book *Dialogues Concerning Natural Religion*. Hume was a skeptic about religion at a time when skepticism could not be publicly acknowledged. So, he never came right out with a profession of disbelief. Instead, he chipped away at the foundations of belief by exposing weaknesses in various theistic arguments. He did not allow *Dialogues Concerning Natural Religion* to be published in his lifetime; it was published after his death, in 1779.

2.3. Evolution and Intelligent Design

As the nineteenth century began, Hume's objections to the Argument from Design were well known, but they were not generally regarded as decisive. Instead, Paley's books were more admired and respected. In the decades to come, Paley's books, not Hume's, would be required reading in British universities. The reason is obvious. The hypothesis of divine creation provided a way to account for the wonders of nature. Hume criticized this hypothesis, but he had nothing substantial to offer in its place. Why should people abandon a useful way of understanding the world when there is none better to be had? Thus, despite any logical weaknesses that the Argument from Design might have, the hypothesis could not be robbed of its appeal until an alternative account was provided. No other explanation was available until Charles Darwin formulated the Theory of Natural Selection in 1859.

How Natural Selection Works. Many people assume that Darwin was the first person to come up with the idea of evolution, but he was not. In the early nineteenth century it was already known that the earth is very old and that different kinds of plants and animals have lived at different times. Many people speculated that the appearance and disappearance of all those species might be explained by evolution (or "descent with modification" as it was then called). But evolution was rejected by scientific thinkers because no one could imagine how one species could change into another. What could the mechanism possibly be? Instead, they accepted the theory of *catastrophism*, according to which a series of great disasters has occurred throughout history—the last, perhaps, being Noah's flood—in which the existing species were destroyed and then replaced by God in a new act of creation. Today catastrophism may seem absurd, but in the early nineteenth century it was the best theory available, and many scientists accepted it. Then Darwin changed everything by proposing a viable theory of how evolution might take place. The Theory of Natural Selection, which he set out in his book *On the Origin of Species* (1859), supplied the mechanism needed to explain how species might evolve over time.

Darwin's genius was in realizing that three well-known facts, taken together, could explain evolutionary change. First, there is the *geometrical increase of populations*. Organisms reproduce in such numbers that, if left unchecked, the members of any one species would soon overrun the earth. (Starting from a few rabbits, there would soon be millions, and shortly thereafter trillions, until we were hip-deep in rabbits.) Second, there is the *heritability of traits*. An organism's descendants tend to resemble it—each individual inherits the characteristics of its parents. Third, there is *variation*. Although individuals resemble their parents, they are not exactly like their parents. There are random small differences between them.

Putting these three facts together, Darwin argued as follows:

(1) Organisms tend to reproduce in such numbers that, if all survived to reproduce again, the members of any one species would overrun the earth. This does not (and could not) happen. No species can continue to multiply unchecked. Each population

reaches a certain maximum size, and then its growth stops.

(2) It follows that a high percentage of organisms must die before they are able to reproduce. Therefore, there will be a "struggle for existence" to determine which individuals live and which die. What determines the outcome of this struggle? What determines which individuals live and which die? There are two possibilities: It could be the result of random causes, or it could be related to the differences between individuals. Sometimes it is random. That is, the reason one organism survives to reproduce while another does not will sometimes be attributable to causes that have nothing to do with their particular characteristics. One may be struck by lightning, for example, while another is not; and this may be mere luck. But sometimes the fact that one individual survives to reproduce while another does not will be due to their different characteristics. It works like this:

- There are differences ("variations") between members of species. Darwin did not know how or why such variations first arise, but today we know it has to do with genetic mutation.

- Some of these differences will affect the organism's relation to its environment, in ways that are helpful or harmful to its chances for survival and reproduction.

- Therefore, because of their particular characteristics, some individuals will be more likely to survive and reproduce than others.

Here are two simple examples of how this happens. Suppose wolves live in an environment that is growing colder. Then the wolves that have thicker fur will be more likely to survive and reproduce. The thicker fur does not appear in response to the weather—it is just a random variation. Nonetheless, it benefits the wolves in the changed environment. Or suppose that a bird like the African finch migrates to an area in which the available food supply consists of nuts. Then, in the same way, the finches with thicker beaks will be more likely to survive and reproduce. They will have an advantage in competing for the limited supply of food, so they will tend to leave behind more descendants.

(3) Organisms pass on their characteristics to their descendants. Again, Darwin did not know exactly how this happens, but it evidently does: An organism's offspring will have most of its particular characteristics. Today, once again, we know this has to do with genes.

(4) Therefore, the characteristics that have "survival value" are passed on and tend to be more widely represented in future generations, while other characteristics tend to be eliminated from the species. Future generations of wolves and finches will, on average, have thicker fur and thicker beaks.

(5) In this way, a species will be modified—the descendants of the original stock will come to have different characteristics than their forebears—and, when enough of these modifications have accumulated, we call the result a new species.

The Theory of Natural Selection made evolution a plausible notion, and it soon replaced catastrophism as the dominant account of why different species have lived at different times. It also provided an alternative to the hypothesis of intelligent design, without appealing to blind chance. Rather than explaining the wonders of nature as God's handiwork, we can account for them as the result of natural selection.

Can Natural Selection Account for Biological Complexity?
When Darwin was enrolled at Cambridge University in the late 1820s, all students were required to read Paley's *Natural Theology*. Darwin later wrote in his *Autobiography* that "I was charmed and convinced of the long line of argumentation." At that time the young Darwin intended to become a clergyman. He abandoned this ambition after completing an around-the-world voyage on the HMS *Beagle* from 1831 to 1835. By 1838 he had formulated the Theory of Natural Selection. After discovering natural selection, Darwin was no longer charmed by Paley's reasoning. Darwin considered the Theory of Natural Selection to be a replacement for the idea that particular aspects of nature

were consciously designed. "The old argument of design in nature," he said, "which formerly seemed to me so conclusive,
fails, now that the law of natural selection has been discovered."

Darwin's views gradually won over the scientific community, but many people have remained skeptical of evolution, or
at least skeptical of the idea that evolution eliminates the need
for a designer. In the 1970s and 1980s, "creation science" came
into vogue in the United States. Creationists accepted the lit-
eral truth of Genesis, and they looked for principles to explain
the diversity and geographic distribution of life. Activists
mounted a campaign to have creation science taught in the
public schools as an alternative to evolution, but they failed
because creation science was so obviously not a science. Today
the campaign has moved on to a more modest claim, namely,
that "intelligent design" should be taught as an alternative to
evolution in explaining the origin of species. In 1996 a scientist
named Michael J. Behe wrote *Darwin's Black Box: The Biochemi-
cal Challenge to Evolution,* in which he argued that some biological systems cannot be the result of natural selection alone
because they are "irreducibly complex." Intelligent design,
Behe said, is a more plausible explanation of such systems,
and the activists have taken this as their new rallying point.
Christianity Today named *Darwin's Black Box* its "Book of the
Year." Behe's next book, *The Edge of Evolution: The Search for the
Limits of Darwinism,* in 2007, pursued similar themes.

Why is natural selection supposedly inadequate? Behe's arguments are too technical in their scientific detail for us to consider. However, it is fair to say that they have not yet convinced
many scientists. Typically, the proponents of "intelligent design" point out that complex organs such as the eye are constructed of numerous parts, each of which appears to be useless
except when working together with the others. How are we to
conceive of the evolution of all these parts? Are we to imagine a
rudimentary eye, a rudimentary tear duct, a rudimentary lid,
and all the rest developing alongside one another? The Theory
of Natural Selection says that such complex organs are the result of small variations that "add up" to the mature organ after
many generations of evolutionary modification. However, even
though it is easy to see that the fully developed eye is useful to
its possessor, of what use is a half-eye that still has many generations to go before it is complete? Why should a half-eye be

"selected for" and preserved for further development? These problems, say the critics, are insuperable.

But this problem is not new. Darwin himself was aware of it. To address it, he made two points. First, he emphasized that a bit of anatomy may originally be preserved by natural selection because it serves a different adaptive purpose than the one it eventually comes to serve. Later, this bit of anatomy may come to play a part in some complex structure because it just happened to be present. Nature may jury-rig a complex structure out of whatever materials happen to be at hand. Second, Darwin called attention to what present-day theorists call the *intensification of function*. A biological structure that originally conferred a certain benefit, might later confer that same benefit to a much greater degree. To explain the eye, Darwin appealed to both of these points:

> To suppose that the eye, with all its inimitable contrivances for adjusting the focus to different distances, for admitting different amounts of light, and for the correction of spherical and chromatic aberration, could have been formed by natural selection, seems, I freely confess, absurd in the highest possible degree. Yet reason tells me, that if numerous gradations from a perfect and complex eye to one very imperfect and simple, each grade being useful to its predecessor, can be shown to exist . . . then the difficulty of believing that a perfect and complex eye could be formed by natural selection, though insuperable by our imagination, can hardly be considered real.

All we have to imagine is that a nerve only slightly sensitive to light confers on an organism some small advantage in the competition for survival. Then we can understand the establishment of the first rudimentary eye. From that simple thing will eventually come our complex eyes.

> In living bodies, variation will cause the slight alterations, generation will multiply them almost infinitely, and natural selection will pick out with unerring skill each improvement. Let this process go on for millions on millions of years; and during each year on millions of individuals of many kinds; and may we not believe that a living optical instrument might thus be formed as superior to one of glass, as the works of the Creator are to those of man?

If the eye itself can be formed in this way, then so can the tear ducts, the eyelid, the bone, and the rest. Take the lid, for example: Imagine that a rudimentary eye has been established and that in some organisms a slight variation has resulted in a small fold of skin that somewhat protects it. The skin is not there *in order to* protect the eye; it originally developed because it conferred a different benefit. But now that it is there, it can serve this new "purpose," and this new feature will be selected for, and further modified, in the usual way. Darwin's analysis has withstood the test of time. Today it forms the basis for scientific thought about these matters. Scientists are not impressed by the challenges of the religious critics.

After Darwin, the Best-Explanation Argument was finally refuted. Hume and the other philosophical critics of the Argument from Design had pointed out its logical deficiencies, but they could not supply a better way of understanding the apparent design of nature. After taking away design as an explanation, they left nothing in its place. It is no wonder, then, that in the early nineteenth century even the brightest people continued to believe in design. But Darwin did what Hume could not do: He provided a detailed alternative, giving people something different they could believe. The Best-Explanation Argument had considered only two ways of explaining the wonders of nature: chance and design. After Darwin there was a third way.

2.4. The First Cause Argument

Today we know—or at least we think we know—that the universe began in a "Big Bang" almost 14 billion years ago and that the earth was formed about 4.5 billion years ago. But, we may ask, what caused the Big Bang? What accounts for the fact that there is a universe at all, rather than nothing? This question requires some sort of answer, and here, once again, it may be suggested that the hypothesis of divine creation provides what we need. We may conjecture that God was the "first cause" of the universe.

This thought can be developed in various ways. The First Cause Argument can take at least three forms.

The Idea That God Was the First Cause in the Long Chain of Causes. One line of reasoning appeals to the principle that *everything that exists must have a cause.* My watch was made by watchmakers working with metals extracted from the earth. Where did the watchmakers and the metals come from? The watchmakers came from their parents, while geological processes explain how the metals came to exist. The chain of causes can be traced back further: Those parents descended from other people, who descended from still other people; the earth itself was formed from matter moving through space; and so on. If we trace everything back far enough, we eventually come to the Big Bang, which in turn must have been caused by something. But, it may be said, the chain of causes must stop somewhere. We must come eventually to the First Cause of Everything. The argument goes like this:

(1) Everything that exists must have a cause.

(2) The chain of causes cannot reach back indefinitely; at some point we must come to a First Cause.

(3) The First Cause we may call God.

As a statement of faith, this line of thought may be appealing. But if it is intended to provide rational support for belief in God, it fails. The main problem is that this reasoning is self-contradictory. It begins by saying that everything must have a cause, but then it goes on to posit the existence of something, God, that has no cause. We must choose: Do we seriously believe that everything must have a cause, or not? If we seriously believe that everything must have a cause, we must ask what caused God, and so on. On the other hand, if we believe that "the chain of causes must stop somewhere," why not say that it stops with the Big Bang? After all, the Big Bang is as far back as science can go, so it is as good a place to stop as any.

The Idea That God Caused the Universe "as a Whole" to Exist. There is a way to avoid these problems. We may think of God not as just another member of the chain of causes, but as the source of the entire chain itself. The "chain of causes and effects" occurs within the universe—indeed, the universe *consists of* the whole series of causes and effects, reaching back to the Big Bang. But now we want an explanation of the whole thing— why does the universe exist at all? Science, it may be said, deals only with causes and effects within the universe, and so science cannot tell us why the universe itself exists. For that, we need religion.

Thus, a different form of the argument might be:

(1) Everything that exists within the universe is part of a vast system of causes and effects.

(2) But the universe itself requires an explanation—why does it exist?

(3) The only plausible explanation is that the cause of the universe is God.

(4) Therefore, to explain the existence of the universe, it is reasonable to believe in God.

But this line of thought has its own problems. It is very much like the Argument from Design in that it attempts to infer the cause of the universe from the existence of the universe itself. The universe exists—that's for sure—and we are invited to infer what its cause was. Because of our religious tradition, we may be disposed to say that God must have caused it. But Hume's observations are again relevant. To infer the cause of something, we need a certain kind of background information. (To infer the cause of a watch, we need general information about what causes watches to exist.) But we do not have the relevant sort of background information about universes. We do not know what causes them to come into existence, and it is mere hand-waving to pretend that we do.

Some people have wanted to give the name "God" to whatever caused the universe. But even if we agreed to this, we would not thereby have provided any reason to think that "God" is the all-powerful, benevolent deity of traditional theism. The word "God" might (for all we know) now be serving as the name of an incredibly dense point of mass and energy that preceded the Big Bang. Once this idea is appreciated, it becomes clear that there is no reason to use the word "God" in this way. Doing so only creates confusion.

The First Cause Argument is like a lot of other philosophical arguments in that we start with a promising idea—in this case, that divine creation might explain the origin of the universe—but run into problems when we try to formulate it into an explicit chain of reasoning. We might now be tempted to give up on the original thought, concluding that it was not such a good idea after all. But before we give up, there is one further thought that we should consider.

2.5. The Idea That God Is a Necessary Being

Peter van Inwagen is a distinguished contemporary philosopher who converted to Christianity as an adult, after he had already done first-rate work in philosophy. Van Inwagen writes that, after he became a Christian, the world seemed like a very different kind of place to him. Before his conversion, he says, "I can remember having a picture of the cosmos, the physical universe, as a self-subsistent thing, something that is just *there* and requires no explanation." But now he can no longer think of the world in that way:

> I can still call the image to mind (I *think* it's the same image), and it still represents the whole world, but it is now associated with a felt conviction that what it represents is not self-subsistent, that it must depend on something else, something not represented by any feature of the image, and which must be, in some way that the experience leaves indeterminate, radically different in kind from what the image represents. . . . [I]t is now impossible for me to represent the world to myself as anything but dependent.

If the universe is not "self-subsistent," then it cannot exist by itself. It must be sustained by something else. But what sort of "something else" could sustain the whole universe? The obvious candidate for this peculiar status is God. God, according to traditional religious thought, is self-sufficient. He is the cause of everything else, but he himself has no cause. He exists eternally, without cause and without beginning or end.

What sort of being could be "self-sufficient"? What could be the cause of everything else and yet not itself require a cause? It all sounds very mysterious. But, according to some philosophers, there is a kind of being that could have these characteristics, namely, a *necessary* being. A necessary being is a being that, by its very nature, could not fail to exist.

If we accept this distinction between (a) things that exist but whose existence depends on something else and (b) things that exist necessarily, then we can formulate one final version of the First Cause Argument. That argument would go like this:

(1) The universe is a dependent thing. It cannot exist by itself; it can exist only if it is sustained by something else—something that is not dependent.

(2) God, a necessary being, is the only thing that is not dependent.

(3) Therefore, the universe is sustained by God.

Does this argument provide good reason to believe that God exists? It is certainly full of puzzling notions. It is puzzling why the universe must be dependent. Why couldn't it exist without being supported by something else? It is puzzling why the universe could be created only by something self-sufficient—why couldn't it be created by something that depends on something else? But perhaps the most puzzling thing is the notion of a being whose existence is necessary. What sense can be made of this?

The idea of God as "a necessary being" goes back at least as far as St. Anselm (1033–1109), the English monk who is sometimes called the father of medieval scholasticism. Anselm suggested that we should conceive of God as "that than which none greater can be conceived." God, in other words, has every possible perfection: He is perfect in knowledge, in power, in goodness, and in every other way imaginable. There is no conceivable way in which he could be made better. Anselm maintained, moreover, that this is true *by definition*—trying to imagine God as having an imperfection is like trying to imagine a married bachelor or a triangle with five sides. You can certainly imagine a being *similar* to God that lacks some perfection, but then you are not thinking of God. The concept of God *is* the concept of a perfect being, just as the concept of a bachelor is the concept of an unmarried man or the concept of a triangle is the concept of a three-sided figure.

But Anselm noticed that something remarkable seems to follow from this: If any being is by definition perfect, then that being must exist. After all, if it did not exist, it would not be perfect. (Beings that do not exist are, at least in this respect, inferior to beings that do exist.) Hence, it is impossible that God not exist, and this is what we mean by a "necessary being." A necessary being is a being that *could not fail* to exist. You and I are not necessary beings, because if history had gone differently, we might not have existed. But God is different. He could not have not existed.

This line of reasoning is known as the Ontological Argument. The Ontological Argument is unlike the Argument from Design or the First Cause Argument in that those arguments frequently occur to ordinary intelligent people. Any reflective person, considering the wonders of nature and the origin of the universe, is apt to wonder whether divine creation is needed to explain them. The Ontological Argument, on the other hand, may sound like a philosopher's trick. How can the existence of anything follow from its definition?

Yet the Ontological Argument has persuaded a number of thinkers. René Descartes (1596–1650), whom we will meet again in this book, and Gottfried Wilhelm Leibniz (1646–1716), the philosopher-scientist who along with Newton discovered calculus, both believed that the Ontological Argument is sound. Others, however, have disagreed.

In Anselm's own day, a monk named Gaunilo argued that if this argument proves that God exists, it must also prove that a perfect island exists. Suppose we say that "Islandia" is the name for our concept of a perfect island. Islandia, by definition, is perfect—it cannot be improved on. It follows, then, that Islandia must exist, because if it did not exist, it would not be perfect. By the same method, we could prove that a perfect banana exists, or that a perfect man exists. But this, Gaunilo observed, is absurd. Therefore, the Ontological Argument cannot be sound.

Gaunilo's reasoning shows that the Ontological Argument is mistaken, but it does not explain the nature of the mistake. That was left to Immanuel Kant (1724–1804), considered by many to have been the greatest philosopher of the modern period. Kant observed that whether a thing is perfect depends on its properties—whether an island is perfect, for example, depends on its size, climate, natural beauty, and so on. Existence, however, is not a property in this sense. Whether such an island exists is a matter of whether anything in the world *has* those properties. Thus, we cannot prove that the island—or anything else—exists just by stipulating that it is "by definition" perfect. The definition of "Islandia" tells us only what Islandia would be like if it existed; it cannot tell us whether there really is such a thing. Similarly, the definition of "God" tells us only what sort of being God would be, if he existed. Whether he does exist is another matter.

Conclusion. The whole business of seeking "arguments" for the existence of God might be thought suspect. People rarely believe in God because of arguments. Instead, they simply accept the teachings of their culture, or they believe because of some urgent inner conviction. Arguments seem irrelevant.

But arguments are not irrelevant if we want to know what is reasonable to believe. A belief is reasonable only if there is evidence for its truth. The arguments we have been considering are the most impressive attempts yet made to marshal such evidence. They aim to provide reasons that any thoughtful person should accept. But none of these arguments succeed. They all contain flaws, and so they must be judged failures.

The fact that these arguments fail does not mean that God cannot exist—it only means that these particular arguments do not prove it. There may be other arguments, still to be discovered, that will be more successful. In the meantime, the idea that God has created the universe may continue to play an important part in the thinking of religious believers. Divine creation may be accepted as part of a satisfying worldview, even if it is not rationally necessary. Like van Inwagen many thoughtful people may even find this way of thinking irresistible. But, for the present at least, such beliefs must be regarded as a matter of inner conviction rather than being the sort of thing that every reasonable person must accept. This conclusion will not surprise those religious people who, in any case, have always regarded their convictions as matters of faith, not logic.

CHAPTER 3

The Problem of Evil

Misery's the river of the world.

—TOM WAITS, BLOOD MONEY (2002)

3.1. Why Do Good People Suffer?

Job was a prosperous man with holdings in land and cattle, and he loved all 10 of his children. He was a good man, generous to his neighbors and a leader in the religious life of his community. This combination of riches and virtue made him the most admired man in the region. Then everything went wrong. Foreigners invaded Job's lands, killing his servants and making off with most of his cattle. A fire destroyed the rest, leaving him penniless. Shortly afterward, a storm caused a house to collapse, killing all his children. Then Job himself came down with a disease that left him covered with sores, so disfigured that people could not recognize him.

When Job's friends came to console him, their pity soon turned to accusation. They were pious, and they could not believe that Job had not done something to deserve his misfortunes. Surely, they thought, God would not allow Job to suffer unless he deserved it. "Does God pervert justice?" one asked. "God will not reject a blameless man, nor take the hand of evildoers." Another told him, "Know that God exacts of you less than your guilt deserves." But Job knew himself to be guiltless. Nevertheless, he could not explain why God had abandoned him.

This story is recounted in the Book of Job, an ancient Jewish writing that is included in the Christian Bible. It is the earliest document we have in which the problem of evil is clearly posed. Of course, the existence of evil is not a "problem" if one takes a nonreligious view of the world. From a secular perspective it is not hard to explain why bad things happen. The world isn't designed for our benefit. Lightning causes fires, geological forces cause earthquakes, and microbes cause disease. If we happen to be in the way, it's just our bad luck. This explains part of Job's suffering, and human viciousness explains the rest. From a secular standpoint there is no mystery in any of this, for we do not expect the world to be fair. Disaster strikes the righteous and the wicked alike. We may not like it, but that's the way life is.

The problem arises when we think of the world as under the control of God. There is a tension between (a) the world's being under the dominion of an all-good, all-knowing, all-powerful being, such as God, and (b) the world's containing evil. A perfectly good being would not want bad things to happen. He would not want children to get leukemia, or floods to destroy cities, or terrorists to kill the innocent. Instead, he would want to prevent such things from happening if he could. Moreover, an all-powerful being would be able to prevent such things from happening. But they do happen. How is this to be explained?

Philosophers distinguish the *logical* problem of evil from the *evidentiary* problem. The logical problem is that God and evil appear to be incompatible: If evil exists, then an all-powerful, all-knowing, perfectly good God cannot exist. But it may be replied that there is no contradiction here, because God might have a good reason for permitting evil. (We do not even have to say what the reason is—we might not even know what it is.) That would solve the logical problem. It would show that believing in God is not logically inconsistent with recognizing that evil exists.

The evidentiary problem, however, would remain. The evidentiary problem is that, even if God and evil are logically compatible, the existence of evil is nonetheless *evidence* that God does not exist. Suppose we find someone's fingerprints on a murder weapon—this is strong evidence that he committed the crime, even if it is still logically possible that he was framed. Pending further investigation, the fingerprints make it *likely* that he is the murderer. They point in his direction. In the same way, the existence of evil might count against belief in God, even if it does not conclusively prove that he doesn't exist. The fact that there is *so much* evil in the world makes the existence of God even less likely.

This is the single biggest problem for theistic religious belief. It is certainly the problem that worries religious people the most. Thus, religious thinkers have tried for centuries to answer Job's question: Why would God permit terrible things to happen?

3.2. God and Evil

There is a long and distinguished tradition of philosophers who have defended orthodox religious belief. For the first 1600 years of the Christian era, almost every important philosopher accepted a theistic worldview and worked within it. Following the Enlightenment, however, educated people were drawn to the worldview of modern science, and they began to develop more secular ways of understanding the world. Today philosophical inquiry is generally conducted independently of religion. Although "philosophy and religion" are linked in the popular mind as though they were aspects of a single subject, most philosophers today do not make such a connection. They see philosophy as independent.

Starting about 40 years ago, however, religious thought began to make a comeback in philosophical circles. Alvin Plantinga, a Christian philosopher who now teaches at the University of Notre Dame, was an early leader in this movement. Plantinga distinguishes two kinds of theistic response to the problem of evil, a *defense* and a *theodicy*. A defense is a demonstration that the existence of God is logically consistent with the existence of evil. A defense does not pretend to reveal God's actual plan for creation. But it does aim to show that theists who acknowledge the existence of evil are not guilty of a logical contradiction. A theodicy, on the other hand, is more ambitious. A theodicy attempts to "justify the ways of God to man" by explaining how evil fits into God's actual plan for the world. Plantinga does not believe we can provide a theodicy, because we do not know the mind of God, and moreover, it is presumptuous to think we do. But, he says, a theodicy is not necessary. A defense is all that is needed to permit religious people to continue in their faith.

The problem with this distinction is that a defense requires too little and a theodicy requires too much. As we have seen, a defense is easy to provide—we can simply point out that God might have a reason for permitting evil, even if that reason is unknown to us. It might be all right to stop here if we were concerned only with defending religious belief from the charge of inconsistency. But we are also concerned with the broader question of what it is reasonable to believe. Does the existence of so much evil make it *unreasonable* to believe in God? Is the existence of evil evidence against such belief? To solve this problem, we need more than a mere "defense," but we do not need as much as a full-blown theodicy. Instead, we need something in between. We need a plausible account of why an all-powerful, perfectly good God might permit great evils, even if we cannot be sure it is God's own reason.

Such accounts have, in fact, been offered. Five major ideas have been advanced to explain why God might allow evil to exist. We will consider them one at a time.

The Idea That Pain Is Necessary as Part of the Body's Warning System. "Evil" might seem to be a mysterious notion, and it may be difficult to say exactly what evil is. But it is easy to give examples that everyone would agree with. The most obvious example is pain. Physical pain—especially intense, prolonged pain—is among the worst things in life, and torturers who deliberately inflict such pain are despicable people. But is God among the torturers? Consider a baby born with epidermolysis bullosa, a genetic skin disease that causes blistering all over the body, so that the baby cannot be held or even lie on its back without pain. If God created the world and everything in it, then he created epidermolysis bullosa, and he left babies vulnerable to it. What justification could there be for this?

It may be pointed out that pain has a purpose: It is part of the body's warning system. Pain alerts us to danger. Imagine what would happen if we could *not* feel pain. When you accidentally put your hand on a hot stove, the pain causes you to snatch it away, saving you from being burned. When you twist your arm, it hurts, telling you not to twist it any further. Thus, if you could not feel pain, you would be much worse off. In fact, there are people born insensitive to pain, and they typically lead short and tragic lives. Similar observations hold true of other unpleasant experiences, such as fear. Fear motivates you to withdraw from danger. Faced with an angry grizzly bear, it's good to be afraid. So, it may be said, God has given us pain and fear for our own good.

This argument is persuasive, as far as it goes, but it does not solve our problem. The trouble is that pain and fear are imperfect mechanisms for danger avoidance. They do not look like they were devised for this purpose by a perfect God. Sometimes we need a warning, but there is no pain. Carbon monoxide poisoning can sneak up on us without warning. Eating ice cream should be painful for the obese, but it is not. At other times people suffer terribly even though they cannot improve their situation. The pain that accompanies cancer of the throat may tell us that something is wrong, but the information does us no good—it is not like a hot stove or a grizzly bear, from which we can flee—and so the victim suffers needlessly. At still other times pain may be so great that it is debilitating. Then it may hinder us from escaping, rather than helping: A solitary hiker who breaks his leg in the wilderness may die because he cannot drag the broken limb back to civilization. These facts do not fit the hypothesis that God has created pain for our protection. Pain looks more like the product of a hit-or-miss process of evolution than the work of a perfect designer.

Finally, even if it is a good thing that we can feel pain, this does not explain why God creates *sources* of pain such as epidermolysis bullosa. A mother who asks why God allows her baby to have this disease can hardly be answered by pointing out that pain is part of the baby's warning system. What needs explaining is why the baby's system is being attacked in such a cruel way.

The Idea That Evil Is Necessary So That We May Better Appreciate the Good. St. Augustine (A.D. 354–430) observed that if nothing bad ever happened, we could not know and appreciate the good. The point is partly logical and partly psychological. Logically, without the concept of evil, there could be no conception of goodness, just as there could be no notion of tallness without a notion of shortness. We could not even know what goodness *is* if we did not have evil for comparison. Moreover, psychologically, if we never suffered, we would take good things for granted and enjoy them less. How could we recognize and enjoy health if there were no disease? Thus, it is foolish to wish for a world that contains only good things.

But even if this is true, it explains only why God might permit *some* evil to exist. We might indeed need a few bad things to happen once in a while, just to remind us how fortunate we are. But it does not explain why there is so *much* evil in the world. The problem is that the world contains vastly more evil than is necessary for an appreciation of the good. If, say, only half the number of people died every year of cancer, that would be plenty to motivate the appreciation of health. And because we already have cancer to contend with, we don't really need epidermolysis bullosa, much less AIDS, muscular dystrophy, cerebral palsy, spina bifida, diphtheria, Ebola, heart disease, diabetes, Alzheimer's, and bubonic plague.

The Idea That Evil Is Punishment for Wrongdoing. Job's friends believed he must have done something to merit his suffering, because a just God "will not reject a blameless man." Thus, they concluded, Job must have deserved what happened to him.

The idea that evil is punishment for wrongdoing goes back to the creation story in Genesis, which says that originally humans inhabited a world without evil. But the first humans, Adam and Eve, rebelled against God and as a result were cast out of paradise. The idea expressed in this story is not that you and I are still being punished for Adam and Eve's wrongdoing. That would obviously be unfair. The point is that all of us are sinners, and our existence in a world of evil is somehow to be explained by that fact. We suffer because we bring it on ourselves.

What are we to make of this? It would make sense if there were some correlation between one's moral character and how one fares in life. If evil is punishment for sin, we should expect the worst sinners to suffer the worst disasters. But no such correlation exists. Disaster strikes the righteous and the wicked alike, without apparent regard for their virtue. Some of the best people get Parkinson's disease, while some of the worst people go through life without problems.

And what about innocent babies, who sometimes have terrible diseases and die horribly? The doctrine of original sin was introduced into Christian thought partly to deal with this problem. According to that doctrine, we are all born in sin, so even babies are sinners. But if this is supposed to mean that a newborn baby deserves to have epidermolysis bullosa, we can only marvel at the mentality that would lead anyone to think such a thing.

The deep problem with using the concept of sin in this way is that it separates sinfulness from what a person actually thinks or does. In the ordinary moral sense, what a person deserves depends on his or her behavior. If you deserve ill, you must have *done something* to deserve it. No doubt all of us have behaved badly at one time or another, so perhaps each of us deserves some degree of retribution. But we don't deserve to get a horrible disease unless we have done something pretty awful, and a baby hasn't done anything bad at all. Therefore, while this conception of "sin" might have religious significance, it has little to do with moral desert. As Job knew, it is false that calamities are always deserved.

3.3. Free Will and Moral Character

The ideas we have considered so far—that pain is part of the body's warning system, that evil is necessary for appreciating the good, and that evil is punishment for wrongdoing—are unconvincing. But two other ideas are more promising. Together, they make up the most plausible theistic response to the problem of evil.

The Idea That Evil Is the Result of Human Free Will. God could have made the world, it is said, without people in it. It could have been a beautiful place, with sunsets and waterfalls, with daffodils and bunny rabbits, and God could have been pleased with it. But God went one step further and chose to include us as well. What difference did that make? Humans are not just another kind of animal. Humans are special. We are moral agents, able to choose what sorts of persons we'll be, and so we're responsible for our choices. We are capable of love and friendship, and we can envision and accomplish great things. Thus, without human beings the world would be a poorer place. That is why humanity was part of God's plan—or at least why God might have chosen to create us.

But there is a catch: In order to make us moral agents, rather than mere robots, it was necessary for God to endow us with free will. Freedom makes humans special. In giving us the power of free choice, however, God had to allow that we might sometimes choose badly. He could not have given us free will and at the same time fixed it so that we could never do wrong—we might then have the appearance of free will, but we would not have the real thing.

The result is that human beings have the power to choose evil, and sometimes we do. Therefore, alongside the understanding, love, kindness, and heroism that they bring to the world, humans add murder, cruelty, rape, and war. But God is not responsible for that; we are. God is responsible for the overall design of the world and for creating us. His creation is good. Our contribution to it, however, is not always good.

This line of thought is called the Free Will Defense. The Free Will Defense shows that the best world God could have created might contain evil, because the best world might include creatures with free will. Compare:

(a) A world without humans in it, which would not contain any of the bad things people do, but would also not contain any of the results of human consciousness, creativity, and virtue

(b) A world with humans in it, which would include human wickedness but also the good things that humanity brings with it

If you think that (b) is better than (a), then perhaps the best world God could have made would have evil in it. This vindicates the perfect goodness of God. After all, we could not expect more of him than to create the best world possible.

Still, this cannot solve the problem completely. We need to distinguish two kinds of evil, *moral evil* and *natural evil*. Moral evil is the evil that people cause by their own actions—murder, rape, war, and so on. Natural evil, on the other hand, is the evil that human beings do not cause—disease, earthquakes, droughts, floods, and other natural disasters. Humans may be responsible for babies born addicted to narcotics, but we are not to blame for babies born with epidermolysis bullosa. Thus, even if the Free Will Defense explains why God would allow moral evil, it does nothing to explain why he would create natural evil. Therefore, it can be only part of the story.

The Idea That Evil Is Necessary for the Development of Moral Character. Suppose God decided to make a world that included human beings, with all the capacities of thought and action that make us who we are. This decision would restrict the kind of world God could make, because the world would have to have a suitable environment for creatures like us. What sort of world would that be? What sort of environment would allow us to grow and develop as human beings?

Imagine a world that was "perfect" in the ordinary sense. In this world the temperature would be a balmy 72°F year-round, and nothing bad would ever happen—there would be no destructive earthquakes, fires, or floods and no diseases. There would be no dangerous predators. Moreover, there would be no hunger. Every tree would bear abundant fruit, and the streams would flow with milk and water (and perhaps beer). Everyone would live to a ripe old age in perfect health, and everyone would enjoy life. The environment would be beautiful in a way that we never grow tired of.

This sounds wonderful. You might ask, If God is perfectly good, why didn't he create that sort of environment for us? The answer is that if we lived in *that* sort of environment, we would not be the kinds of creatures we are. In a "perfect" world there would be no problems to overcome, and thus no occasion for the development of moral character. There could be no courage, because there would be no dangers to face. There could be no helpfulness or generosity, because no one would need help. All the other virtues—such as kindness, compassion, perseverance, and creativity—would also go by the wayside, because we develop such qualities only by striving to cope with adversity. If we lived in a perfect environment, there would be no work to be done. We would be slugs—slugs who enjoy life, but slugs nonetheless.

Thus, we have a plausible explanation for natural evil: In order to create human beings as creatures with moral character, God had to place us in an environment in which those qualities could be developed. That means an environment with problems to be solved and evils to be overcome. The world that we actually inhabit seems well suited for the development of people like us. After all, here we are.

A Complete Account? The most plausible response to the problem of evil combines the Free Will Defense with the idea that evil is necessary for an environment in which human beings can develop and flourish. The former explains moral evil, while the latter explains natural evil. Together, they seem to give a more or less complete account of the evils we face. They explain why a perfectly good, all-powerful God might have created a world like the one we actually inhabit. We need not pretend that this account is a "theodicy" in Plantinga's sense—perhaps God actually had other purposes in mind, of which we are not aware. But this account does seem to be the best available way to square the hypothesis of God with the existence of evil.

The picture may be rounded out by adding another familiar idea from the theistic tradition, namely, that human life as we know it is a mere prelude to the eternal life we will enjoy after we die—or rather, after the bodies we inhabit die. As Peter van Inwagen puts it:

> Every human being has an eternal future (and, therefore, the human species has an eternal future). We are now living, and have been living, throughout the archaeologically accessible past, within a temporary aberration in human history, an aberration that is a finite part of an eternal whole. When God's plan of atonement comes to fruition, there will never again be undeserved suffering or any other sort of evil. The "age of evil" will eventually be remembered as a sort of transient "flicker" at the very beginning of human history.

If, indeed, the evil that concerns us is only a feature of a "transient flicker" in human history, then the problem does not seem nearly so pressing.

Should we be content with this and conclude that the problem of evil has been overcome? That is different from asking whether we actually believe the theistic story. Remember that we are not discussing whether God actually exists. We are discussing whether the existence of evil is evidence against belief in him. If evil can be justified within a theistic framework, then the problem of evil has been resolved, regardless of whether we believe the theistic picture to be true.

But three problems stand in the way of such a conclusion. The first has to do with moral evil. The Free Will Defense says that God wants us to be free, so he tolerates the bad effects of human misconduct. This might explain why God doesn't step in to prevent small offenses—perhaps those things should be allowed to occur. But why wouldn't God intervene when people are about to do something particularly awful, like abuse an innocent child? It is not plausible to say, "Intervening would turn the attacker into a robot" or "Respecting the abuser's free will is more important than protecting the child." We would not accept those excuses from a police officer who was passively witnessing the crime, so why should we offer those excuses on behalf of God? The Free Will Defense explains why God doesn't intervene all the time, but it doesn't explain why God allowed the holocaust or why God allows isolated cases of extreme cruelty.

The second problem has to do with the theist's explanation of natural evil. The need to develop moral character might explain why there is *some* evil in the world, but there is far more evil than is necessary for such a purpose: There is stunning, overpowering misery that crushes the life out of people. If we already have AIDS, muscular dystrophy, cerebral palsy, and spina bifida, why do we need Ebola as well? If the people of Guatemala are already poor and hungry, why do they need an earthquake on top of it? Nothing in our account addresses why there is *so much* suffering caused by natural events.

It might also be useful to imagine our account addressed to

> a man who drove a cement mixer truck. He came home one day for lunch; his three year old daughter was playing in the yard, and after lunch, when he jumped into his truck and backed out, he failed to notice that she was playing behind it; she was killed beneath the great dual wheels.

If this man were told the story about free will and character development, he might find it unconvincing, not because he is blinded by grief and guilt, but because he hasn't been told why *this* sort of thing must happen, in addition to all the other troubles that plague us. Even if God needed some evil to accomplish his purposes, there is no reason to believe he would need so much. The amount of evil in the world could be reduced by two-thirds, and there would still be more than we could handle.

The third problem has to do with nonhuman animals. The traditional debate about evil has centered on human beings. But human life and history are only a small part of nature and its history. Countless animals suffered terribly in the millions of years that preceded the emergence of *Homo sapiens,* and none of the ideas we have been considering address their suffering.

Animals are not sinners, they do not have "free will," they do not develop moral character, and they are not going to heaven. What of them? Charles Darwin made this point forcefully:

> That there is much suffering in the world no one disputes. Some have attempted to explain this in reference to man by imagining that it serves for his moral improvement. But the number of men in the world is as nothing compared with that of all other sentient beings, and these often suffer greatly without any moral improvement. A being so powerful and so full of knowledge as God who could create the universe, is to our finite minds omnipotent and omniscient, and it revolts our understanding to suppose that his benevolence is not unbounded, for what advantage can there be in the sufferings of millions of the lower animals throughout almost endless time?

We are left, then, with this conclusion. Our survey of ideas about how to reconcile God with evil has turned up various thoughts that might be useful. But none of them dispel the suspicion that, in the end, God and evil may not be reconcilable. The amount of gratuitous, pointless evil that exists in the world not only poses a serious problem for the believer. It is also a reason why a serious person who is considering whether to accept such a belief might decide against it.

CHAPTER 4

Do We Survive Death?

> No one can prove that this will not happen. But it is easy to see that it is very unlikely.
> —BERTRAND RUSSELL, *DO WE SURVIVE DEATH?* (1936)

4.1. The Idea of an Immortal Soul

On the day of his execution, Socrates and his friends discussed the immortality of the soul. His friends were distressed that he was about to die, but Socrates told them not to worry. After all, he reminded them,

> By death do we not mean simply the departure of the soul from the body? Being dead consists, does it not, in the body having been parted from the soul and come to be by itself, and in the soul having been parted from the body, and being by itself. Can death possibly be anything other than that?

Since the soul continues to exist, what is there to fear? In fact, Socrates says, the soul of a philosopher will be better off separated from his body, because the body is a hindrance to the pursuit of truth. Socrates was confident that he would live on in a disembodied state, and he was eager to see what it would be like.

Today we consider "the soul" to be a religious idea, but Socrates did not. He thought it was a fact, independent of religion, that each human being is composed of a physical body and a nonphysical soul. Similarly, he believed on rational grounds that the soul—the part of you that perceives, thinks, and feels—will never die.

41

Socrates knew that this last claim was open to doubt and that arguments were needed to support it. As Cebes told him:

> Your view about the soul is one that people find it very hard to accept; they suspect that, when it has left the body, it no longer exists anywhere; on the day when a man dies his soul is destroyed and annihilated; immediately upon its departure, its exit, it is dispersed like breath or smoke, vanishing into thin air, and thereafter not existing anywhere at all.

To counter this, Socrates gave several arguments to show that the soul cannot be destroyed. His most plausible argument appeals to the simplicity of the soul.

Destroying something, Socrates says, means breaking it down into its component parts. We could destroy a shirt, for example, by tearing it to bits so that nothing remained except scraps of cloth. But nothing like that can be done to the soul. The soul is not composite. It is simple. It has no parts that can be detached from one another. Moreover, because it is not a physical thing, the soul cannot be burned, crushed, or mangled. Thus, it cannot be destroyed.

This argument has a certain initial plausibility, and Socrates' friends said they were convinced by it. Unfortunately, however, it is not as strong as Socrates thought. First, why must the soul be simple? Couldn't the soul have one part for thinking, another for perceiving, another for feeling, and so on? Second, as Cebes suggests, ceasing to exist need not involve coming apart. The soul might simply vanish. Presumably, a simple soul would have come into being simply by appearing one day, as if by magic: poof! Similarly, one day it might disappear.

But regardless of the strength (or weakness) of Socrates' arguments, his conception of an immortal soul has had an enormous influence. It was adopted by Christian thinkers, and in a modified form it has come down to us through the teachings of the Church. Because of this, many people believe that the immortal soul is a biblical doctrine. They are surprised to learn that the Bible teaches no such thing. Instead, the Bible— or at least the New Testament—holds out the hope that, at some time after our deaths, God will bring us back to life.

These two notions are quite different. According to Socrates, you will survive death because *there is something in you that is indestructible.* Or, to put it another way, *you yourself are indestructible.* To survive, you do not need to be resurrected. You do not need the sustaining power of God, or anything like it. Your soul is immortal by itself, in its own nature. In St. Paul's view, however, there is nothing about you that is indestructible. When you die, you are well and truly dead. Your only hope is that God will restore you to life by resurrecting you, just as Jesus was resurrected. Moreover, there is no suggestion in the Bible that you will ever exist in a disembodied state. Rather than imagining the afterlife as a realm of pure spirit, St. Paul speaks of your getting a new body.

The intellectual climate today is unlike that of Socrates' Athens. The hope of eternal life remains with us, but speculative arguments for the immortality of the soul no longer carry much weight. The reason is that modern science goes against Socrates' idea, in two ways.

First, the idea of a "soul" has disappeared almost entirely from the scientific study of human beings. In modern science the idea that each of us is a body-plus-soul has been replaced by theories that focus on the relation of thought to the brain. Psychologists are apt to talk about behavior, the emotions, cognitive capacities, perceptual systems, genetics, the environment, natural selection, and the brain—but the "soul" does not enter the picture, except perhaps for a brief nod when scientists give popular expositions of their work. Even then, the word will be in quotation marks.

Second, a great deal of evidence suggests that consciousness is not possible unless the person's brain is functioning in the right way. We see this again and again: When you are hit on the head, events occur in your brain that cause you to lose consciousness; if the supply of oxygen to your brain is interrupted, you lose consciousness; if an anesthesiologist "puts you under," you lose consciousness. In each case consciousness is restored only when your brain begins to function normally again. From this we may infer that when you die and your brain shuts down for good, you lose consciousness permanently. The lights go out, and there is no way to turn them back on. Of course, this does not prove that consciousness cannot resume. But it does support a strong presumption that it will not.

Nevertheless, hope remains. The great religions teach that we survive bodily death, and science does not prove them wrong. Many believers are content to let the matter rest there, as a matter of faith. Others, however, want more than religious hope. They look for factual evidence to set against the cold pessimism of science. Does any such evidence exist? Many websites and TV shows say that it does. The purported evidence is of three kinds: near-death experiences, instances of reincarnation, and mediums who communicate with the dead. Under close inspection none of this evidence stands up very well. But it is worth looking at. Much of the purported evidence is pseudo-science, and by examining it we can get an idea of the difference between fake science and the real thing.

4.2. Is There Any Credible Evidence of an Afterlife?

Go into any large bookstore, and near the philosophy section you will find a shelf labeled "Metaphysics" or "New Age," a category that includes books about angels, astrology, earth spirits, and alien abductions. Topics come and go. Books about the mystic powers of pyramids, ancient astronauts, and the Bermuda Triangle are also in this section, but they are not as popular as they used to be. Philosophers are not happy that the word "metaphysics" has been appropriated for these subjects. Since the time of Aristotle, metaphysics has been a sober branch of philosophy that has nothing to do with the occult or the paranormal. Nonetheless, in book marketing this is what the word has come to mean.

These books are collected in one place, not because they share a common subject matter, but because they appeal to a common sensibility. They see the world as having mysterious dimensions, full of significance but ignored by modern science and mainstream religion. In their pages scientists are viewed as a closed-minded elite who refuse to acknowledge the truths discovered by other investigators. Psychics, mediums, and spiritualists have their own "research," and while the establishment may ignore them, their books sell briskly.

Near-Death Experiences. In 1975 a medical student named Raymond A. Moody, Jr., published a short book called *Life after Life*. Moody, who had previously earned a Ph.D. in philosophy, wrote that he had interviewed 50 people who had undergone remarkable experiences when they were near death. Typically, he said, they would hear themselves pronounced dead and feel themselves floating out of their physical bodies. Looking down, they would see the doctors trying to revive them, and then they would move on, perhaps passing through a tunnel toward a bright light where they would be greeted by the spirits of old friends and loved ones. A "being of light" would seem to be in charge. They would feel intense joy and peace. But then, as the doctors brought them back to life, they would be pulled back into their physical bodies. Although Moody disavowed any intention of proving the existence of an afterlife, the title of his book proclaimed otherwise.

Life after Life was an instant best-seller. It has sold more than 13 million copies and has inspired numerous similar books by other authors. There is now a whole "field" of near-death research, with its own professional association and its own journal. Some of the other books report additional experiences like the ones Moody describes. Others detail further aspects of "the light," such as its healing powers. One book even suggests that we now know enough about "the other side" to make plans for what to do when we get there—it is called *What to Do When You Are Dead: Living Better in the Afterlife*. Moody, meanwhile, went on to become a "past-life therapist," helping people overcome their psychological problems by facing traumas from their previous lives. He has also developed a method for communicating with the dead by gazing into mirrors. Moody explains that he discovered this last technique after "studying ancient writings as well as an archaeological site in Greece."

What are we to make of all this? Setting aside the sillier aspects of these books, do near-death experiences provide evidence of an afterlife? There are several obvious problems. For one thing, it is hard to judge how frequent these experiences are and what they are really like. Even in the most favorable circumstances, people are bad at remembering their dreams. Moreover, psychologists know from long experience that people will say whatever they think will please the interviewer, or they will fudge what they say so as to make themselves appear more interesting.

"Investigator bias" is also a problem, even for the best researchers. It is hard for anyone to avoid emphasizing evidence that supports one's own theory while playing down evidence that goes against it. In conducting interviews this bias may take the form of asking leading questions, interpreting the responses to fit one's preconceptions, and then writing summaries that leave out material that contradicts the preferred theory. Mainstream scientists are aware of these dangers and take precautions against them. One precaution is to let other scientists review the tapes and transcripts of their interviews. Moody has never let anyone see the interviews on which his book was based, so no one knows how much investigator bias crept into his work.

This might not matter so much if impartial investigators could reproduce Moody's results. *Life after Life* got a lot of publicity, and as a result physicians with no axes to grind began to note the experiences of their own patients. They found that in most cases the dreams of patients undergoing medical crises have little to do with happy reunions or feelings of peace. An editorial in the *Lancet* (the official publication of the British Medical Association) commented that "Of male survivors of cardiac arrest, 80 percent had dreams of violence, death, and aggression, such as being run over by a wheelchair, violent accidents, and shooting their way out of the hospital only to be killed by a nurse." Even when patients did dream about peace and light, the details varied with their education level. Less-educated patients dreamed of being met by friends and loved ones, while better-educated patients did not. This suggests that the dreams are just dreams, reflecting the individual's preconceptions, and not experiences of real events.

But even if we set these problems aside and grant that people have the experiences Moody describes, a further issue arises: What is the *best explanation* of those experiences? Contact with the "next world" is one hypothesis. Here are some others:

- *Influence of drugs.* The drug ketamine, sometimes used as an anesthetic, produces all the characteristic features of near-death experiences. Moreover, Ronald K. Siegel, a UCLA psychologist, compared the accounts of near-death experiences with the statements of people undergoing drug-induced hallucinations and found them virtually identical.
- *Oxygen deprivation.* Even without drugs, we know that oxygen deprivation, which occurs when the heart stops beating, causes hallucinations.

- *Commonplace dreaming and hallucinating.* More mundanely, we all know what it's like to lie in bed half-awake and have strange thoughts, partly connected with the world around us and partly hallucinatory. We are familiar with dreams and nightmares, and we know that people's dreams are sometimes similar, often because they incorporate common religious and cultural symbols.

With these other explanations available, there is no need to postulate anything as radical as "contact with the next world" to explain the experiences.

For these reasons most philosophers, like most scientists, have little interest in Moody's work. In 1988, however, philosophers were startled when one of their own reported a near-death experience. A. J. Ayer was an enormously respected figure who had no patience with supernatural notions. His best-known book, *Language, Truth and Logic* (1936), argued that metaphysics and religion are nonsense and that the scientific method is the only reliable guide to truth. Throughout a long and distinguished career, he never abandoned that creed.

One year before his death, Ayer was hospitalized for pneumonia. While he was in intensive care, his heart stopped beating for four minutes. Upon awakening, he said to a friend: "Do you know that I was dead? The first time I tried to cross the river I was frustrated, but my second attempt succeeded. It was most extraordinary, my thoughts became persons." Ayer, who was later amazed that he had said such things, interpreted these statements as reflecting his classical education—the "river" was obviously the Styx of Greek mythology. But he also reported having had another experience while unconscious: "I was confronted by a red light, exceedingly bright, and also very painful, even when I turned away from it. I was aware that this light was responsible for the government of the universe." Reflecting on this remarkable vision, Ayer concluded that the explanation was probably naturalistic: "The most probable hypothesis," he said, "is that my brain continued to function although my heart had stopped." Nevertheless, he added that "My recent experiences have slightly weakened my conviction that my genuine death, which is due fairly soon, will be the end of me, though I continue to hope that it will be."

Reincarnation. According to the hypothesis of reincarnation, each of us has lived before, and each of us will live again. Perhaps you are the reincarnated spirit of a seventeenth-century Frenchman, and perhaps, someday, a twenty-third-century soldier will be the reincarnation of you.

Could this sort of thing be true? There are some obvious difficulties. One problem is that, if reincarnation occurs, why aren't babies born with adult personalities? After all, a baby is supposed to "be" someone who was 60 or 70 years old. If the baby has the old person's psyche, why doesn't the baby have the old person's knowledge and experience? The philosopher Paul Edwards comments that "It is little less than scandalous that no reincarnationist has ever attempted to reply to this argument. It is as if Christian theologians had never attempted to face the problem of evil."

A different problem, also pointed out by Edwards, is connected with the size of the human population. Could each person be the reincarnation of someone who lived before? In 8000 B.C., before the rise of civilization, there were only 5 million humans scattered around the world. By the time of Jesus, the number had grown to 200 million. In 1650 there were about 500 million of us, and by 1850 there were 1 billion. Now the population has passed the 6.5-billion mark. There simply weren't enough people in previous generations for each person in subsequent generations to "be" one of them. When the population grows, "new" people must be created.

But such objections would be swept aside if there was good empirical evidence that reincarnation occurs. Is there any such evidence? We might begin by noting what really good evidence would be like, if it existed. Suppose a great many people, in all cultures, could remember having lived before, at different times and places. Suppose you, for example, could remember having lived through an entire life in seventeenth-century France. You remember the language you spoke, the clothes you wore, the things you did, and the people you knew; furthermore, you remember these things in the same vivid way you remember earlier events in your present life. Moreover, your memories are historically accurate—we can verify that there really was a person such as you remember being. And let's say that one of your friends in the seventeenth century was Pierre, and, living today, there is someone who remembers being Pierre. You get together with him, and it is exactly what you would expect in seeing an old friend—you reminisce about the old days and catch up with what's been going on lately. Suppose this sort of thing was so common that no one thought it remarkable.

That is what we would expect life to be like if reincarnation took place. But in reality almost no one has such memories. Even in India, where belief in reincarnation is widespread, people rarely claim to remember a specific past life. Believers in reincarnation have searched far and wide for such cases, and they have turned up only disappointing examples.

The most famous case of apparent reincarnation was Bridey Murphy. In 1952 a Colorado businessman and amateur hypnotist named Morey Bernstein placed Virginia Tighe, a Chicago housewife, into a hypnotic trance. While in the trance Mrs. Tighe began talking in an Irish brogue and said that her name was Bridey Murphy and she was born in Ireland in 1798. In subsequent sessions Mrs. Tighe provided impressive details about her life as Bridey, from her marriage to a barrister in 1818 to her death on a Sunday in 1864. The newspapers got hold of the story, and soon everyone knew who Bridey Murphy was. Bernstein, who had long been an enthusiast of reincarnation, eventually wrote a book, *The Search for Bridey Murphy* (1956), that rose to the top of the best-seller lists.

While Bridey's picture of nineteenth-century Irish life enthralled ordinary people, it did not impress the experts. W. B. Ready, an Irish scholar at Stanford University, said that she depicted "an Ireland that never was, save in the minds of the uninformed and the vulgar." But because of the high level of public interest, attempts were made in Ireland to verify the details of her story. The results were unexciting. No record of Bridey's birth or death could be located, despite the existence of birth and death registries in the cities where she supposedly lived. Cork city directories are virtually complete from 1820 on, but no mention of her family, including her barrister husband, could be found. Bridey said her husband taught law at Queens University, but no record of that could be found, either. On the other hand, it could be said that she knew the names of various places in Ireland, and she had heard of Queens University.

The public discussion of the Bridey Murphy case ended on a bizarre note when the *Chicago American,* a Hearst newspaper, published an exposé "revealing" that when Virginia Tighe was a girl, she would visit a neighbor, an Irish woman named Mrs. Bridey Murphy Corkell, who would tell her tales of the old country. After this story had been circulated and, as a result, people had lost interest in Bridey, the *American*'s story was itself exposed as a hoax.

The leading contemporary defender of reincarnation is Dr. Ian Stevenson (1918–2007), a psychiatrist who taught for many years at the University of Virginia Medical School. Dr. Stevenson devoted his life to collecting and investigating cases of alleged reincarnation. Many involve stories told by small children about their previous lives. These cases almost always occur in countries where belief in reincarnation is widespread, and the children almost always stop telling the stories at age 7 or 8. Sometimes the child's family will seek out the child's "other" family, from the previous life, to verify the child's report. Dr. Stevenson was convinced that this research proves the reality of reincarnation.

It is hard to evaluate such evidence, but we might note the assessment of Champe Ransom, who was Stevenson's research assistant for three years—an experience he describes as "interesting but painful." In a report written for Dr. Stevenson, Ransom described a number of problems with the Stevenson team's research methods. While he did not publish or circulate the report beyond the Stevenson laboratory, he did provide a summary for Paul Edwards. Ransom's comments read like a checklist of precautions that any scientist would think obvious:

> Three notable [flaws] are that leading questions were being asked, that the questioning period for each case was quite brief . . . and that the time elapsed between the alleged occurrence of the event and the investigation was quite long, frequently years. Stevenson's cases seldom, if ever, contain any study or discussion of the child's storytelling inclinations to get attention. Similarly, there is no investigation of the playmates of the subject and the extent of *their* knowledge of the events in question. Still another set of factors Stevenson neglects concerns human fallibility. There are subtle distortions of memory; there is the tendency to unintentionally "fill in" a story in order to make it complete; there is a general lack of caution of many people in reporting what they have observed; there is the general unreliability of detail of personal observation; there is witness bias; and there is witness suggestibility.

These are not arcane matters of scientific technique. After all, science is not an exotic art; it is just the persistent use of human intelligence in the attempt to figure out the truth about the world. Ransom's points are "scientific" because, as scientists are aware, no technique of investigation that ignores them has much chance of finding the truth.

As for confirming the children's memories by checking with the families from their previous lives, Ransom notes:

> [I]n only 11 of the approximately 1,111 rebirth cases had there been no contact between the two families before investigation was begun. Of those 11, seven were seriously flawed in some respect. What this means is that in the great majority of cases, the two families had met years before a scientific investigation began, and that the likelihood of independent testimony was quite small.

Psychics Who Claim to Communicate with the Dead. No one doubts Ian Stevenson's integrity, though many question the quality of his research. When we turn to the psychics, however, we enter a world of fakery and fraud. Modern spiritualism began in 1848 in Hydesville, New York, when two girls, Katie and Maggie Fox, claimed to communicate with a ghost by means of mysterious rapping sounds. The Fox sisters were a sensation, and soon a host of others were making similar claims. In later years Katie and Maggie admitted it was just a trick—they had made the sounds by knocking or kicking anything handy. (They had initially fooled their mother by dropping an apple to the floor.) Later, spiritualists would develop more sophisticated techniques. Trumpets would float while spirits made music; ghostly images would appear on exposed film; tables would levitate; strange breezes and odors would waft through the room; and otherworldly visitors would inhabit the bodies of mediums and scrawl messages on slates.

To professional magicians, it was plain that the spiritualists were using tricks of the trade. Harry Houdini was among those who exposed the frauds as a professional service. But as the spiritualist craze spread to Europe, scientists and members of learned societies declared the psychics to be genuine. William James, the brother of Henry James and one of America's most distinguished psychologists and philosophers, wrote of one medium: "I should be willing now to stake as much money on Mrs. Piper's honesty as on that of anyone I know."

It should not be surprising that intelligent people can be taken in by fakery—the presumption that sincere-seeming people are honest is very strong, and even a clumsy magician can produce startling illusions. Why should training in psychology or physics make someone immune to the magician's art? James Randi, a magician who regards psychics as unethical practitioners of his trade, put the point well. If you want to catch a cheat, he said, give the job to a magician, not to a scientist.

The most common technique used by spiritualists today is "cold reading," a method by which the psychic appears to produce information when in fact the information is being provided by the client. As the medium "makes contact" with someone in the spirit world, she will make vague statements, and the "sitter," as the client is called, will react to them. The medium might say, "I feel like there's a G- or J-sounding name attached to this . . . does that mean anything to you?" Or, "He's pointing to his head . . . there's something about a head here . . . does that mean anything to you?" The sitter will think of something significant suggested by these references, and then the process is repeated as the medium extracts details. If the psychic is addressing a group, achieving results is even easier: Only one member of the group needs to come up with a "G- or J-sounding name."

When the medium gets a hit, she builds on that information. If she doesn't get a hit, she quickly moves on, making other vague references, until the sitter responds to something. The sitter will usually be eager to help, and it is easy to get hits. Nearly anyone can react to the mention of a common object such as a hat or a key, and the sitter's recollection can then be interpreted as a hit. If things aren't going well, the medium may suggest that the sitter is having trouble remembering. Sometimes, with a show of confidence, she may suggest that the sitter write down the question and think about it later. In any case, when the medium's performance is later recalled, only the hits will be remembered.

A good psychic doing a cold reading can make surprisingly specific suggestions and get positive responses. To show how easy this is, one investigator carried out a survey in which

> [m]ore than 6,000 people were asked to state whether quite specific statements were true of them. More than one third of people endorsed the statement "I have a scar on my left knee" and more than a quarter answered yes to the statement "Someone in my family is called Jack."

The results produced by "hot reading," in which the medium has advance information, can be even more impressive. Advance information is not hard to get. One technique used in stage shows is for the psychic's confederates to circulate in the audience before showtime, talking to members of the audience and eavesdropping on conversations. Then, during the show, when the psychic tells a member of the audience that her niece named Jocelyn is in the hospital for an operation, onlookers will conclude that the psychic's powers must be real. But sometimes hot reading can backfire. John Edward, a popular "psychic medium" with his own syndicated TV show, appeared on NBC's *Dateline* to demonstrate his abilities. Referring to the spirits with whom he was communicating, Edward said, "They're telling me to acknowledge Anthony." When the cameraman indicated that that was his name, Edward acted surprised; but later he admitted he'd already met the cameraman and knew his name. Even then, he insisted he was merely repeating what the spirits were telling him.

4.3. Hume's Argument against Miracles

When it comes to the question of life after death, many mainstream scientists may seem closed-minded and uninterested in examining the evidence. Why should that be? Part of the answer is that they have better things to do. Life is short, and once it becomes clear that an area of research is rife with error and fraud, scientists naturally lose interest in it. But there is another reason for the lack of interest, connected with Hume's argument against miracles.

David Hume, the great Scottish philosopher of the eighteenth century, did his most important work in his early twenties. In later life he gained fame for a long series of books and essays on philosophy, history, psychology, religion, and morals. Hume worked as a tutor, as secretary to the British ambassador in Paris, and as a librarian at the University of Edinburgh. But the university professorship that he coveted was denied him, partly because of his scandalous views about religion and morals. One example of these views is the essay on miracles that he included in his book *An Enquiry Concerning Human Understanding* (1748).

Hume did not say that miracles can't occur, but he did argue that it is never reasonable to believe in them. Suppose, for example, someone tells you that a dead man came back to life. Should you believe it? Hume says:

> When anyone tells me that he saw a dead man restored to life, I immediately consider with myself whether it be more probable that this person should either deceive or be deceived, or that the fact which he relates should really have happened. . . . If the falsehood of his testimony would be more miraculous than the event which he relates, then, and only then, can he pretend to command my belief or opinion.

In other words, we have to ask which is more likely:

(a) That a dead man came back to life

(b) That the report is mistaken

Of course it is more likely that the report is mistaken. "We frequently hesitate concerning the reports of others," Hume notes, because we know that often people get things wrong, make mistakes, exaggerate, and even lie. These are common occurrences. On the other hand, we have never known someone truly dead to return to life. Therefore, a reasonable person will conclude that the report is probably mistaken.

Hume said he hoped that this argument would be "an everlasting check to all kinds of superstitious delusion," and it seems to apply to the matters we have been discussing. Suppose someone says he knows of a really strong case of reincarnation. We must ask which would be more likely:

(a) That when we die our spirits go to an astral world, where they reside for an indefinite period, until they reenter the world and invade the uterus of a pregnant woman, there uniting with the fetus she is carrying, and in the process losing the memories and personality that make us the distinctive people we are

(b) That there is some defect in the evidence

The first is incredible, while on the basis of experience, the second would not be at all surprising. Thus, a reasonable person will think (b) more likely; in fact, he or she will think it is *much* more likely. This is the underlying reason why mainstream scientists don't want to pore over an endless amount of "evidence" concerning postmortem existence.

CHAPTER 5

The Problem
of Personal Identity

> When I consider my own individual life from inside, it seems that my existence in the future or the past—the existence of the same "I" as this one—depends on nothing but itself. To capture my own existence it seems enough to use the word "I," whose meaning is entirely revealed on any occasion of its use. "I know what I mean by 'I.' I mean *this!*"
>
> —THOMAS NAGEL, *THE VIEW FROM NOWHERE* (1986)

5.1. The Problem

Can we possibly survive death? The answer depends on what "we" are. Is a person the sort of thing that can survive the disintegration of the body? Most people in our culture seem to think so; they believe that after you die, your body rots in the ground, but you wake up in heaven (or somewhere else you don't want to be). Does that belief make sense? *Could* the person who dies on earth be the same person who wakes up in heaven? To answer these questions, we must grapple with the problem of personal identity. We must think about what persons are.

A Thought Experiment. Suppose scientists invented a machine that could make a perfect copy of anything. It worked by scanning an object's atomic structure and then assembling identical atoms in the same pattern. The Duplicator successfully copied various items, starting with paper clips and ashtrays, and then a computer that ran perfectly. It made a chocolate cake that tasted fine. When a painting by Picasso was duplicated, there was some inattention afterward, and now no one knows which painting is the original. The ultimate challenge, however, was to reproduce life. Preliminary tests went well—a mouse was duplicated, and the copy was every bit as frisky as the original.

Now the scientists want to conduct one final test. They want to duplicate a human being, and they have picked you for the honor. If you agree, a copy of you will be made that will have your memories, your beliefs, your desires, and your personality. It will believe it is you, and no one—not even your closest friends and family—will be able to tell the difference. It will, for all practical purposes, *be* you. There is only one catch: We can't have two of you running around, so after the procedure is completed, the original "you" will be destroyed and the new "you" will carry on as before. For your trouble, you will be paid a million dollars.

Would you agree? There are two ways to think about this. On the one hand, you might be impressed by the fact that your life will go on exactly as before, and no one, not even "you," will be able to tell the difference. So you should take the money. Few of us, however, would think that way. Instead, we would think: *I'll be dead.* It doesn't matter that the duplicate will act like me and have my memories and emotions. Nor does it matter that the duplicate will believe it is me—the fact is, it won't be. I'll be dead, and it will merely be a copy of me.

Now consider the afterlife. According to traditional belief, when you die you will lose consciousness and your body will decay. Here on earth, it will seem like you no longer exist. Meanwhile, in another world, someone will appear with your beliefs and memories. That person will believe she is you. But will she really be you? Why won't she just be your duplicate? This question is important. All of us want to go to heaven, but few of us care whether our duplicate gets to go.

5.2. Personhood at a Moment

The problem of personal identity is the problem of what we are. It has two aspects. First, there is the question of what a person consists in at a particular moment. What does it mean to be you, right now? Second is the question of what makes someone the same person at different times. The child at your seventh birthday party, blowing out the candles, was the person who is now reading this sentence. How should we explain that fact?

These questions—of personal identity at a time and over time—are related. We'll take them up in turn.

The Bundle Theory and the Soul Theory. What does a human being like you consist in, at a given moment or over a brief stretch of time? Two points should be uncontroversial. First, you have a physical body. Second, you have a mental life that takes place in, and is sustained by, your physical body.

Your mental life includes perceptions, thoughts, memories, emotions, and other such items, which are connected with one another in various ways. The individual items come and go. Some, such as your awareness of this sentence, are short-lived. Others, such as your memories of your parents, may persist for a long time. Some of them may be related to one another by cause-and-effect while others are not. When you go to sleep, many (if not all) of them cease to exist; and when you wake up, they are succeeded by a similar parade of mental items, many of which resemble and are caused by the earlier ones.

Does anything more need to be added? One hypothesis is that you consist simply of your body together with this collection of mental items. This is the Bundle Theory. Many people, however, think that it leaves out something important. They believe something like this:

> Within each person is a kernel that may be called the *soul* or the *ego* or the *self.* It is the subject of all the person's experiences. It is simple and indivisible. And it is present throughout the person's life.

Call this the Soul Theory. The Bundle Theory denies that there is any such soul. On the Bundle Theory, *the parade of mental items is all that exists,* so far as the "mind" is concerned.

The Bundle Theory may be hard to accept, because you may feel that, in addition to the various experiences you have, there is the being who *has* the experiences—and that being is *you.* David Hume (1711–1776) understood this problem. He said, "[Human beings] are nothing but a bundle or collection of different perceptions"; and when asked whether there mustn't be a "self" that has those perceptions, he replied that there is no reason to think such an entity exists:

> [W]hen I enter most intimately into what I call *myself,* I always stumble on some particular perception or other, of

heat or cold, light or shade, love or hatred, pain or pleasure. I never can catch *myself* at any time without a perception, and never can observe any thing but the perception.

Consider this analogy: A car consists of an engine, a body,
a transmission, wheels, an electrical system, and so on. Suppose
we listed all the parts of a car and asked: "But isn't the car itself
something separate from all these parts? After all, it is the car
that *has* an engine, a transmission, and so on." Obviously, this is
silly—the car is not some mysterious thing in addition to all its
parts. The car is simply the collection of parts arranged in a certain way. Similarly, a "self" may simply be a bundle of mental
items, combined with a body, and nothing more.

Split Brains. How can we decide between the Bundle Theory
and the Soul Theory? Hume's point was that the Bundle Theory is faithful to what we actually observe. We observe the parade of mental items, but not the unified "self" that supposedly
underlies them. This eighteenth-century observation accords
well with our present-day scientific view of the person. In a scientific account of human beings, we are apt to talk about behavior, the brain, various mental phenomena, and the relations
among them; but scientists do not talk about a separate, simple
"self" or "ego." And we may add to the scientific picture an
amazing discovery about the brain.

In 1981 Roger W. Sperry was awarded the Nobel Prize in
medicine for his work on split brains. Earlier in his career,
Sperry had demonstrated that different parts of the brain serve
different functions. Then in the 1960s he and his co-workers
studied what happens when the brain's two hemispheres are
split apart.

In a normal human being, the left hemisphere of the
brain contains the "language center" and does mathematics
and other kinds of analytical thinking. The right hemisphere
specializes in other matters, such as spatial comprehension,
map reading, and recognition of faces. The right side can do
simple calculations—it can perform addition, but only up to
about 20. The right side of the brain controls the left side of the
body, and vice versa.

With this much specialization, you might think that the
two hemispheres would sometimes interfere with each other,
with signals from one side contradicting signals from the other

side. Normally, however, this does not happen, because the hemispheres communicate with each other through a bundle of nerves called the corpus callosum. Trouble starts when the corpus callosum is severed, as is sometimes done to treat epilepsy. Then the hemispheres cannot communicate, and strange things happen:

- If a split-brain patient is asked to reach into a bag and identify an object, such as a pencil, she will be able to identify the pencil with her right hand but not with her left hand.
- When the words "Give me the pencil" are shown to the left side of her visual field, she will insist that she cannot see anything. At the same time, her left hand will be picking out a pencil from a collection of objects and offering it to you.
- Similarly, if an odor from a clove of garlic is fed into her right nostril, the patient will deny that she can smell anything; but if she is asked to point to what she has smelled, the left hand will point to the garlic.

What are we to make of all this? It looks as if the patient has split into two people who are at odds with each other. Sperry himself concludes that each side of the brain is "a conscious system in its own right, perceiving, thinking, remembering, reasoning, willing, and emoting, all at a characteristically human level, and . . . both the left and the right hemisphere may be conscious simultaneously in different, even in mutually conflicting, mental experiences that run along in parallel."

The Oxford philosopher Derek Parfit saw a connection between these results and the Bundle Theory. Parfit considered this case: A split-brain patient is shown a blue patch in the left side of his visual field and a red patch in the right side. Pencils are placed in each of his hands, and he is asked to write down how many colors he sees. The left hand writes "only one" and the right hand writes "only one." So far, so good. But when asked what color he sees, one hand writes "blue" while the other hand writes "red."

We have here two streams of consciousness. In one, blue is experienced and reported; in the other, red is experienced and reported. The two streams do not interact. How many persons are there under these circumstances? If we assume that a person is a soul or a "self" that underlies experience, then the question is surprisingly hard to answer. "One person" sounds wrong, because each stream seems to have its own "self"—the self associated with one stream has no access to the experience or behavior of the self associated with the other stream. But if we say that there are two selves, we invite a barrage of embarrassing questions: Where did the extra self come from? Is one of the selves the same as the original person? If so, which one? And if neither is the original, where did the original person go? Did he die?

The split-brain case exposes the weakness of the view that people consist of simple souls. The Bundle Theory, however, provides a neat description of what is happening in these cases. There are two streams of consciousness that do not interact. Each stream contains familiar sorts of elements. That is all there is to it. Parfit concludes that the answer to the question of how many selves there are is the same as the answer to the question of how many selves are normally present in us—none.

This is an unsettling conclusion. If the Bundle Theory is correct, then we are not what we thought, and we may not like what we are. Common sense says that, when we die, it is at least possible that we will go to heaven. But if the Bundle Theory is true—if we are just a body and a parade of mental items—then how could we survive the destruction of our body, the disabling of our brain, and the disruption of our conscious experiences? A belief in heaven seems to presuppose that a person is a kernel, or a soul, that could shed both the body and the mind.

5.3. Personhood over Time

If the Soul Theory were true, then it would be easy to say what makes you the same person at different times—the same kernel is present at each time. If that little kid at the birthday party was you, then this is because you and he have the same soul (or better yet, you and he *are* the same soul). Admittedly, it would be hard to know whether the same kernel was present at different times; the soul can't be seen or touched or detected in any normal way. However, we would at least know what personal identity over time would consist in.

If, on the other hand, the Bundle Theory is true—if a person is a body plus a collection of mental items—then a fundamental problem remains. Which part of the bundle is crucial for your continued identity? Obviously, you could lose your left leg and still be you, but could you survive the loss of your memories, or your brain, or your personality? Different theories give different answers.

Numerical and Qualitative Identity. There are two ways in which someone might be "the same person" at different times. On the one hand, you are the same person you used to be if you have the same personality—your character hasn't changed, your sense of humor is the same, and so on. Suppose my old college roommate, John Smith, was a decent, funny man who was the son of Bill and Mary Smith and who went to high school in Atlanta. But over the years he has become mean and humorless. I might complain that this new John Smith is not the person I roomed with; he has changed. If I said this, everyone would know what I meant. John Smith is *qualitatively* not the same as he used to be.

In another sense, however, he *is* the person I roomed with—he is still John Smith, the son of Bill and Mary, and the graduate of an Atlanta high school. He has not been replaced by an imposter. If the sheriff comes looking for the man who signed our lease, there he is. John Smith might have changed over the years, but that doesn't matter—*the same person* who was decent and funny is now grim and unpleasant. He is *numerically* the same individual.

Is personal identity important? Does it matter whether someone in the future will be *you*? Remaining the same person qualitatively is a good thing only if you are a good person; otherwise, it might be better if you changed. But we all want there to be a future person who is numerically identical with us. Otherwise, we will not exist. What does it take to be the same person, at different times, in the numerical sense?

5.4. Bodily Continuity

There are various ideas about what makes someone the same person at different times. One is the Same-Body Theory:

> *The Same-Body Theory:* X, who exists at an earlier time, and Y, who exists at a later time, are the same person (numerically) if and only if they have the same body.

Years ago, when I last saw my roommate, someone could have (in theory) started observing him, and they could have traced the long, unbroken path through space and time that led him into my presence again today. That path connects the person then with the person now and makes them the same. Of course, his body may have undergone some changes. He may have gained a little weight and lost a little hair. But that does not matter. Physical objects can change, within limits, and yet remain the same physical objects.

In everyday life the Same-Body Theory works well enough. Sameness of body and sameness of person always go together, so it is natural to think they are the same thing. But this criterion seems to rule out the possibility of postmortem existence. If my roommate dies and his body is rotting in the ground, then he cannot be in heaven. Someone else might be there, with "his" memories and personality, but it cannot be him.

The Prince and the Cobbler. Is the Same-Body Theory a satisfactory account of our identity over time? John Locke (1632–1704), the first major philosopher to discuss personal identity, argued that "sameness of body" cannot be the correct measure of whether two individuals are the same person.

Suppose, Locke said, we imagine that the mind of a prince is magically transferred into the body of a cobbler. The prince wakes up one morning, looks around, and is horrified to find himself in the cobbler's humble bed. He looks in the mirror and is even more horrified to see the cobbler's face staring back at him. Pulling himself together, he marches off to the palace, tells the guard that he is the prince, and orders him to open the door. Meanwhile, in the palace, the cobbler's mind has been transferred into the prince's body. Upon awakening, he is frightened to find himself in the prince's bed, and he tries to leave before he is discovered.

Now consider the individual who has the cobbler's body but the prince's memories and personality. Who is this person? Is it the prince or the cobbler? If the body is what matters, it must be the cobbler. But Locke thought otherwise: "Everyone sees he would be the same person with the prince, accountable only for the prince's actions." Therefore, Locke concluded, we need a different sort of criterion.

The Ship of Theseus and the Human Body. Plutarch, an ancient Greek writer, told a riddle about an ordinary ship. This ship, the Ship of Theseus, was composed of wooden planks, and once in awhile a plank would get damaged or become rotten and then be replaced. Eventually, *all* of the ship's planks had been replaced. This raises a question: Is the new Ship of Theseus the same ship—*numerically* the same—as the old Ship of Theseus? It would seem not. A ship is composed of a bunch of planks; once the planks have been removed, the ship is gone. Gradually, it seems, the Ship of Theseus was disassembled.

Now consider the human body. It gets disassembled, too. Our bodies are composed of cells, and new cells are constantly being created to replace the old. This process is called "cell regeneration" or "cell turnover." After about nine years, most of the cells in the human body have been replaced. To put this another way: the body of a 60-year-old is composed mostly of cells less than nine years old.

These facts create another problem for the Same-Body Theory. If our bodies get replaced, bit by bit, then no human body lasts more than nine years or so. Thus, no human *being* survives more than nine years, if we are our bodies. The John Smith of today cannot be the person I roomed with many years ago because these two individuals have different bodies. This implication of the Same-Body Theory is certainly odd, if not downright absurd.

Now consider some other facts about human biology. The main type of brain cell is the neuron. Although our cells are constantly being replaced, most of our neurons never get replaced. Some do, but most do not. An old man had most of his neurons when he was an infant. Thus, even if our bodies don't exist more than nine years, our brains do. And perhaps the persistence of the brain is enough to ensure one's continued existence. The brain, as the seat of higher functioning, does occupy a special place in the human body. This suggests a new theory:

> *The Same-Brain Theory:* X, who exists at an earlier time, and Y, who exists at a later time, are (numerically) the same person if and only if they have the same brain.

This theory could be defended from the Ship of Theseus example. In the actual world our neurons do not get replaced like the planks of Plutarch's ship. We retain the same brain through-out our lives.

As promising as the Same-Brain Theory is, we will not try to assess it. However, I will mention one problem. When a person dies, her brain has ceased functioning in important ways. Nevertheless, her brain may still exist because it takes time for one's body to decompose. Suppose, for example, that a healthy person drowns over a 10-minute period. At the end of those 10 minutes, she no longer exists (on earth, anyway), but her brain is still there. Those who believe in the Same-Brain Theory will be hard-pressed to explain how she has ceased to exist while her brain is still around. In its simplest form, then, this theory fails.

5.5. Memory

A different theory of personal identity focuses on mental connections, especially the connections of memory. I am certain that I am the person who went to the movies yesterday, sat in the third row, and talked to his wife, because I *remember* going to the movies, sitting in the third row, and talking to my wife. I am certain that I was John Smith's roommate because I remember living with him. Where the connections of memory are strong, personal identity seems certain.

So we might pose this theory:

> *The Memory Theory:* X, who lived at an earlier time, is the same person (numerically) as Y, who lives at a later time, if and only if Y can remember doing what X did, feeling what X felt, thinking what X thought, and so on.

If this theory is correct, it explains why the individual in the cobbler's body is really the prince. He is the prince because he remembers living in the palace, giving orders to the servants, and so on. This theory also accommodates the idea of an after-life—if the person in heaven has your memories, then that person is you.

This was Locke's theory. Locke wrote:

> Consciousness alone unites actions into the same person . . . it is plain, consciousness, as far as ever it can be extended— should it be to ages past—unites existences and actions very remote in time into the same person, as well as it does the

existences and actions of the immediately preceding moment: so that whatever has the consciousness of present and past actions, is the same person to whom they both belong.

As it now stands, the Memory Theory is open to a decisive objection. We forget things all the time. An hour ago, I had thoughts that I now have no recollection of. On the Memory Theory, we cannot say that I am the same person who had those thoughts. This seems absurd.

Thomas Reid (1710–1796), the Scottish "philosopher of common sense," brings up another problem for the Memory Theory, based on the fact that we forget things:

> Suppose a brave officer to have been flogged when a boy at school, for robbing an orchard, to have taken a [battle flag] from the enemy in his first campaign, and also to have been made a general in advanced life; suppose, also, which must be admitted to be possible, that, when he took the [flag], he was conscious of his having been flogged at school, and that, when made a general, he was conscious of taking the [flag], but had absolutely lost the consciousness of his flogging.

This is a common turn of events. When he is 25, a man may remember being 12; and when he is 60, he may remember being 25 but not remember being 12. If we think about this scenario in light of the Memory Theory, we get a strange result: The boy is the same person as the young man, and the young man is the same person as the general, but the boy is not the same person as the general.

What is wrong with this? The problem is that the relation "same person as," in the numerical sense, is *transitive*. This means that if A is the same person as B, and B is the same person as C, then A must be the same person as C. For example, if Lee Harvey Oswald is the person who killed John Kennedy, and the person who killed John Kennedy is the person who was shot by Jack Ruby, it follows that Lee Harvey Oswald is the person who was shot by Jack Ruby. On the Memory Theory, however, it turns out that the same-person relation is not transitive. Therefore, the Memory Theory cannot be right.

However, the Memory Theory can be revised to get around both of these problems. Rather than ask whether the later person *remembers* the earlier person's life, we can ask whether a *chain of memories* connects the two individuals. When Y remembers X's life directly, then the chain is short: Y and X are the same person because Y remembers being X. However, in other cases the chain may be longer. In Reid's example the young man connects the general to the boy. The general is the same person as the young man because the general remembers being the young man; the young man is the same person as the boy because the young man remembers being the boy; and so, the general is the same person as the boy. In my earlier example, though I don't remember what I was thinking an hour ago, I do remember what I was thinking five seconds ago; and five seconds ago I remembered what I was thinking ten seconds ago; and so on. Thus, we have:

> *The Memory-Links Theory:* X, who lived at an earlier time, is the same person (numerically) as Y, who lives at a later time, if and only if a chain of memories links X and Y.

This theory has an interesting implication about dreams. Most of us have forgotten our dreams by the time we wake up in the morning. Does this mean that we were not the ones who had the dreams? According to the Memory-Links Theory, the key is whether a chain of memories can link "Morning Person" to "Dream Person," thus establishing their identity. When you dream, you sometimes dream about real events or real people. If so, a chain can be found: Dream Person and Morning Person may both remember something that happened before the dream. So, the link would go: Morning Person → Earlier Person → Dream Person, and all three are the same person. If, however, Dream Person remembered nothing about Earlier Person, then no link would exist. In that case Morning Person would not have been the one who had the dream. Rather, Dream Person would have existed only during the dream.

Memory and Responsibility. Locke favored the Memory Theory not only because it explains how we might survive death but because it fits with our beliefs about responsibility and punishment. In discussing the prince and the cobbler, Locke notes that the individual with the prince's memories will be held accountable for the prince's past actions; and from this he concludes that the individual with the prince's memories *is* the prince, even though he has the cobbler's body. Personhood follows the memories, not the body.

This argument is complicated. Let's consider it in its most general form:

(1) Memory always goes with responsibility. (Whether you should be held responsible for an action depends on whether you can remember doing it.)

(2) Responsibility always goes with identity. (You are always responsible for what you do; you are never responsible for what others do.)

(3) Therefore, memory always goes with identity.

(4) Therefore, some version of the Memory Theory is true.

What are we to make of this? In defense of the first premise, responsibility does seem to depend on memory. Suppose my old roommate, John Smith, committed a crime—say, he robbed a bank—but then he suffered amnesia. When he is now shown the surveillance video of the robbery, he is amazed. In these circumstances it would indeed seem strange to blame him. Because he cannot remember committing the crime, he no longer seems to be a proper target of our indignation.

However, this line of thought is too weak to justify the first premise. It does not show that memory *always* goes with responsibility, as the premise states. Suppose that, after many years in prison, a murderer serving a life sentence has changed—perhaps he has become religious, or has written a remorseful autobiography, or has simply matured. If we are convinced that the transformation is genuine, we may conclude that it is no longer appropriate to keep him behind bars. The prisoner *remembers* committing the act, but he is no longer responsible for having done it. In this scenario memory doesn't go along with responsibility. Also, responsibility does not go along with identity, in violation of the second premise: The prisoner is the person who committed the crime, but he is no longer responsible for it.

The idea here is that responsibility seems to depend on sameness of person in the *qualitative* sense only. After his transformation the murderer is a "different person" in the sense that his character has changed fundamentally. That is why it may seem wrong to keep him locked up. We have "statutes of limitation" on many crimes partly for this reason: If someone shoplifted in 1979, we might wonder whether she is still the "same person" today, or whether her character has changed significantly in the intervening years. None of these thoughts need affect our belief that the reformed individual is the person who committed the crime—the *numerical-identity* claim holds true.

Is the Memory Theory Trivial? We have already cast some doubt on the Memory Theory—it looks as if memory may be relevant only to qualitative identity, not numerical identity. But there is another problem.

Memory is notoriously unreliable. We "remember" things that never happened, and we fail to remember things that did happen. Even when our recollections are mostly accurate, our memories will add fictitious details to fill in gaps, and we will be certain those details are true. For example, people almost universally believe they know what they were doing when they heard that President Reagan was shot, or that Princess Diana had died, or that the World Trade Center had collapsed. Psychologists call these "flashbulb memories." People have great confidence in them. But are they accurate? In 1986, when the space shuttle *Challenger* exploded, psychologist Ulric Neisser saw an opportunity to test the veracity of such memories. On the day after the disaster, he asked a group of people to write down what they had been doing when they heard the news. Two and a half years later, the same people were contacted and asked again what they had been doing when the disaster occurred. They were also asked how certain they were of their memories. They expressed great confidence in their memories, but Neisser's experiment showed that their confidence was an illusion. Only 3 of his 44 subjects gave answers that matched their earlier statements in detail, while over half the subjects gave answers that were simply wrong. Neisser, who had spent years studying memory, was not surprised.

The Memory-Links Theory says that X and Y are the same person if a chain of memories connects X and Y. But what do we mean by a chain of *memories*? We must distinguish real memories from apparent memories. Real memories are accurate representations of things that really happened to us, while apparent memories include the false "recollections" that sometimes mislead us. When Y remembers doing what X did, is the memory real or apparent? Obviously, the theory cannot be referring to apparent memories. If it were, then it would imply that any lunatic who "remembered" writing *Hamlet* would be Shakespeare. So the theory must be referring to real memories—X is the same person as Y if a chain of *accurate* memories links X to Y. This seems correct, but only because it is an empty statement. Of course, if Y accurately remembers doing something X did, then he was X—this follows from what "accurate" means. Bishop Butler, the British moralist, noticed this problem in 1736: "[O]ne should really think it self-evident," he wrote, "that consciousness of personal identity presupposes, and therefore cannot constitute, personal identity." In other words, a theory focusing on memory cannot explain why X and Y are the same person, if the notion of memory presupposes that X and Y are the same person.

Conclusion. The Same-Body Theory and the Memory Theory are the most obvious attempts to define personal identity over time. However, there are others. We have already mentioned the theory that emphasizes the brain. Other theories focus on personality, on causal connections, or on some combination of features. Different philosophers favor different approaches.

What is most striking in all this is what philosophers today seem to agree on. They agree that the Bundle Theory, not the Soul Theory, is the correct view of personal identity at a moment. And so they think that identity over time has to do with the continuation of certain bodily or mental features, not with the ongoing existence of a soul, or an ego, or a self, or a kernel.

If these philosophers are right, then we might have to reevaluate our attitudes about life and death. Right now we care far more about ourselves than about others, and we regard our own deaths with horror. These attitudes seem to go along with the Soul Theory: If I am a kernel—if my identity consists in a simple and indivisible entity that is *me*—then naturally I will care especially about that kernel, and I will not want it to be snuffed out for all eternity. However, on the Bundle Theory, both my life and my death appear different. I am just a body combined with certain mental states. There is nothing special about what I am, except for the trivial fact that no two people are exactly alike. When I die, nothing magical will happen.

In the future there will be other minds and other bodies, but none of those minds and bodies will bear the right relation to me in order for us to say that I am one of them.

As Derek Parfit has noted, these changes in our outlook might be liberating. We might care more about others, and we might worry less about our own death. Meanwhile, the question of whether the individual in heaven is you or is only your duplicate may suddenly seem trivial. There are a limited number of relevant facts: We know that you, on earth, have various thoughts, memories, and so on; and we know that the individual in heaven has similar thoughts, memories, and so on. In addition, we may have information about the kind of cause-and-effect relations that obtain between the earthly mental states and the heavenly mental states. But these are all the facts there are. If we ask whether the individual in heaven is *you*, and we mean to be requesting some further information, we are going to be disappointed. The person in heaven has no soul, and neither do people on earth.

CHAPTER 6

Body and Mind

> How it is that anything so remarkable as a state of consciousness comes about as a result of irritating nervous tissue, is just as unaccountable as the appearance of the Djinn when Aladdin rubbed his lamp.
> —T. H. HUXLEY, *LESSONS IN ELEMENTARY PHYSIOLOGY* (1866)

6.1. Descartes and Elizabeth

Like Socrates, René Descartes (1596–1650) believed that the body and the soul are different kinds of things. Using traditional terminology, Descartes said that they are different *substances.* The body is a material substance. It is like a machine, with parts that work together according to the laws of physics; and, like a machine, a body is incapable of thought and feeling. The soul, on the other hand, is an immaterial substance. It weighs nothing and has no measurable dimensions. But it does have thoughts and feelings. One's entire mental life is the life of the soul. A human being is therefore a compound entity, a combination of a body and a soul.

Mind–Body Dualism. The mind–body problem arises because there seem to be two radically different kinds of facts about human beings. On the one hand, there are *physical facts:* A woman may be five feet tall, with green eyes, a heart, a brain, and two big toes. On the other hand, there are *mental facts* about her: She has beliefs, desires, and intentions. The problem is to explain the nature of the mental facts and their relation to the physical facts.

Mind–Body Dualism is one attempt to solve this problem. This theory says that the mind and the body are different kinds of things: The body is physical, while the mind is nonphysical.

71

So, physical facts are facts about the body, while mental facts are about the mind. To prove that the body and mind are different, Descartes observed that we can imagine the body without the mind, and the mind without the body. We can imagine a human robot—someone who was physically like us but had no consciousness or inner life. And we can imagine spirits—creatures with emotions and desires but no bodies. If two things can exist without each other, then they are not the same thing. Thus, body and mind are distinct. This has been called The Conceivability Argument.

Descartes also emphasized two differences between mental states and physical states.

Privileged access: Each person has special access to his or her own mental states. Mental facts and physical facts are known in different ways. Physical facts are known by observation and experiment. Thus, they are publicly available: Anyone can look at you and see how tall you are. You yourself have no special access to such information. You learn your height in the same way that everyone else does, by looking and seeing. In fact, other people may know more about your body than you know. A physiologist may know that your heart has four chambers, even if you are ignorant of that fact. Your doctor may know that your blood has a high sugar-content, while you know nothing about it.

The situation with respect to mental facts is different. Mental states are private. Each person has special access, through introspection, to his or her own thoughts. You know that you are thinking of Marilyn Monroe simply because you are aware of having those thoughts, while other people will know only if you tell them.

Infallibility: Each person is infallible with respect to his or her own mental states. We can easily be mistaken about physical facts, including facts about ourselves. A woman might believe she is five-feet-one when really she is only five feet. You might believe you have an appendix, because you have forgotten the operation you had as a child. Of course, we may believe some things about ourselves with a high degree of confidence. You may feel certain, for example, that you have two arms. But, at least in principle, you could be wrong about even that. You could be crazy, or, as Descartes says, an evil demon could be deceiving you.

But, once again, the story about mental facts is different. Each of us, Descartes said, is infallible when it comes to the contents of our own minds. If you think you are feeling pain, then you are. You cannot be mistaken, not even in principle. (Imagine that, when you tell your doctor you need a painkiller, she replies: "I'm sorry, but you're mistaken—you really aren't feeling anything." That would be crazy.) Similarly, if you sincerely believe you are thinking about a blonde-haired woman, then you are.

Of course, you may be mistaken about the causes of your mental states. You may believe you are hearing a flute when in reality you are only hearing a computer-generated simulacrum. But *that you are hearing sounds of a certain nature* is beyond doubt. Similarly, you may have false beliefs about Marilyn Monroe— you may be thinking of the star of Alfred Hitchcock's *The Birds*, believing it was Miss Monroe, when really you are thinking of Tippi Hedren. But *that you are thinking of a woman with a certain appearance* is undeniable. Descartes' point was that we can never be mistaken about what our current experience is like.

Elizabeth's Objections. Born into a well-to-do French family, Descartes took a law degree when he was 20 and then joined the army of Bavaria, which, he said, would give him the free time he needed for his intellectual work. After a couple of years he quit the army and moved to Paris. Later, when his writings became controversial, he lived for 20 years in Holland, a country with a long history of providing safe haven for radical thinkers and persecuted minorities. He became a favorite of royal ladies. In 1649 Sweden's Queen Christina invited him to Stockholm to teach her philosophy. There he died of pneumonia, brought on, legend has it, by having to give her lessons at 5 A.M.

Another royal lady who played a part in Descartes' life was Princess Elizabeth of Bohemia (1618–1680). Elizabeth was a gifted woman who might herself have become a great philosopher, had social customs been different. As it was, she spent her life in genteel poverty, and in later life she became the abbess of a Protestant convent. She never married, she said, because she preferred intellectual pursuits. In 1642 she read Descartes' *Meditations on First Philosophy* and began a correspondence with him that lasted until his death. In these letters she identified one of the main difficulties with Mind–Body Dualism.

The problem is that it seems inconceivable how a non-physical mind could interact with a physical body. It is obvious that mental events can cause physical events—you decide to do something, and your body responds. It is equally obvious that events in your body cause events in your mind—when light waves of a certain length strike your eye, you see red; when you step on a tack, you feel pain. But if the body is physical and the mind is nonphysical, how is this interaction possible? Elizabeth put the question bluntly:

> I beg of you to tell me how the human soul can determine the movement of the animal spirits in the body so as to perform voluntary acts—being as it is merely a conscious substance. For the determination of movement seems always to come about from the moving body's being propelled—to depend on the kind of impulse it gets from what sets it in motion, or again, on the nature and shape of this latter thing's surface. Now the first two conditions involve contact, and the third involves that the impelling thing has extension; but you utterly exclude extension from your notion of soul, and contact seems to me incompatible with a thing's being immaterial.

Descartes did not have a good answer. He wrote back and suggested, somewhat lamely, that the mind might work like gravity. At that time, before Newton, gravity was thought of as something inside objects that causes them to move toward the center of the earth. Similarly, the mind might be something inside a human body that causes it to move.

Elizabeth was unimpressed. "I cannot see," she replied, "why this should convince us that a body may be impelled by something immaterial." Instead of thinking that gravity is an "immaterial cause," she said, we should search for a better understanding of what gravity is. She also expressed puzzlement about what "immaterial substances" are supposed to be. She complained that immaterial substances are always defined in terms of what they are *not:* An immaterial object has no mass, it does not occupy space, and so on. But what *is* it? Elizabeth was perplexed: "[T]he immaterial . . . I have never been able to conceive *that,* except as a negation of matter, which can have no communication with matter."

Faced with such a trenchant and unyielding critic, Descartes was out of ideas. With nothing further to offer, he concluded the exchange by assuring the princess that the subject was very difficult and telling her that she should not spend too much time worrying about it.

Radical Emergence. Another problem for Mind–Body Dualism is to explain why the immaterial mind exists at all. In the womb, a human being begins as a purely physical thing. But then one day, after the brain has reached a certain level of complexity, poof!— a new kind of substance pops into existence. Why? And remember that human beings are not the only conscious animals. Life existed on earth for hundreds of millions of years before a species evolved that could think and feel. So, for millions of years, there were only physical systems on earth. And then one day, seemingly out of nowhere, consciousness comes on the scene. Why? This is called *the problem of radical emergence.* On Dualism, as Huxley said, the emergence of mind from matter seems inexplicable, like the emergence of the genie from the lamp.

Despite the objections, Mind–Body Dualism remained popular well into the twentieth century. The theory finally faded away because it did not fit the emerging scientific picture of what people are like. As the scientific understanding of human beings advanced, Cartesian immaterial substances came to seem more and more like ghosts and ectoplasm. The result is that, while Mind–Body Dualism still has some defenders, the theory has largely disappeared from science and philosophy.

6.2. Materialist Theories of the Mind

A human being is a vast collection of atoms, organized in a complicated way, obeying the laws of physics, chemistry, and biology. Materialism claims that this is *all* we are—we have no ghostly, nonphysical parts. Materialism is, of course, a controversial doctrine, and the debate over materialism is often taken to be a debate about religion. Here, however, the issue is not religion but the nature of mental facts. Materialist theories of the mind attempt to explain those facts in purely physical terms. Is any such theory defensible?

There are two ways to proceed. A materialist theory could focus on what we can observe about people from the outside—their speech and behavior. Or it could focus on what goes on inside the person—occurrences in the person's brain. Each of these possibilities has been tried.

The First Materialist Theory: Behaviorism. Can we explain the nature of thoughts and feelings purely in terms of behavior? Intuitively, this seems to get things backwards—behavior is explained by reference to thoughts and feelings. When someone shouts at us, we say it is because she is angry; when someone grabs a sandwich, we say it is because he is hungry.

For ordinary purposes such explanations may do just fine. However, according to a school of thought known as Behaviorism, which flourished among academic psychologists during the middle of the twentieth century, such "mentalistic" explanations have no place in a scientific account of human behavior. Psychologists John B. Watson (1878–1958) and B. F. Skinner (1904–1990) were the leading figures in this movement.

Science, they said, deals with what is publicly observable, and private inner states do not qualify. So, rather than saying "Jane shouted because she was angry," behaviorists would focus on Jane's situation and the events that triggered her outcry. She shouted, for example, because she was surrounded by noisy children, and one of them squirted water in her ear. According to Watson and Skinner, the science of psychology looks for patterns of stimulus and response—physical responses (shouting) to physical stimuli (noise, water in the ear)—and formulates general laws about how behavior is shaped by physical inputs. Private mental episodes are irrelevant.

Watson and Skinner were *methodological* behaviorists. They did not deny that private mental states exist; they said only that such states have nothing to do with science. Internal mental states play no part in causing behavior, and so for scientific purposes they can be ignored. It is not that the noisy children and the water in her ear caused her to be angry, and that being angry caused her to shout. Instead, the noisy children and the water in the ear caused her to shout.

It was only a small additional step to say that private mental states do not exist at all, and philosophical behaviorists such as Gilbert Ryle (1900–1976) took that step. Ryle's book *The Concept of Mind* (1949) was, for a brief time, the most widely discussed book of philosophy in the English language. Ryle argued—or anyway, he has been interpreted as arguing—that so-called mental states are really nothing more than behavior. Some mental states consist in patterns of current behavior: To be angry is to be aggressive, to shout, to use harsh words, to strike out, or to turn one's back on someone. (There is a wide range of behavior associated with anger, rather than one specific behavior. That is typical.) Other mental states consist in a tendency to behave in certain ways on suitable occasions. You may want a donut, for example, even though you are currently doing nothing about it. Nonetheless, if you want it, you must be disposed to seek it when it is available, and (if you want it badly enough) you must be disposed to celebrate like Homer Simpson when you get it. Similarly, to be afraid of something is to be disposed to tremble and flee from it when you are in its presence. So Jane's being angry does not cause her to shout; rather, her anger *consists in* her shouting. This version of Behaviorism was called *Analytical Behaviorism* because it tries to "analyze" mental states in terms of behavior.

Ryle ridiculed Descartes' view as "the dogma of the Ghost in the Machine," and the image stuck. By exorcising the ghost, behaviorists avoided the problems that had plagued Mind–Body Dualism. Gone were the problems of explaining what nonmaterial substances are, why they came to exist, and how they interact with physical bodies. These were problems for those who believe in ghosts.

The ideas of privileged access and infallibility also fell by the wayside. The behaviorists noted that an outside observer can often see that someone is angry, or afraid, or in love, just as easily as, or perhaps even more easily than, the person herself. As for infallibility, only a little reflection is needed to realize how often we are wrong about our own mental states. Someone who is depressed, or afraid, or resentful, will often think otherwise; and what you want may sometimes be more obvious to other people than it is to you. So it looks as if our "mental" states are in fact publicly observable, which makes it unnecessary to understand them as private "inner" episodes.

The Failure of Behaviorism. Behaviorism was appealing because of its no-nonsense, scientific stance. Nonetheless, after enjoying almost a half-century of popularity, it was ultimately abandoned by most psychologists and philosophers. In psychology the behaviorist research program was replaced by cognitivist projects, while in philosophy Analytical Behaviorism could not be defended against a number of objections.

First, Analytical Behaviorism seems false on its face. At any given moment, each of us is aware of having perceptions, thoughts, and so on, even if no behavior is occurring. While sitting in my armchair, all sorts of mental activity may be going on: I can see the green wall in front of me; I can feel the chair's fabric beneath my hand; and all the while I am thinking about how no one except a few astronauts has ever seen the dark side of the moon. It just seems false to say that this mental activity consists of nothing but behavior or possible behavior. The stream of consciousness seems to have a reality of its own, independent of its connection (or lack of connection) to behavior.

Second, not every mental state can be understood as a pattern of behavior or as a disposition to behave. So long as we concentrate on examples such as fear and desire, the behaviorist analysis seems plausible. But consider a different sort of example, say, the experience of listening to Chopin's Nocturne in C Minor—what pattern of behavior is this sublime experience supposed to consist in? And is this behavior different from the behavior associated with listening to Bach's Mass in B Minor? To put the matter even more simply, think of how a major chord sounds and how a minor chord sounds. Is the difference between them supposed to be a difference in behavior? The idea of trying to explain the difference between these experiences by reference to different behavior is too far-fetched to take seriously.

Third, it seems possible for two people to behave in exactly the same way and yet have different mental states. In the seventeenth century John Locke suggested that one person's sense organs might differ from another's, so that in the same circumstances in which one person sees red, the other sees blue. In stopping at a traffic light on a clear day, one person would see the sky as blue and the light as red, while the other would see the sky as red and the light as blue. However, their behavior would be indistinguishable—they would both *say* "That's red" when looking at the light, because each of them would have learned to call that color "red." This example is known as the "inverted spectrum." If this happened, their visual experiences would be different, but their behavior would be the same. This seems to show that, whatever a mind is, it is not behavior.

With the failure of Behaviorism, scientifically minded philosophers looked for an alternative explanation of mental facts.

The Second Materialist Theory: Mind–Brain Identity. Events in the brain cause mental experiences. This can be experimentally confirmed in various ways. One way was discovered by Wilder Penfield, a Canadian physician who developed techniques for operating on the brain while the patient is awake, using only a local anesthetic. He started doing this in the 1930s and 1940s in order to treat patients with severe epilepsy. Epileptic seizures, he thought, must be triggered by events in a diseased part of the brain. Therefore, if he could surgically remove the diseased part, he might be able to stop them. But how could the precise bit be identified? The key turned out to be that patients reported seeing lights and hearing sounds at the onset of the seizures. Penfield reasoned that, if he could locate the part of the brain that caused these experiences, he would know what part to cut out.

So, while his patients were fully conscious, Penfield would use an electric probe to stimulate their brains, and the patients would report what they were experiencing. One patient said he was sitting in a railway station. Another said he was snatching a stick from the mouth of a dog. Others said they were watching a circus wagon or hearing the music from the Broadway show *Guys and Dolls*. The patients did not say they were *remembering* these experiences; they said they were *having* them. Feelings such as fear and loneliness were also reported. In each case the experience could be repeated by restimulating the same spot in the brain.

Penfield was not trying to prove any philosophical theory, but his results strengthened the conviction that, in some important sense, the mind *is* the brain. Penfield seemed to have identified, in a crude way, the location in the brain of particular conscious experiences. Today we often see the identity of the mind and the brain asserted as one of the main findings of twentieth-century neurology. But is this identification to be taken literally? Many philosophers argued that it is literally true. Mental events, they said, are not ghostly; nor are they behavioral. Instead, they are neurological. Each of a person's mental states is identical with the firing of particular neurons, or cells, in the brain.

The Mind–Brain Identity Theory, as it was called, was developed by a number of thinkers, including psychologist U. T. Place in England and philosophers J. J. C. Smart and D. M. Armstrong in Australia and David Lewis in the United States. Armstrong gave the following argument for the theory:

> Behaviourism is certainly wrong, but perhaps it is not altogether wrong. Perhaps the Behaviourists are wrong in identifying the mind and mental occurrences with behaviour, but perhaps they are right in thinking that our notion of a mind and of individual mental states *is logically tied to behaviour.* For perhaps what we mean by a mental state is some state of the person which, under suitable circumstances, *brings about* a certain range of behaviour. Perhaps mind can be defined not as behaviour, but rather as the inner *cause* of certain behaviour.
> . . . [I]f our notion of the mind and mental states is nothing but that of a cause within the person of certain ranges of behaviour, then it becomes a scientific question, and not a question of logical analysis, what in fact the intrinsic nature of that cause is. . . . [T]he verdict of modern science seems to be that the sole cause of mind-betokening behaviour in man and the higher animals is the physico-chemical workings of the central nervous system. And so, assuming we have correctly characterised our concept of a mental state as nothing but the cause of certain sorts of behaviour, then we can identify these mental states with purely physical states of the central nervous system.

To see how this works, consider an example such as *being in pain*. Pain is a good example of a mental state: It feels a certain way, subjectively, and, as Descartes said, each of us is aware of our own pain in a way that others are not. But what is pain? There is, first of all, a necessary connection between pain and behavior. If someone is in pain, she will be disposed to flinch, tighten her muscles, wince, cry out, and take action to stop the pain. She will also be disposed to say things like "That hurts" or to respond positively when asked if it hurts. If someone has no inclination to behave in any of these ways, then it follows, logically, that the person is not in pain.

Therefore, "being in pain" may be defined as the state of the person that causes that sort of behavior. But what, exactly, causes that sort of behavior? This is where science comes in. Science tells us that this behavior is caused by particular neurological events. Therefore, we may conclude, pain *consists in* those neurological events. And we may hypothesize that other mental states are identical with other neurological states, even if we don't know which neurological states they are.

Of course, mental states do not *seem* like brain states. Being in pain, listening to Mozart, or thinking about Paris seems very different from neurons firing. But it is common in science to discover that a familiar kind of thing actually consists in something surprising and unfamiliar. Water, for example, is H_2O; lightning is an electrical discharge; and heat is molecular motion. Those who believe in the Mind–Brain Identity Theory thus have a ready answer to Descartes' Conceivability Argument. The idea that the mind and brain could exist without each other, they say, is an illusion. It is like the belief that water could exist without H_2O, or lightning could occur without electrical discharge, or heat could occur without molecular motion.

Advantages of the Mind–Brain Identity Theory. A philosophical theory gains credibility when it explains what needs explaining without falling into the problems that beset its rivals. From this perspective the Mind–Brain Identity Theory was a clear advance over both Mind–Body Dualism and Behaviorism. First, the Mind–Brain Identity Theory explained the nature of mental facts without any reference to ghostly "nonmaterial" entities. Mental facts are facts about the brain. Second, there is no problem in explaining how mental events cause physical events, and vice versa. Because mental events are occurrences in the brain, all causal interactions are interactions between physical things. Third, the theory can explain how thought occurs without any behavior occurring. Things can be happening in your brain— neurons fire as you think of Paris—even though there is no outward behavior.

Finally, the Mind–Brain Identity Theory helps us understand how introspection works. If mental events are occurrences in the brain, then introspection—which, after all, is just another mental event—is also an occurrence in the brain. Introspection is an "inner" process because its neural firings are not connected with inputs from the eyes and ears and other senses. Instead, they are connected internally with the brain events that constitute the thoughts being introspected. As a result, introspection gives us a special kind of access to our own mental states.

For all these reasons, the Mind–Brain Identity Theory seemed right. Here was a plausible, scientifically respectable view, free of the problems that plagued the other theories.

A Third Theory: Functionalism. There was a catch. The Mind–Brain Identity Theory holds that conscious experiences such as "being in pain" are identical with neurological occurrences in the brain. But suppose there was a life-form that had developed on another planet with a different biochemistry. Those beings might not have neurons like ours. According to the Mind–Brain Identity Theory, then, they could not feel pain. But that seems wrong. Why couldn't pain have some other physical basis for them? Perhaps, for them, being in pain would consist in contact between alien brain-particles that are different from the particles in our brains. In defining pain as identical with particular features of our brains, the Mind–Brain Identity Theory seems committed to an unfortunate sort of human chauvinism.

To bring this point into focus, it will help to distinguish between *tokens* and *types*. Suppose you and I each have a $20 bill in our pockets. We both have the same type of thing—a $20 bill—but the particular bill (the "token") in my pocket is not the particular bill in your pocket. The distinction may be obvious, but consider some further examples: *The Godfather* and *Casablanca* are tokens of the type "movie"; the Sears Tower and the Empire State Building are tokens of the type "skyscraper"; Everest and Kilimanjaro are tokens of the type "mountain."

"Neuron firing" is also a type that can have various tokens. The neuron firing that occurs in my brain at a particular time is one token of this type, while the neuron firing that occurs in your brain at a different time is another token of this type. The same goes for pain: The particular pain that I am feeling now is one token; the pain that you felt yesterday is another. Now, with this in mind, let us look again at the Mind–Brain Identity Theory. It turns out that there are two different theses that may be distinguished, only one of which is plausible:

1. *Type–type identity:* This is the idea that being in pain (considered as a type of thing) is identical with a particular sort of neuron firing (considered as a type of thing). It would follow from this that no one could

be in pain—no token of pain could exist—unless neurons were firing. This is implausible because, as we have seen, it would rule out any experience of pain in beings with a biochemistry different from ours.

2. *Token–token identity:* Each instance of pain is identical with some particular physical state. For example, the pain that I am feeling now is identical with the neuron firing that is now occurring in my brain, while the pain you felt yesterday was identical with the neuron firing that occurred in your brain at that time. Perhaps, for the extraterrestrial being we mentioned, the pain he felt on a certain occasion was identical with the specific instance of alien brain-particle contact that took place at that time. Token–token identity is the most plausible form of mind–brain identity.

The upshot is that, even if particular instances of pain may be identified with particular bodily states, the Mind–Brain Identity Theory provides no general understanding of what pain is. If we ask, "What is pain?" and we want to know, not about this or that particular pain, but about the nature of pain in general—that is, pain as a type of thing—then the Mind–Brain Identity Theory has no good answer.

These thoughts pointed the way to a new theory of the mind, which today is accepted by many philosophers, psychologists, and cognitive scientists. The new theory, Functionalism, still identifies pain (the type) with the activation of physical features of systems. But it does not characterize those features by reference to their physical composition. Instead, pain is identified with *whatever* physical features of a system serve a certain function within that system. As a first approximation, we may say that *pain is the activation of any feature of a physical system that serves the same function, in that system, as the neuron firings serve in us.* (Remember that pain is just an example; similar accounts will also be given for other mental states.)

What, exactly, is the "function" that the neuron firings serve in us? We may think about this in terms of inputs, outputs, and relations to other mental states. The inputs are the physical occurrences that impinge upon your sense organs—for example, a hammer falls on your foot. The outputs include your speech, behavior, and other physical reactions—for example, you wince, grab at your foot, and cry out. These are the outward manifestations of pain. The relations to other mental states include the fact that pain makes it hard for you to concentrate on other things. Now we ask what happens inside you that processes the inputs and produces the outputs and relations to other mental states, so that one causes the other. One answer, of course, is that you feel pain, but that isn't the answer we are looking for. We are looking for the feature of your physical system that mediates the inputs and outputs. There is a lot going on inside you, but as we develop a comprehensive theory to explain what is happening, we focus on the crucial part played by the neuron firings—these firings link these particular sorts of inputs with these particular sorts of outputs. That is their function in the system as a whole.

We can now say more precisely what pain is. According to Functionalism, being in pain is identical with the activation of any feature of a system that serves this function—that links these kinds of inputs, outputs, and relations to other internal states. For you, therefore, a particular token of pain may be a neural firing, while for an extraterrestrial a particular token of pain may be the activation of a different internal mechanism. The physical character of the mechanism doesn't matter. All that matters is that the mechanism serves the appropriate function. I should add that, strictly speaking, the mechanism does not *have to be* physical. A nonphysicalist Functionalism is possible: Mental events could be nonphysical, provided that they played the appropriate causal role within the overall system. But I leave this possibility aside and assume that the most sensible version of Functionalism is a form of Materialism.

A Problem with Functionalism. Functionalism has joined the Mind–Brain Identity Theory as a leading theory of the mind. It seems to incorporate the insights of the earlier theories while avoiding their problems. But is it successful?

Functionalism implies that any sufficiently complex system will have a mind and that the physical composition of the system doesn't matter. We humans are made of flesh and blood, but the flesh and blood are not essential—we could be made of other stuff, like the extraterrestrials, and still be "thinking things." We could even be made of silicon chips, like a computer.

For this reason researchers in the field of artificial intelligence (AI) are strongly attracted to Functionalism. Functionalism supports the idea, common in AI circles, that the mind may be understood as a type of digital program. The relation between body and mind, it is said, is like the relation between hardware and software. A computer is an inert, lifeless thing until a program starts running. Then it accepts inputs, performs operations on them, and produces outputs. A human brain works in the same way: It accepts inputs, performs operations, and produces outputs. Thus, what we call the mind is simply the program running in the brain. Of course, human minds are enormously more complicated than any computer program yet written. Nonetheless, if a self-correcting, "learning" program running on a computer operated at the same level of complexity, accepting the same inputs and yielding the same outputs, it would have the same mental states that we have. And it would have those mental states for the same reason we have them.

But while this implication of the theory makes it attractive to many people, it is also a source of weakness. Functionalism says that the physical composition of a system doesn't matter; all that matters is how it operates. Is that true? Suppose we imagine a system consisting of a vast collection of beer cans connected by wires and pulleys and powered by windmills, so that the beer cans' clanking against one another exactly parallels the firings of neurons in someone's brain. Would this contraption be conscious? Functionalism implies that it would be, but critics of Functionalism think this is absurd.

6.3. Doubts about Materialist Theories

Each theory we've considered has its own particular problems. But there are two additional problems that threaten all materialist approaches.

Subjectivity. Think of "what it is like" to see a green lawn or to taste a plum. Don't think of anything that merely accompanies the experience, like playing golf or being at your grandmother's farm, but think of the experience itself: the way green looks and the way the plum tastes. These experiences have a subjective character; there is something that it is like to see that color and taste that fruit. More generally, there is something that it is like to be you, to move through the world perceiving it from your point of view, experiencing the sights, sounds, smells, touches, and emotions that make up your life. This is what makes you so different from a mere physical object, such as a brick. There is nothing it is like to be a brick. It would be impossible to see the world from the brick's point of view, because the brick has no point of view.

Being the subject of experiences is the essence of what it is to have a mind. Therefore, above all else, this is what we should expect a theory of the mind to tell us about. Yet the subjective character of experience is missing from the materialist theories we have been considering. Those theories talk about behavior, brain states, and system functionings. But nothing in all this matches the look of green or the taste of the plum. How can a brain state or a computational process be the taste of a plum? To assert that they are identical seems more like a statement of the problem than a solution to it.

Could some different materialist theory, not yet devised, do better in this regard? Or could a modification of one of the familiar theories enable it to explain subjectivity? Of course, it is impossible to say that this could not happen. But the problem cuts very deep. None of the available physical facts—facts about behavior, neuron firings, and the rest—seems to be the *kind* of thing that could be the look of green or the taste of a plum, because the latter have a subjective character that the former lack.

Intentionality. Materialist theories also seem unable to accommodate what Franz Brentano (1838–1917) called the "intentionality" of mental states. Brentano was a German philosopher whose best-known work is *Psychology from an Empirical Standpoint* (1874), in which he addresses the nature of mental states.

Mental states, Brentano says, are always *about* things other than themselves. My desire to see Paris is about Paris; your belief that seawater is salty is about seawater; the math student's bafflement is about the square root of minus 1. This simple feature of mental states, which you may think is too obvious to mention, poses a formidable problem for materialist theories of the mind. How can a physical state, considered simply as a physical state, be "about" anything? How can a group of firing neurons be about Paris, seawater, or the square root of minus 1?

There are a couple of ways in which we might try to understand how physical objects could be intentional, but neither works very well. One idea is that a physical object can be about something by *resembling* it. A picture of Queen Elizabeth, for example, is "about" the queen because it looks like her. But this idea does not get us far, for several reasons.

First, resemblance is a symmetrical relationship—the picture resembles the queen, but the queen also resembles the picture. Yet the queen is not "about" the picture. So the relation of "being about" cannot be the same as the relation of "resembling." Second, brain states do not look like Paris, or seawater, or Queen Elizabeth, or much of anything else. To the naked eye the brain looks like squishy reddish grey stuff; under a microscope a neuron looks like a little clump with lots of stringy appendages. If "aboutness" consisted in resemblance, neurons could be about lightning bolts or bushes, but not much more. Third, we can think about the square root of minus 1 and have beliefs about it, but no physical state could resemble it, because the square root of minus 1 does not look like anything. The notion of resemblance, therefore, is no help.

Another idea, popular among philosophers, is that brain states can be about objects if the brain state is *causally related* to the object in some appropriate way. For example, a certain state of my brain may have been produced by my having seen Queen Elizabeth, and that is what makes it about her.

The evaluation of this idea involves some complex issues; nonetheless, there is one fairly simple reason why all causal theories of "aboutness" are implausible. Many of our thoughts are about things that do not exist—unicorns, Martians, honest politicians—and nonexistent things cannot participate in the causal chains that make our neurons fire. Moreover, other objects of thought, such as the square root of minus 1, could not possibly enter into causal relations.

It does not look as if physical states could be intentional. This seems to show that, whatever mental states are, they are not states of the brain. But we should not be too eager to draw this conclusion. Intentionality is a puzzling notion. It is the subject of ongoing debate and study, and no one has yet produced an account that satisfies even the majority of investigators. Moreover, intentionality is not just a problem for materialism; it is a problem for any theory of the mind. If you believed, like Socrates and Descartes, that the mind is immaterial, you would still face the problem of explaining how fluctuations in an immaterial substance can be about the queen, or about Paris, or about a unicorn. The problem would be just as difficult for you as for the Mind–Brain Identity theorists. A more prudent course, therefore, might be to await further developments. For now, no one knows how to solve the mind–body problem.

CHAPTER 7

Could a Machine Think?

Philosophers have been dreaming about AI for centuries.
—DANIEL C. DENNETT, *BRAINCHILDREN* (1998)

7.1. Brains and Computers

In 1637 René Descartes considered the question of whether machines could think, and he decided they could not. The sign of intelligence, he said, is the ability to understand language, but machines could never do that:

> It is indeed conceivable that a machine could be made so that it would utter words, and even words appropriate to the presence of physical acts or objects which cause some change in its organs; as, for example, if it was touched in some spot that it would ask what you wanted to say to it; if in another, that it would cry that it was hurt, and so on for similar things. But it could never modify its phrases to reply to the sense of whatever was said in its presence as even the most stupid men can do.

Descartes was right about the machines he was familiar with. No assembly of levers, cogs, and pulleys could chat with you about the latest fashions. But the modern computer is different. As computational power increases, it seems inevitable that a computer will be able to "modify its phrases" to chat with you about clothes, or baseball, or anything else.

If this happened—if a computer could respond appropriately to any question you asked—would the computer really be intelligent, or would it be just a clever electronic trick? The intelligent robots in science-fiction stories and movies (there are many to choose from) can talk fluently. Should we think of them as conscious beings, with an inner life of thoughts and feelings, or should we think of them only as mechanical contrivances that mimic human sounds and movements?

7.2. An Argument That Machines Could Think

The idea that machines could have conscious thoughts may seem unremarkable to generations raised with computers and science-fiction stories about intelligent robots. Nonetheless, it is a controversial thesis. Here is a line of thought that supports the idea.

The Piecemeal-Replacement Argument. This argument involves a bizarre, unrealistic story. Such stories are called "thought experiments," because you're merely invited to think about them—you couldn't possibly set them up in a lab.

Our story begins by supposing that a small piece of your brain becomes diseased, and as a result you go blind. But luckily, there is a new biomedical technique that can restore your sight. Scientists have developed a tiny silicon chip, too small to be seen with the naked eye, that duplicates the functions of the diseased part of your brain. They can cut out the diseased bit and replace it with the chip. After the operation you can see again. Otherwise, you cannot tell any difference. You are as good as new.

A little later, however, a different bit of your brain becomes diseased. This time you lose your ability to remember names. But once again, scientists are able to replace that bit with another tiny chip that does the same job, and when the surgery is over, you can tell no difference except that now you can remember names again.

Now imagine that this happens over and over, until your entire brain has been replaced. At each step in the process, you can detect no difference from before, except that a problem has been corrected. At the conclusion of the process, however, you no longer have an organic brain. Instead, you have an artificial brain, a patchwork of silicon chips that functions in exactly the same way as the original organic model.

If this story is possible, then not only could a machine think, but *you* could become that machine. If you doubt this, go back to the first step for a moment. Suppose you really did go blind, and scientists offered to restore your sight by implanting a device that would replace the function of the faulty part of your brain. Would you refuse, on the grounds that no artificial device could actually produce human sight? Would you prefer to remain blind? Most of us would grab the chance to have our sight restored in this way. But once the process of piecemeal replacement has begun, there is no point at which we may draw the line and say that *now* human consciousness has been extinguished. Nor may we say that consciousness is being extinguished a little bit at a time. After all, you can still see, remember names, and so on. If the replacement brain can do everything the original could do, and there is no point at which you feel "different," then we must conclude that the artificial brain is sustaining the same mental life as the original.

There is one further step in the argument. Suppose nothing goes wrong with your brain, and you undergo no operations. Instead, scientists assemble the same parts in the laboratory and put them into a robot. Would the robot be a conscious, thinking thing? If we grant that this collection of parts could sustain a mental life inside your skull, there is no reason why it should not do the same inside the robot's head. Thus, the robot would be a thinking being in the same sense that you are a thinking being.

The Objection That Computers Can Do Only What They Are Programmed to Do. At this point a familiar objection may be raised. Computers, it will be said, can do only what they are programmed to do. They can never go beyond their programs or display any genuine creativity. A chess-playing computer, for example, is just making moves mechanically, according to its program, without understanding anything about chess. Indeed, when we say it is "playing" chess, we are speaking metaphorically—it is really just a mechanical contrivance that, when supplied with certain physical inputs, gives back certain physical outputs. It has no awareness of what is happening or of its significance for chess. And if your brain were replaced by a computer that could play chess, you would be no better off.

This may look like a simple objection, but it raises a host of complex issues. The objection is partly true, partly false, partly irrelevant, and partly question begging.

The true part is that present-day chess computers are not conscious of what they are doing. They are relatively simple machines that merely process inputs and return outputs according to their programs. Moreover, the main method used by these computers—the brute-force search of a billion moves per second—bears no relation to how human chess masters think.

Nonetheless, it is not true that computers cannot "go beyond" what their programmers put into them. In carrying out their instructions, even present-day computers have produced new, unexpected knowledge. The best-known achievement of a chess-playing computer came in 1997 when Deep Blue, an IBM machine, defeated world champion Garry Kasparov in a six-game match. The victory of "machine over man" was highly publicized, but the chess community shrugged it off. It was a different result that got chess players talking. Certain endgames that had been considered draws were shown by computer analysis to be wins. The two-bishops-and-king versus knight-and-king endgame, for example, was proved to be a win for the side with the two bishops—but the proof consists of long, massively branching lines of analysis that no human being could master. When this endgame arises in human tournaments, there is no telling whether the game will end in a win or a draw.

The limitations of present-day computers, however, are irrelevant to the question of whether computers may someday be conscious. Current chess-playing computers might not be aware of what they're doing because they only play chess; perhaps we could add some other features to them that would make them conscious. To say that this is impossible because a computer will always be executing programs, and nothing more, begs the question. Perhaps *we* are only executing programs, but of a very complex kind. Maybe, or maybe not—but the simple assertion that we must be doing something more does not advance the discussion.

The Tipping Point Objection. There is a better objection to the Piecemeal-Replacement Argument. The argument assumes that nothing dramatic will happen as your brain is gradually replaced by silicon chips. In particular, it assumes that no single change will cause the lights to go out—no replacement will result in the immediate loss of whatever consciousness you have left.

That assumption can be questioned. Normally, we think of the world as changing gradually: Dust accumulates on the TV set; hairlines recede; our bank balance drifts down from the moment we get paid. However, a great many processes hit thresholds, or *tipping points:* One more drop of water causes the pitcher to spill over; one more banana peel causes the compost heap to catch fire; one more soldier allows the defensive line to be held and the battle to be won. Couldn't a tipping point be reached in the case of piecemeal brain replacement? Some small change might pull the plug on whatever system in the brain undergirds consciousness. If so, the Piecemeal-Replacement Argument might get its appeal merely from our ignorance—our ignorance of which part of the brain can't be replaced without the immediate loss of consciousness.

7.3. The Turing Test

Most researchers in the field of artificial intelligence (AI) believe that they would be creating a conscious machine if they could program a computer to do everything a human being can do. Any protests about human "uniqueness" would be empty metaphysics and of no interest to science. This belief was expressed by one of the twentieth century's great figures, the British mathematician Alan Turing.

In 1936 the 24-year-old Turing published a paper called "On Computable Numbers, with an Application to the *Entscheidungsproblem*" in the *Proceedings of the London Mathematical Society.* The purpose of the paper was to solve a problem in mathematical logic, but in the course of doing so, Turing described, for the first time, the idea of a digital, stored-program, general-purpose computer. At that time no such machines existed, but Turing understood what they would be like and how they would work.

When World War II broke out, Turing joined the team of code breakers at Bletchley Park, outside London, where he played a key part in deciphering German codes. In the first few years of the war, when the outcome was in doubt, the work at Bletchley was critical. Without it, for example, ships bringing supplies from America could not evade German submarines. To help crack the codes, one of the first electronic computers, the Colossus, was built. Years later, I. J. Good, a member of the

Bletchley team, told an interviewer: "I won't say that what Turing did made us win the war, but I daresay we might have lost it without him." You might expect Turing to have been hailed as a hero after the war. But the work done at Bletchley remained top secret for many years, and Turing's contribution remained unknown.

Turing realized that the development of the computer raised a new philosophical question—or at least, it posed an old question in a new, more urgent way. In 1950 he published a paper called "Computing Machinery and Intelligence" in the philosophical journal *Mind*. It began with the words "I propose to consider the question, Can machines think?" At that time the question struck most people as absurd, but Turing predicted that by the end of the century computers would have developed to the point where their "thinking" would no longer seem out of the question. Turing was a smart man.

Turing approached the issue of machine thought by asking how we might *tell* whether a machine was thinking. The basic idea of the Turing Test is this: Take two humans and a computer, and put them in different rooms, allowing them to communicate with one another only by typing messages. One of the humans—the interrogator—will ask questions of the other two and try to figure out, from their responses, which is the person and which is the computer. The interrogator can ask anything he likes—he can initiate discussions of poetry, religion, love, or the latest fashions. He can try to trip up the computer any way he can. The computer, meanwhile, will deny it is a machine. Turing imagines the following exchange:

Q: Please write me a sonnet on the subject of the Forth Bridge.
A: Count me out on this one. I never could write poetry.
Q: Add 34957 to 70764.
A: (Pause about 30 seconds and then give as answer) 105621.
Q: Do you play chess?
A: Yes.
Q: I have K at my K1, and no other pieces. You have only K at K6 and R at R1. It is your move. What do you play?
A: (After a pause of 15 seconds) R–R8 mate.

Is the responder a human or a machine? The pauses suggest it is a person who needs time for calculating. But the machine might be pausing in order to mimic a human being. After all, it doesn't want to give away that it is a machine.

To make the test fair, we must repeat the experiment several times, with different people involved. After each session the interrogator guesses which responder is the computer and which is the human being. If no more than half of the guesses are correct (the number that random guessing would produce), then the machine has passed the Turing Test. The computer's responses are indistinguishable from those of a human being.

Turing argued that if a machine passes this test—if we can tell no difference between its performance and that of another person—then the machine must have the mental properties of a person. After all, you take what I say as proof that I am conscious and intelligent. To be consistent, mustn't you also say that a computer giving the *same* verbal performance is equally conscious and intelligent? Of course, the machine does not look like a person, and it is made of different stuff. But so what? As one commentator put it, "If trees could converse with us as fluently as they do in some fairy tales, wouldn't you unhesitatingly say that trees can think?"

When Turing wrote his original paper, there were only four primitive electronic computers in existence, two in England and two in the United States. Of course, none of them could pass the test. Even today, the Turing Test remains out of reach. Despite the ubiquity and power of present-day computers, none can come close to passing it. Indeed, after a half-century of research in artificial intelligence, it is clearer than ever how difficult it would be to create and program a machine that matches or mimics human intelligence.

One famous AI product, Eliza, can converse in English, but only in a limited way. Eliza is a program developed at MIT that conducts therapeutic interviews with human beings. Here is a sample conversation between Eliza and a young woman. Eliza's comments are in capital letters:

Men are all alike.
IN WHAT WAY
They're always bugging us about something or other.
CAN YOU THINK OF A SPECIFIC EXAMPLE

Well, my boyfriend made me come here.
YOUR BOYFRIEND MADE YOU COME HERE
He says I'm depressed much of the time.
I AM SORRY TO HEAR THAT YOU ARE DEPRESSED
It's true that I am unhappy.
DO YOU THINK COMING HERE WILL HELP YOU
    NOT TO BE UNHAPPY
I need some help, that much seems certain.
WHAT WOULD IT MEAN TO YOU IF YOU GOT
    SOME HELP
Perhaps I could learn to get along with my mother.
TELL ME MORE ABOUT YOUR FAMILY
My mother takes care of me.
WHO ELSE IN YOUR FAMILY TAKES CARE OF YOU
My father.
YOUR FATHER
You are like my father in some ways.
WHAT RESEMBLANCE DO YOU SEE
You are not very aggressive but I think you don't want me
    to notice that.
WHAT MAKES YOU THINK I AM NOT VERY
    AGGRESSIVE
You don't argue with me.
WHY DO YOU THINK I DON'T ARGUE WITH YOU
You are afraid of me.
DOES IT PLEASE YOU TO BELIEVE I AM AFRAID
    OF YOU
My father is afraid of everybody.
WHAT ELSE COMES TO MIND WHEN YOU THINK
    OF YOUR FATHER
Bullies.
DOES THAT HAVE ANYTHING TO DO WITH THE
    FACT THAT YOUR BOYFRIEND MADE YOU COME
    HERE

Mostly, Eliza just turns people's words back on them. This doesn't look very impressive, and Eliza is not hard to trip up—the program can easily be tricked into producing gibberish. Joseph Weizenbaum, the program's creator, was alarmed at how easily some people would come to depend on Eliza, as though she were a human therapist. People would call him demanding Eliza's help. Articles appeared in professional journals suggesting that the program be made more widely available as a diagnostic aid. Weizenbaum's secretary began to insist that others leave the room so that she could talk to Eliza in private. Weizenbaum, who had never intended that the program be taken seriously, concluded that AI is dangerous and should be abandoned.

But Eliza lives on. Today, copies of the program are easily available on the Internet. In one celebrated instance, a businessman accidentally got connected to Eliza on his company's computer system and, thinking he was talking to a human, had a conversation that he found insulting. He learned only later that he had been talking to a machine. When this happened, it was half-seriously suggested that Eliza had passed the Turing Test. Of course, it had not. Neither Eliza nor any other presently existing computer program could pass a serious Turing Test.

Alan Turing did not live to see the advances that his work made possible. In 1952 it was discovered that he was a homosexual. For this the man who had broken the German codes was hauled into a British court, stripped of his security clearance, and forced to endure a hormone "treatment" that made him physically grotesque and impotent. In 1954 he committed suicide.

7.4. Why the Turing Test Fails

Is the Turing Test really a valid criterion of mentality? Would passing the test prove that a machine was conscious? There are some strong reasons to think not.

First, the test is an application of Behaviorism, a discredited theory of the mind. Behaviorism flourished at mid-century, when Turing's "Computing Machinery and Intelligence" was published. Behaviorism held that mental concepts such as "thinking," "being worried," and so on refer to behavior or behavioral dispositions. But it is now generally accepted that this idea is wrong. Behavior is an expression of mental states, but it is not identical with them. Thought can occur without behavior, and vice versa. Thus, it is possible for a zombie to behave like a person but be mindless. Machines that pass the Turing Test may be such zombies.

Also, John Searle's Chinese Room Argument seems to show that a computer could pass the Turing Test but have no mental states at all.

The Chinese Room Argument. A man is locked in a room filled with books. In the door is a slot through which slips of paper may be passed. Occasionally, a piece of paper will come through the slot with marks on it, but the marks mean nothing to the man—as far as he is concerned, they are just meaningless squiggles. However, he has been told that, each time a slip of paper comes in, he must send back another slip with different markings on it. The books will tell him what marks to make. The books contain elaborate instructions that say this: Whenever you see a squiggle of such-and-such shape, draw a different squiggle of such-and-such shape. The man does this, hour after hour.

Meanwhile, outside the door a woman from Beijing is writing messages in Chinese and passing them through the slot. Each time she does this, there is a pause, after which she receives a response in Chinese. The responses make perfect sense, and in this way she carries on a conversation for several hours. Naturally, she believes that there is someone on the other side of the door who understands Chinese, but she is wrong—there is only the man following the instructions in the books.

We could not create a Chinese Room in the real world because we could not write down all the instructions that would be needed in those books. But suppose we could. What would we think about this situation? Obviously, the man in the room does not understand Chinese. He manipulates symbols according to the instructions he has been given, but he has no way of attaching meaning to those symbols. This seems to show that the Turing Test is unsound. After all, the man in the room passes the Turing Test for understanding Chinese, yet he does not understand Chinese.

Notice that the elements of the Chinese Room correspond to the main parts of a computer: The man is the central processing unit (CPU), the instructions in the books are the program, and the slips of paper are the inputs and outputs. The whole system is doing just what a computer would be doing if a program could be written for conversing in Chinese. The Turing Test says that a computer running such a program would have mental states, including understanding its own words. The Chinese Room Argument seems to show that this is false.

It seems strange that such a simple argument could be so devastating. Yet the many philosophers and cognitive scientists who are skeptical of it have not produced a convincing rebuttal. Perhaps the most popular reply is to suggest that, although the man in the room does not understand Chinese, the whole system of which he is a part does understand it. This strains credulity. If the man does not understand Chinese, how could the man plus the books understand it? Has the simple interaction between the man and the books somehow generated a new consciousness? Suppose the man memorized all the instructions and so could discard the books. The man would then be the system, but still he would not understand Chinese. Are we to suppose that his body is now inhabited by a second consciousness, of which he is unaware? These lines of thought do not seem promising.

The Chinese Room Argument draws its strength from the distinction between *syntax* and *semantics*. Syntactical rules are rules for manipulating uninterpreted symbols. Semantic rules, on the other hand, are rules for interpreting those symbols, for attaching meaning to them. The core of the Chinese Room Argument is this: To have a mind, a system must have more than a syntax. It must also have a semantics. The Turing Test can be satisfied by a system that has only a syntax. Therefore, the Turing Test is not a valid criterion of mentality.

The "What More Do You Want?" Objection. The Chinese Room Argument has been debated for more than 25 years. Some philosophers are convinced by it, others are not, and some—especially researchers in AI—think it is just silly. Those in the last group are apt to express their frustration like this: If we could create a machine like the ones in the science-fiction stories—a machine that was indistinguishable in its speech and behavior from human beings—what more could you possibly want? We would have done everything that could be done. We would have as much evidence that the machine thinks as that a human thinks. If the machine can pass any test you can devise, but still you insist that human beings are different, that is just empty metaphysics, of no interest to science.

This is an impressive objection. Yet we would *not* have the same evidence that a machine thinks, as that a human being thinks, even if the machine passed the Turing Test. To understand a language—to think and to have a semantics—requires consciousness. And our belief that humans are conscious is not merely a deduction from behavior, as it would be for the machine. I know that I am conscious because I am immediately aware of it. Lying in my hammock, I know that I am thinking of Paris simply because I am aware of those thoughts. Moreover, I know that you, as a fellow human being, are in a position similar to mine. I could not be sure that a computer was in the same position, even if it passed the Turing Test.

So, there is something more that we should want. We should want additional evidence that computers can be conscious. How could we get such evidence? First, we need to understand what it is about our brains that enables us to be conscious. Right now we know a lot about the brain, but not enough to answer that question in detail. Once we have that information, we can ask whether a computer could have similar features that would enable *it* to be conscious. That would put us on firm ground in thinking about whether machines can think. Unfortunately, that firm ground is not yet available.

I hope we can settle this issue before intelligent robots become a reality. If 200 years from now robots seem to have all the thoughts and feelings of humans, how they are to be treated will be a pressing matter. Would they be capable of suffering? Would they have moral rights? Would it be murder to kill them? Technological advances in AI may create new ethical questions, and we'd better be prepared to answer them.

CHAPTER 8

The Case against Free Will

A small part of the universe is contained within the skin of each of us. There is no reason why it should have any special physical status because it lies within this boundary.
— B. F. Skinner, *About Behaviorism* (1974)

8.1. Are People Responsible for What They Do?

In 1924 two Chicago teenagers, Richard Loeb and Nathan Leopold, kidnapped and murdered a boy named Bobby Franks just to prove they could do it. The crime caused a sensation. Despite the brutality of what they had done, Leopold and Loeb did not appear to be especially wicked. They came from rich families and were both outstanding students. At 18 Leopold was the youngest graduate in the history of the University of Chicago, and at 19 Loeb was the youngest ever to have graduated from the University of Michigan. Leopold was about to enroll at Harvard Law School. How could they have committed a senseless murder? Their trial would receive the same kind of attention as the O. J. Simpson trial 70 years later.

The parents hired Clarence Darrow, the most famous lawyer of the day, to defend them. Darrow was known as a champion of unpopular causes—he had defended labor organizers, communists, and a black man accused of killing a member of a racist mob. Three years later, in his most celebrated case, he would defend John Scopes of Tennessee from the charge that he had taught evolution in a high school classroom. Darrow was also the country's best-known opponent of the death penalty. In 1902 he had been invited by the warden to give a talk to the inmates of the Cook County Jail in Chicago, and he told the prisoners:

> I really do not in the least believe in crime. There is no such thing as a crime as the word is generally understood. I do not believe there is any sort of distinction between the real moral conditions of the people in and out of jail. One is just as good as the other. The people here can no more help being here than the people outside can avoid being outside. I do not believe that people are in jail because they deserve to be. They are in jail simply because they cannot avoid it on account of circumstances which are entirely beyond their control and for which they are in no way responsible.

These ideas would figure prominently in Darrow's defense of Leopold and Loeb.

The public wanted blood. As the trial began, the *Chicago Evening Standard* carried this headline:

DARROW PLEADS FOR MERCY: MOBS RIOT
BAILIFF'S ARM BROKEN AND WOMAN FAINTS AS FRENZIED MOB STORMS PAST GUARDS; JUDGE CALLS FOR 20 POLICE; FEARS SOME WILL BE KILLED

Leopold and Loeb had already admitted their guilt, and so Darrow's job was just to keep them from the gallows. There would be no jury. The judge would listen to the lawyers' arguments and then decide whether the defendants would hang.

Darrow spoke for more than 12 hours. He did not argue that the boys were insane; nevertheless, he said, they were not responsible for what they had done. Darrow appealed to a new idea that psychologists had proposed, namely, that human character is shaped by an individual's genes and environment. He told the judge, "Intelligent people now know that every human being is the product of the endless heredity back of him and the infinite environment around him."

> I do not know what it was that made these boys do this mad act, but I do know there is a reason for it. I know they did not beget themselves. I know that any one of an infinite number of causes reaching back to the beginning might be working out in these boys' minds, whom you are asked to hang in malice and in hatred and injustice, because someone in the past sinned against them.

Psychiatrists had testified that the boys lacked normal feelings, because they showed no emotional reaction to what they had done. Today a psychiatrist might say that Leopold and Loeb suffered from "antisocial personality disorder," commonly known as "sociopathy" or "psychopathy." Darrow seized upon this idea:

> Is Dickie Loeb to blame because out of the infinite forces that conspired to form him, the infinite forces that were at work producing him ages before he was born, that because out of these infinite combinations he was born without [the right kind of emotions]? If he is, then there should be a new definition for justice. Is he to blame for what he did not have and never had?

Darrow portrays Loeb as having had a childhood bereft of the affection that boys need, spending his days studying and his evenings secretly reading crime stories, fantasizing about committing the perfect crime and fooling the cops. Leopold, meanwhile, was weak and without friends. He grew up obsessed with Nietzsche's philosophy of the "superman," disdaining other people and desperately wanting to prove his own superiority. Then the two boys found one another and committed the crime. But they were just playing out the hand nature dealt them. "Nature is strong and she is pitiless," Darrow concluded. "She works in her own mysterious way, and we are her victims. We have not much to do with it ourselves."

The judge deliberated for a month and then sentenced Leopold and Loeb to life in prison. Twelve years later, Richard Loeb was killed in a dispute with another prisoner. For his part Nathan Leopold spent 34 years behind bars. During that time he taught other prisoners, volunteered for malaria testing, ran the prison library, and worked in the prison hospital. After his release on parole, he moved to Puerto Rico, where he continued his lifelong effort to "become a human being again," largely through jobs that involved helping others. He died in 1971.

8.2. Determinism

Clarence Darrow was the first lawyer to use the defense that people are never responsible for what they do, because their actions are caused by forces beyond their control. However,

Darrow was not the first person to doubt that we control our own destinies.

Aristotle worried that the laws of logic might imply that we have no control over what we do. Every proposition, he reasoned, must be true or false. So at this moment it is either true or false that you will drink a Diet Coke tomorrow. If it is true, there is nothing you can do to prevent it—after all, *it will happen*. If it is false, there is nothing you can do to make it happen, for *it will not happen*. Either way, the future is fixed, and you have no power to change it. This became known as the problem of Fatalism. Theologians from St. Augustine onward realized that the assumption of God's omniscience creates a similar difficulty. If God knows everything, he knows what you will do tomorrow. But if God already knows what you will do, then you cannot do otherwise.

As serious as the problem of Fatalism is, it is not the most worrisome challenge to human freedom. A greater threat is posed by Determinism, which was known in the ancient world but came into its own with the rise of modern science. To say that a system is deterministic means that everything that happens within it is the result of prior causes and that, once the causes occur the effects must follow, given the surrounding circumstances and the Laws of Nature. You probably regard the building you live in as a deterministic system. If the lights go out, you will think there must have been a cause; you will assume that, once the cause occurred, the effect was bound to follow. If an electrician told you "It just happened," for no reason, that would violate your conception of how things work.

With the rise of modern science, it became common to think of the whole universe as one giant deterministic system. Nature consists of particles that obey the laws of physics, and everything that happens is governed by the invariable laws of cause and effect. This idea was vividly expressed by the French mathematician Pierre-Simon Laplace (1749–1827), who said in 1819 that if a supremely intelligent observer knew the exact location and velocity of every particle in the universe and all the laws of physics, he could predict with certainty every future state of the universe. Nothing would surprise him; he would know everything before it happened. Of course, we cannot make such predictions, but that is only because we lack the necessary information and intelligence.

The universe includes us. We are part of nature, and what happens inside our skins is subject to the same physical laws as everything else. The movements of our arms, legs, and tongues are triggered by events in our brains, which in turn are caused by other physical occurrences. Thus, Laplace's perfect observer could predict our actions in the same way that he predicts everything else. In fact, by tracing the causes far enough back, he could have predicted whether you will drink a Diet Coke to-morrow even before you were born. It may seem to us that we make our choices freely and spontaneously. But Laplace argued that our "freedom" is only an illusion created by our ignorance. Because we aren't aware of the underlying causes of our behavior, we assume that there aren't any.

What, exactly, are "the underlying causes of our behavior"? As Clarence Darrow observed, the "ultimate" causes may stretch far back in time. But the immediate causes are events in our brains. Neurological events cause both our mental states and the motions of our bodies. This last claim is not mere speculation. Brain surgery sometimes takes place under only a local anesthetic, so that the patient can tell the surgeon what he or she is experiencing as various parts of the brain are probed. This technique was pioneered more than a half-century ago by Dr. Wilder Penfield, who described it in his book *The Excitable Cortex in Conscious Man* (1958). Neurosurgeons have been using Penfield's technique ever since. They know that if you probe in one place, the patient will feel a tingle in her hand; probe in another place, and the patient will smell garlic; and, in one patient, probing in still another place made her hear a song by Guns n' Roses.

Actions can also be induced by electrical stimulation of the brain. Jose Delgado, who did his research at Yale University four decades ago, discovered that by stimulating various regions of the brain he could cause all sorts of bodily motions, including frowning, the opening and closing of the eyes, and movements of the head, arms, legs, and fingers. When he first tried this using cats and monkeys, he noticed that the animals showed no surprise or fear when their bodies moved. Apparently the animals experienced the movements as if they were voluntary. In one instance, stimulating a monkey's brain caused the monkey to get up and walk around. The effect was repeated several times, and each time the animal strolled around, without surprise or discomfort, as if it had just decided to take a walk.

Some philosophers would say that Delgado's procedure produced not actions, but only bodily movements. Actions involve reasons and decisions, not just motions. But there is more. When Delgado tried his experiment on humans, they were even more compliant than the animals—not only did they act out the movements without surprise or fear, but they also produced reasons for them. In one subject electrical stimulation of the brain produced "head turning and slow displacement of the body to either side with a well-oriented and apparently normal sequence, as if the patient were looking for something." This was repeated six times over two days, confirming that the stimulation was actually producing the behavior. But the subject, who did not know about the electrical stimulation, considered the activity spontaneous and offered reasons for it. When asked "What are you doing?" he would reply, "I am looking for my slippers," "I heard a noise," "I am restless," or "I was looking under the bed."

Are our *decisions* also produced by neural firings? There are some experimental results about this, too, due to the German scientist H. H. Kornhuber. Suppose you sit quietly, and some time during the next minute you spontaneously move your finger. Subjectively, you may feel quite certain that the decision to move your finger was entirely within your control. But now suppose we attach some electrodes to your scalp and ask you to repeat the action. A technician watching an electroencephalograph would be able to observe a characteristic pattern of brain activity when you move your finger. The brain activity begins up to one-and-a-half seconds before the movement, and *it begins before you make your decision*. So the technician, watching his monitor, knows that you are going to move your finger before you do. He is, in a small way, like Laplace's perfect observer. Kornhuber first performed this experiment in the 1970s.

8.3. Psychology

It may seem odd that the primary argument against free will appeals to the principles of physics. After all, psychology, not physics, studies human behavior. So we might wonder what psychology has to say. Do psychological theories about human behavior have room for the notion of free will, or do they support Determinism?

Before turning to psychology, however, let me mention some of the ways in which our commonsense understanding of human beings already contains elements favorable to Determinism. Each of us was born to particular parents at a particular time and place, and only a little thought is needed to realize that if those circumstances were changed, we would have turned out different. A young man "chooses" to become a stockbroker—is it a coincidence that his father was a stockbroker? What would he choose if his parents had been missionaries? What would he choose if he had been born into a different culture?

We also know from statistics that social conditions influence us in ways we don't realize. Consider, for example, the names we give to our children. White parents tend to choose different names than black parents—this is not a "moral" observation, it is just a fact. In California in the 1990s, for example, girls named "Imani" and "Ebony" were overwhelmingly African-American, while girls named "Molly" and "Amy" were overwhelmingly white. Social differences between the white and black communities resulted in different names being popular. Socioeconomic status also influences our naming decisions. Again in California, the most common names given to rich white girls in the 1990s were Alexandra, Lauren, Katherine, and Madison; poor white girls were most often called Amber, Heather, Kayla, and Stephanie. These trends change over time. Sometimes "rich names" become more popular among the poor, which in turn causes the rich to abandon them. Individually, parents may always seem to be making free, independent choices. But when social circumstances change, so do the popularity of the names.

Consider another example: The United States has the highest rate of imprisonment in the world. Over 2 million Americans are currently in jail or prison, and 7 million more are on probation or parole. Perhaps some of these individuals would break the law no matter what, but some offenders would be law-abiding in different circumstances. Here are some social factors that have been shown, statistically, to be predictive of criminal behavior: having an uneducated mother, growing up poor, being raised in a single-parent household, and having a teenage mother. Considered as individuals, it may seem that each person "freely decides" to break the law. And perhaps that is right. Still, it is sobering to realize how many people feel morally superior to criminals even though they themselves would be in jail under different circumstances.

When we set aside statistics and try to understand in more detail why individuals behave as they do, we always seem to end up with explanations in which "free choice" plays little part. Darrow's explanation of how Leopold and Loeb came to kill Bobby Franks is one example. For another, consider Eric Rudolph, who committed a series of bombings in Georgia and Alabama in the 1990s. I heard one of the explosions from my office—the bomb killed a policeman and critically wounded a nurse at an abortion clinic in Birmingham, Alabama. Rudolph was caught in 2003, and today he is serving five consecutive life sentences.

Why would he have done such a thing? Why did he kill the policeman and maim the nurse in Alabama? We might suppose that Rudolph hated abortion so much that he was willing to use any means to stop it. That may be true, but a lot of people oppose abortion without planting bombs. Why would this particular man turn deadly?

According to *Newsweek*, "He is perhaps best understood as the product of a paranoid fringe of white supremacists, religious zealots and government haters. Rudolph's mind and motives are hard to fathom, but extremism seems to run in the family." When he was 13, Eric's father died, and his family moved from Miami to rural North Carolina. They lived on a gravel road near a sawmill owner named Tom Branham. Branham, a survivalist who had been arrested on federal weapons charges and who believed that the government had no authority over him, took an interest in Eric and his brother Daniel and became a substitute father to the boys. His mother, meanwhile, moved to the Missouri Ozarks to join a community of white separatists. By the time he was in the ninth grade, Eric was writing in a class paper that the Holocaust never happened, using as his "research" pamphlets issued by hate groups. As much as we might detest what he became, it is hard to believe that the little boy had a chance.

Classical Psychology. Whenever we try to understand extraordinary behavior, some deterministic explanation always seems to come to mind. "He just decided to do it" doesn't sound like any explanation at all. Thus, determinism is a hard-to-avoid by-product of the search to explain behavior. As B. F. Skinner (1904–1990), a behaviorist who taught at Harvard for many years, put it:

> If we are to use the methods of science in the field of human affairs, we must assume that behavior is lawful and determined. We must expect to discover that what a man does is the result of specifiable conditions and that once these conditions have been discovered, we can anticipate and to some extent determine his actions.

As the science of psychology has developed, one theory after another has competed for acceptance. But none of them has had much use for "free will."

During the first two-thirds of the twentieth century, Behaviorism vied with Freudian ideas for dominance among psychologists. Freud sought to understand human conduct by identifying the unconscious motives of action. Conscious processes of thought and deliberation are, on his view, only rationalizations for deeper forces hidden within the psyche. Long-forgotten events of infancy and early childhood created in each of us unconscious desires and impulses that control us even as adults. For example, a woman has a series of relationships with abusive men. Each time she rids herself of one, she swears never to make that mistake again; but she does, over and over. How can she keep making the same mistake? She appears to choose freely each time she begins a new relationship, but she does not. She has a masochistic personality, formed as a child when she was battered by an abusive father; now, as an adult, she helplessly reenacts her relationship with her father again and again. She will not be able to break the pattern until she confronts her repressed memories and feelings about her father, possibly after years of psychoanalysis.

The behaviorists would have none of this. On their view unconscious thoughts play no part in explaining behavior. In fact, no thoughts of any kind enter the picture. Instead, a person's behavior is explained by reference to the process of conditioning that produced it. We tend to repeat behavior for which we are rewarded, and we tend not to repeat behavior when we are punished. Suppose you get an electric shock every time you touch a fence; you will soon stop touching it. Or suppose a child is fed when he says "please" and not fed when he does not say "please." He will soon be saying "please" whenever he is hungry. These are simple examples. The real world is complex, but the principle is the same for all behavior.

B. F. Skinner once explained how the process of conditioning can be demonstrated in the laboratory. First, we place a pigeon in a cage for a few days, always feeding it from a small tray that is opened electrically. Then, after the pigeon has become accustomed to eating from the tray, "We select a relatively simple bit of behavior which may be freely and rapidly repeated, and which is easily observed and recorded. . . . [T]he behavior of raising the head above a given height is convenient." Whenever the pigeon raises its head above the given height, the food tray is opened. "If the experiment is conducted according to specifications, the result is invariable: we observe an immediate change in the frequency with which the head crosses the line. . . . In a minute or two, the bird's posture has changed so that the top of the head seldom falls below the line which we first chose." Of course, the pigeon is not aware of why its posture has changed. The alteration in its behavior is just a mechanistic reaction to a stimulus.

The behaviorists argued that all our conduct is like this. In theory everything we do can be explained as a response to prior conditioning, including our proudest and noblest actions as well as our most shameful ones. Of course, in practice we don't know enough about the causal chains to actually supply the explanations. In the same year that Clarence Darrow was defending Leopold and Loeb, John B. Watson, often called "the father of Behaviorism," wrote:

> Give me a dozen healthy infants, well-formed, and my own specified world to bring them up in and I'll guarantee to take any one at random and train him to become any type of specialist I might select—doctor, lawyer, artist, merchant, chief, and, yes, even beggar-man and thief, regardless of his talents, penchants, tendencies, abilities, vocations, and race of his ancestors.

Many readers complained that such ideas violate our sense of freedom and dignity. In response Skinner titled one of his books *Beyond Freedom and Dignity.*

Is "Character" a Matter of Luck? When we reflect on other people's misfortunes, we sometimes think, "There but for the grace of God go I." It is worth pausing over the idea that luck might account for most of the moral differences between people. Some of the most famous experiments in social psychology suggest that any of us might behave badly if we were unlucky enough to be in the wrong circumstances.

In one experiment Philip Zimbardo and his colleagues set up a simulated prison in the basement of a Stanford University building. Twenty-four volunteers were arbitrarily assigned to be guards or prisoners. The experiment was supposed to last two weeks, but it had to be called off after five days because the "guards" treated the "prisoners" so brutally.

In another study Stanley Milgram asked volunteers to operate a device that administered increasingly severe electric shocks to someone in an adjoining room. The person in the other room was supposed to be "learning" by being punished for giving wrong answers to questions. (He was, in reality, an actor who was only pretending to be shocked.) Milgram was surprised to discover that every single volunteer was willing to continue shocking the other person even when the levels were labeled as extremely dangerous and the other person could be heard crying and begging the volunteer to stop.

When people hear about these experiments, they invariably feel that *they* would not have acted so badly. This feeling is hard to avoid, yet the participants in the experiments were ordinary people like you and me. Zimbardo comments that, after the guards-and-prisoners experiment was over, the "prisoners" insisted that they would not have been so abusive if they had been guards. But, Zimbardo emphasizes, there was no difference between those who were made guards and those who were made prisoners—the assignment was random. The natural conclusion is that the only difference between them was in their circumstances. Apparently, all of us—or at least the great majority of us—have the inner capacity to behave badly if we are in the relevant position.

I will mention one other study that makes a similar point: the "Good Samaritan" experiment of J. M. Darley and C. D. Batson. In Luke's gospel the Good Samaritan is presented as a model of decent behavior:

> "And who is my neighbor?"
> Jesus replied, "A man was going down from Jerusalem to Jericho, and he fell among robbers, who stripped him and beat him, and departed, leaving him half dead. Now by chance a priest was going down the road; and when he saw him he passed by on the other side. So likewise a Levite, when he came to the place and saw him, passed by on the other side.
> "But a Samaritan, as he journeyed, came to where he was; and when he saw him, he had compassion and went to him and bound his wounds, pouring on oil and wine; then he set him on his own beast and brought him to an inn, and took care of him. And the next day he took out two denarii and gave them to the innkeeper, saying, 'Take care of him; and whatever more you spend, I will repay you when I come back.' Which of these three, do you think, proved neighbor to him who fell among the robbers?"
> He said, "The one who showed mercy on him."
> And Jesus said to him, "Go and do likewise."

The traditional interpretation of this story is that the Samaritan was a man of better moral character—he "had compassion," while the priest and the Levite did not. (Samaritans, incidentally, were people of low standing, while priests and Levites played important roles in the Temple.) Is this right? Darley and Batson decided to investigate the circumstances in which we would be Good Samaritans, using Princeton theology students as their subjects.

In the study the theology students first filled out forms giving pertinent information about themselves, including their ethical and religious beliefs. Then half of the students were told to prepare a lecture on ethics, and half were told to prepare a lecture on job opportunities. All the students were told to go to another building to give their lectures. Some were told they needed to hurry over, while others were told they had plenty of time. It had been arranged that on their way to the other building they would pass by someone slumped in a doorway, obviously in distress. Would they stop to help?

Some stopped and some did not. But it turned out that their ethical and religious views had nothing to do with it, nor did it matter whether they had ethics or job opportunities on their minds. All that mattered was whether they thought they had time to stop. This small change in circumstances determined who would be heroic and who would be heartless.

8.4. Genes and Behavior

There aren't many Freudians or behaviorists around these days. Behaviorism went out of fashion partly because it explained behavior too much in terms of the environment—as it turns out, the human personality is not as malleable as Watson and Skinner thought. Researchers now believe that our genes are equally important in shaping our personalities, and our genes cannot be changed by conditioning—no matter how vigorous.

To what extent do our genes determine the kind of people we are? There is no uncontroversial way of measuring this, nor is there any uncontroversial way of understanding how genes exert their influence. Educated people commonly assume that organisms are products of genes-plus-environment, but that is too simple. As the biologist Richard Lewontin tells us, the picture must also accommodate *developmental noise,* "a consequence of random events within cells at the level of molecular interactions." For example, there is considerable variation from cell to cell in the rate and number of molecules synthesized, and this changes the times at which cells divide or migrate. This can affect the development of the organism in unexpected ways. "Developmental noise" is about neither genetics nor environment. Of course, from the point of view of "free will," it doesn't matter whether one's personality is influenced by genes or by developmental noise, since neither is controlled by the individual.

Twin Studies. Some researchers have tried to devise ways of estimating the influence of genes on human behavior. One strategy is to study identical twins, especially those raised in different environments. To the extent that such twins are alike, their genes may be responsible (but not necessarily, since there may still be similarities in their environments); and to the extent that the twins are different, other factors must be at work.

Such studies may provide a rough idea of how much our genes influence our personalities.

At the University of Minnesota, there is an ongoing research project, started in 1979, called the Minnesota Study of Twins Reared Apart. When such twins are located, they are invited to the university for a week of tests. The researchers have found that identical twins reared apart resemble each other very closely. In some cases the similarities are so striking that they sound like something out of science fiction.

Among those tested were the "Giggle Sisters," both of whom laughed all the time. Both had the habit of pushing at their noses, which they both called "squidging"; both claimed to have weak ankles as a result of falling when they were 15; both had met their husbands at dances when they were 16; and, although both shunned controversy, both had worked as polling clerks.

There were also brothers named Jim, who drove the same model car and smoked the same brand of cigarettes. Both had elaborate workshops at home where they made miniature furniture as a hobby. Both liked to leave little love notes for their wives lying around the house. And they had named their sons James Alan and James Allan.

But perhaps the most remarkable were Jack Yufe and Oskar Stöhr, whose home environments had been as different as could be imagined. One twin was raised in Trinidad by his Jewish father, the other in Germany by his Nazi grandmother. Oskar was in the Hitler youth; Jack served in the Israeli navy. When reunited, both were wearing rectangular wire-frame glasses and blue two-pocket shirts with epaulets. Both had small mustaches. Both liked to read magazines from back to front, and both flushed toilets before using them. And both liked the same odd practical joke of startling people by sneezing in elevators.

These are arresting anecdotes, but they are only anecdotes, and we can draw no firm conclusions from them. In the first place, an enormous amount of data would have to be gathered and analyzed before we could know what, if anything, to conclude. Take the blue-shirt-with-epaulets story, for example. How many such shirts were owned by men in the areas where Jack and Oskar lived? What are the chances of two men wearing that shirt on the same day? Or, more generally, in any group of males drawn from the same population, what are the chances that any two selected at random will be dressed similarly? Most important of all, what are the chances that there will be *some* striking similarity between two such men, even if it is not how they are dressed? In any case critics also object that the anecdotes themselves should be taken with a grain of salt because the stories are likely exaggerated. Also, some of the twins, it turns out, had met one another before they were studied by the Minnesota researchers.

The researchers do not, however, base their conclusions on such anecdotes. Instead, the reared-apart twins are given standard psychological tests for such traits as flexibility, tolerance, conformity, self-control, conscientiousness, openness, tough-mindedness, social dominance, alienation, authoritarianism, and aggressiveness. They are found to be remarkably alike in all these ways. They have similar senses of humor and levels of optimism or fearfulness. They share (or lack) similar talents, and they have similar mental illnesses and disabilities. On the basis of such studies, researchers have concluded that the major components of our personalities are about 50 percent due to our genes.

Are Some People Born Bad? The idea that traits like aggressiveness are linked to our genes will come as no surprise to neurologists and clinical psychologists, who have long known about the connection between biology and violence. Experiments with cats have shown that if a small section of the hypothalamus is removed, the animals will turn savage. Humans with head injuries sometimes experience fits of uncontrollable rage. Meanwhile, for people who are "naturally" prone to violent behavior, effective treatments include lithium and beta-blockers. The genes–neurology–violence connection was further confirmed in 1995 when geneticists discovered that turning off the gene responsible for producing nitric oxide—a neurotransmitter in both mice and humans—causes normally sociable mice to become vicious. So the fact that there is *some* sort of connection between genes, neurology, and violence is well established.

Some researchers believe that this tells us something important about crime, although this idea is controversial. The general notion of "crime" is too socially variable to be of much use—fornication, gambling, and heresy, for example, are sometimes counted as "crimes" and sometimes not. But suppose we focus on violent crimes—for example, murder, assault, and rape. Is it "in the genes" for some people, but not others, to do violence? There is evidence that it is.

Various dispositions, including a propensity to violence, contribute to socially unacceptable behavior. Darrow believed that Leopold and Loeb were "born bad" because they were born without such feelings as pity and sympathy. There is no way for us to know the precise truth about Leopold and Loeb as individuals, but on the more general issue Darrow might have been right. Psychologist Judith Rich Harris puts it like this:

> Though we no longer say that some children are born bad, the facts are such, unfortunately, that a euphemism is needed. Now psychologists say that some children are born with "difficult" temperaments—difficult for their parents to rear, difficult to socialize. I can list for you some of the things that make a child difficult to rear and difficult to socialize: a tendency to be active, impulsive, aggressive, and quick to anger; a tendency to get bored with routine activities and to seek excitement; a tendency to be unafraid of getting hurt; an insensitivity to the feelings of others; and, more often than not, a muscular build and an IQ a little lower than average. All of these characteristics have a significant genetic component.

It is easy to understand why such ideas arouse controversy. It sounds like we are being told that some children are beyond help—they're born bad, and bad they'll stay. Moreover, in the context of discussions of crime, such remarks ignore the influence of environmental factors like poverty and racism. Behaviorism, with its upbeat message "Improve the environment, and improve the child" seems more in line with a progressive social outlook.

But the idea that such traits as aggressiveness and insensitivity "have a significant genetic component" does not imply that some children are lost causes or that education and social conditions don't matter. No social scientist believes that genes determine everything. Your genes might incline you, in certain environments, to act in certain ways, but whether you actually behave in those ways will depend on other things. Thus, education and the elimination of poverty and racism are still important. The research about genes only helps explain why virtue comes easier to some people than to others.

To avoid such misunderstandings, social scientists often take pains to point out that they are not endorsing Determinism. Anthropologist John Townsend writes:

> Many misinterpret biosocial explanations. They assume that such explanations are deterministic: that we are saying human beings are like animals, that we are "wired" for certain behaviors, and that these instinctive behaviors will emerge whether we want them to or not. . . . All of these assumptions are false. As human beings we have inherited certain predispositions from our evolutionary past, but that does not mean we have to act on them.

Despite such reassurances, however, there remain at least two reasons to worry about what this means for our freedom.

First, even if we are not "wired for certain behaviors," we are being told something disturbing—that we come equipped by nature with deep-seated desires that we can resist only with difficulty. If, in some people, these desires prove irresistible, it is hard to see this as their fault. Moreover, these desires might be with us forever, and they play a significant role in explaining our behavior. This may not be Determinism in the strict sense, but it sounds suspiciously close to it.

Second, we need an explanation for why some people, but not others, are able to resist the impulses that nature has given them. Why do some people end up murderers while others do not? Is it a matter of choice? Or is there some further aspect of their situations that makes the difference? Perhaps where genes leave off, the environment takes over. One man, who was brought up in a certain way, is violent; another man, who was brought up differently, is not. Thus, even though genetic explanations are not deterministic by themselves, when we combine them with other plausible ideas, we end up with an overall picture in which "free will" plays a vanishingly small part. To say that biology does not determine us, because the environment also plays a part, is little consolation.

Conclusion. Psychologists and other investigators have developed a number of ideas that help explain human behavior. Each is supported by impressive evidence, and each seems to be at least part of the truth. We don't yet know how to combine these ideas into a comprehensive account. Nonetheless, as far as free will is concerned, the overall trend is not encouraging. Each new discovery chips away a bit more of our confidence. The more we learn about the sources of human conduct, the less room there seems to be for the idea of free choice.

CHAPTER 9

The Debate over Free Will

Man's life is a line that nature commands him to describe on the surface of the earth, without his being able to swerve from it, even for an instant. . . . Nevertheless, in spite of the shackles by which he is bound, it is pretended he is a free agent.

—PAUL HENRI BARON D'HOLBACH,
THE SYSTEM OF NATURE (1770)

Sir, we *know* our will is free, and *there's* an end on it.

—DR. JOHNSON, IN BOSWELL'S
THE LIFE OF SAMUEL JOHNSON, LL.D. (1791)

9.1. The Determinist Argument

When asked about his philosophy of life, novelist Isaac Bashevis Singer (1904–1991) liked to tell his friends: "I believe in free will. I have no choice." Singer's little joke makes a serious point: It is hard to avoid thinking you have free will. When you are deciding what to do, the choice seems entirely yours. The inner feeling of freedom is so powerful that we may be unable to give up the idea of free will, no matter how much evidence there is against it.

And there is a lot of evidence against it. The more we learn about the causes of human behavior, the less likely it seems that we freely choose our actions. No one piece of evidence forces this conclusion. Nonetheless, many different strands of evidence point in this direction, and the cumulative effect is that "free will" looks more and more like part of a prescientific way of thinking.

119

We may call this the Determinist Argument:

(1) Everything we do is caused by forces over which we have no control.

(2) If our actions are caused by forces over which we have no control, we do not act freely.

(3) Therefore, we never act freely.

This is a disturbing line of thought because of what it seems to imply about individual responsibility. If we are not free, then it seems that we are not responsible for what we do.

But is the Determinist Argument sound? It is plausible, but it can be disputed. We will look at two responses to the argument that defend free will in different ways. One theory, Libertarianism, denies the first premise of the argument and holds that our actions are not causally determined. Another theory, Compatibilism, denies the second premise and holds that we are free *even if* our actions are causally determined. We will consider these views one at a time.

9.2. The Libertarian Response

Libertarianism is the view that at least some of our actions are free because they are not, in fact, causally determined. According to this theory, human choices are not constrained in the same way that other events in the world are constrained. A billiard ball, when struck by another billiard ball, must move in a certain direction with a certain velocity. It has no choice. The laws of cause and effect determine precisely what will happen. But a human decision is not like that. Right now, you can decide whether to continue reading or to stop reading. You can do either, and nothing makes you choose one way or the other. The laws of cause and effect have no power over you.

Several arguments have been given in favor of this theory.

The Argument from Experience. We may begin with the idea that we know we are free because *each of us is immediately aware of being free* every time we make a conscious choice. Think again of what you are doing at this moment. You can continue reading, or you can stop. Which will it be? Think of what it is like, right now, as you consider these options. You feel no constraints.

Nothing is holding you back or forcing you in either direction. The decision is up to you. The experience of freedom, it may be said, is the best proof we could have on the matter. As Samuel Johnson told his friend Boswell, "You are surer that you can lift up your finger or not as you please, than you are of any conclusion from a deduction of reasoning."

The problem is that the evidence against free will tends to undermine our confidence in our experience. Jose Delgado found that he could cause people to do things by electrically stimulating their brains—they would look over their shoulder, for example—and then they would offer reasons why they had done so, such as "I was looking for my comb." Delgado's subjects, who did not know that their brains were being stimulated, would *experience* the movements as voluntary. Perhaps we are like Delgado's subjects. What is the difference between us and them, except that in the experimental setting we know about the electrochemical event that causes the action, while in everyday life we are ignorant of what is happening in our brains? In the face of such evidence, it is hollow to insist, with Dr. Johnson, that we simply know we are free. If freedom is to be defended, a better argument is needed.

The Argument That the Universe Is Not a Deterministic System. Determinism, it may be said, is out of keeping with present-day science. In the heyday of Newtonian physics, it was thought that the universe operates strictly according to laws of cause and effect. The Laws of Nature were believed to be causal laws that specify the conditions under which one state of affairs must follow another—the motion of balls on a billiards table was a model for the whole universe. But Newtonian physics has been replaced by a different view of nature.

According to quantum mechanics, a cornerstone of present-day physics, the rules that govern the behavior of subatomic particles are irreducibly probabilistic. The laws of quantum theory do not say, "Given X, Y *must* follow." Instead, they say, "Given X, there is *a specific probability* that Y will follow." Thus, the Laws of Nature may tell us that under certain conditions a certain percentage of radioactive atoms will decay, but they do not tell us which atoms will decay. The fact that a certain percentage will decay may be determined, but the fact that a particular atom will decay is not determined.

Some scientists believe, on philosophical grounds, that quantum theory must eventually be superseded by a different, as yet unknown theory that is deterministic. They find the idea that the universe operates according to principles of chance to be abhorrent. Albert Einstein, who famously said, "God does not play dice with the universe," was one such scientist. Yet no replacement theory is in sight, and quantum theory is the best thing going.

Does this mean that we don't need to worry about Determinism? Quantum theory has sometimes been hailed as good news for free will. If not everything is causally determined, it is said, then we may be free after all, because our actions may be among the things that are not determined.

However, quantum physics does not really offer much help in defending free will, for two reasons. First, quantum physics interprets nature as containing a lot of randomness—it is random and unpredictable which radioactive atoms will decay. However, these random events occur everywhere in nature, not just in human bodies. Is free will supposed to pervade every bit of matter, in every corner of the universe? No, because freedom is not the same thing as randomness. Second, the implications of quantum indeterminacy for human behavior are likely to be very small. Compare the implications of quantum theory for computers. A computer's outputs are determined by its inputs and its program. Quantum mechanics does not imply that we should stop trusting computers—the computer's operations are, if not completely determined, close enough as to make no difference. We will still get the expected outputs, given the right program and the right inputs. Something similar could be true of human beings. If so, that would be enough for the Determinist Argument.

The Argument That We Cannot Predict Our Own Decisions. A different sort of argument for Libertarianism turns on the idea that anything that is causally determined is predictable. The tree outside my window is leaning, and sooner or later it will fall. If I knew all the Laws of Nature, and if I knew everything about the tree and its physical environment, I could predict exactly when it will fall. Of course, I can't actually do that, because I don't know all those things. We might say that causally determined events are predictable *in principle*, if not always in practice.

If human actions are causally determined, then it should be possible, in principle, to predict them, too. We would need only to know the pertinent facts about the person, the person's circumstances, and the relevant causal laws. However, you could not always predict your own actions, even in principle. For example, suppose you were trying to decide between going out for pizza with your friends and staying home and having leftovers. Could you, in principle, predict what you'll do? Even if you knew everything about your brain, you couldn't do it. The problem is that, once you formulated the prediction, you could change your mind, just to keep things interesting. If you predict that you'll go out with your friends, then you could decide to stay home, just to prove a point about free will. This seems to show that there is a big difference between predicting human behavior and predicting other events in the physical world.

We may summarize the argument like this:

(1) If human behavior is causally determined, it is in principle predictable.

(2) But a prediction about what someone will do can be thwarted if the person whose behavior is being predicted knows about the prediction and chooses to act otherwise.

(3) Therefore, not all human actions are in principle predictable.

(4) And so not all human actions are causally determined.

This is a clever argument, but is it sound? Unfortunately, the argument fails once we examine what the word "predictable" means. There are two types of predictability:

(a) Predictable by a hypothetical ideal observer who stands outside the system and observes events but does not interfere with them

(b) Predictable by you in the real world

Determinism implies predictability in sense (a) but not in sense (b). Consider again the case where you predict that you'll have pizza, and then you decide against it. Your prediction was indeed proved wrong. However, an ideal observer might have known exactly what was going to happen—she might have been able to predict your prediction as well as your decision to do the opposite. Everything might still be determined.

This argument, then, does not prove that our behavior is not determined. But there is one more argument to consider.

The Argument from Accountability. The assumption that we have free will is deeply engrained in our ordinary ways of thinking. In responding to other people, we cannot help but think of them as the authors of their actions. We hold them responsible, blaming them if they behave badly and admiring them if they behave well. For these attitudes to be justified, people must have free will.

Similarly, in thinking about ourselves, we assume that we have free will. Someone who hits the winning basket or aces a test may feel proud, while someone who chokes or cheats may feel ashamed. These feelings of pride and shame would be baseless if our actions were always due to factors beyond our control. Yet these feelings are inescapable. Thus, once again, we must think of human beings as free.

We might therefore reason as follows:

(1) We cannot help but admire or blame people for what they do, nor can we avoid sometimes feeling pride or shame for what we do.

(2) These responses—admiration, blame, pride, and shame—would not be appropriate if people did not have free will.

(3) Therefore, we must believe that people have free will.

(4) Since we must believe it, we do: People have free will.

The problem with this argument is obvious: Our attitudes might be unjustified or misleading, even if they're inescapable. Step 4 is therefore unwarranted. The argument engages in a kind of wishful thinking.

Is Libertarianism Coherent? Finally, we may consider whether Libertarianism makes any sense as a positive view of human behavior. To understand our behavior, we need more than just the denial that our actions are determined. We need, in addition, a positive account of how we make decisions.

If our actions are not causally determined, how are they supposed to come about? What, exactly, produces our decisions? We might imagine that there is, inside each of us, a sort of "mental being" whose decisions are not constrained by the laws of cause and effect—a ghostly controller who makes choices independently of the happenings in the brain. But this is not credible. It goes against what science tells us about how things work. There is no evidence for any sort of "mental energy" at work within us, disconnected from the operation of our neurological systems. And even if we set science aside, this speculation looks like nothing more than a fairy tale.

But if we are not to suppose that there is a disconnected mental entity inside us calling the shots, what are we to think? That some part of the brain operates outside the causal network of the world? It sounds silly, but it is hard to come up with anything better. There seems to be no plausible account available that makes sense of Libertarian "freedom." Without such an account we must look elsewhere for a solution to the problem of free will.

9.3. The Compatibilist Response

Compatibilism is the idea that an act can be both free and determined at the same time. This may sound like a contradiction, but according to this theory it is not. Contrary to what you might think, we can accept that human behavior is causally determined and yet go right on thinking of ourselves as free.

Compatibilism has always enjoyed a following in philosophy. In one form or another, it was the theory of Hobbes, Hume, Kant, and Mill; and it is defended by many writers today. This usually comes as a surprise to people who are not familiar with the philosophical literature, because free will and Determinism seem obviously *in*compatible. How are they supposed to go together? How can an act be free and determined at the same time?

According to Compatibilism, some actions are obviously free, and some are obviously not free. The trick is to see the difference between them. Here are some examples of when your action is not free:

- You hand over your wallet because a robber holds a gun to your head.

- You attend the company picnic because your boss tells you to.
- You report for induction into the army because you've been drafted and if you don't you'll be arrested.

In these cases you are not acting freely because you are being forced to do things you don't want to do. On the other hand, here are some cases in which you do act freely:

- You contribute money to a charity because you've decided the charity deserves your support.
- You urge your company to sponsor a picnic because you think it would be a great thing for the employees. You're delighted when your boss agrees, and you volunteer to help organize the event. On the day of the picnic, you arrive early because you're so excited about it.
- You join the army because the prospect of being a soldier appeals to you.

These actions are free because your choice is based on your own desires, without anyone else telling you what you must do. *This is what it means to do something "of your own free will."* But notice that this is perfectly compatible with your actions being causally determined by your past history, by events in your brain, and so on. It is even compatible with your *desires* being caused by factors beyond your control—the theory says freedom is about acting according to your desires, but it says nothing about where those desires came from. Thus, free will and Determinism are compatible.

The basic idea of Compatibilism may be summed up by saying that "free" does not mean "uncaused." Rather, it means something like "uncoerced." Thus, whether your behavior is free does not depend on *whether* it is caused; it only depends on *what causes it.*

Free Will as Involving Determinism. Is Compatibilism a viable theory? The basic argument for it goes as follows.

The whole worry over free will begins with the thought that *if an action is part of the great causal chain, it cannot be free.* In other words, if human actions are like other events, subject to prior causes and controlled by the laws of physics, then we are no more free than a feather tossed about by the wind. Without this assumption, no problem of free will arises. The question, then, is whether this assumption is true.

If it were true, then in order to be free, an act would have to be outside of the great causal nexus. The act would have to be uncaused. But consider what that would mean. What would it be like for *any* event to be uncaused? Imagine that billiard balls stopped obeying the laws of cause and effect. Their motions would then be unpredictable, but only because they would be random and chaotic. They might go off at odd angles, leap into the air, or suddenly stop. When struck by the cue ball, they might not move at all, or they might explode or turn to ice. Anything at all could happen.

Similarly, if a person's actions were suddenly disconnected from the network of causes and effects, they would become random, chaotic, and unpredictable. A man standing on a street corner might step into the traffic rather than wait for the light to change. Or he might take off his clothes, attack the person next to him, jump up and down, or recite the Magna Carta. This is what it would be like for behavior to be uncaused. But it is not what we mean by "free." You would not think that someone who began behaving in this way had suddenly acquired free will—you would think he had gone crazy. Free actions are not random and chaotic. They are orderly and thoughtful.

This line of thought may be taken one step further. Free will is not only compatible with Determinism; free will *requires* Determinism. In a random, chaotic world, no one would be free. But in a world that operates in an orderly fashion, according to the laws of cause and effect, free and rational actions are possible. In such a world a person's character and desires will control what he does.

In the causally determined world, however, people's actions would be *predictable*. Does this undermine the notion that they would be free? Consider an example. I have a friend who sees lots of movies, and I know exactly what sorts of movies she likes. I have been observing her moviegoing habits for years. If she is picking a movie to go to tonight, and I know what's playing, I can predict fairly well what she will choose.

But does the fact that I can predict her choice mean that she is not free? Not at all—she looks at the newspaper listings, thinks over what she wants to see, and decides accordingly. No one is holding a gun to her head. No one is manipulating her or tricking her. No one has planted a remote-control device in her brain. Thus, she chooses "of her own free will." The fact that, knowing her as I do, I can predict her choice changes nothing. Indeed, if I could *not* predict that she will prefer *The Remains of the Day* to *Rush Hour 3*, something would be wrong.

The Problem with Compatibilism. In the opinion of most philosophers today, Compatibilism has the best chance of saving free will and protecting the notion of moral responsibility from the onslaught of Determinism. Yet there is a serious problem with Compatibilism. Compatibilism says we are free if our actions flow from our own unmanipulated character and desires. The problem is that our characters and desires are themselves ultimately caused by forces beyond our control. This fact by itself is enough to bring our "freedom" into doubt. Peter van Inwagen puts the point like this:

> If Determinism is true, then our actions are consequences of the laws of nature and events in the remote past. But it is not up to us what went on before we were born, and neither is it up to us what the laws of nature are. Therefore, the consequences of these things (including our present acts) are not up to us.

Compatibilists agree that our present characters and desires are not up to us. But that concession seems to give away the game.

9.4. Ethics and Free Will

Many philosophers and theologians see the deterministic implications of modern science as a crisis. Our freedom, they say, is essential to our dignity as moral beings. It separates us from the animals. If we start thinking of ourselves as mere robots, pushed and pulled about by impersonal forces, we lose our humanity.

But before we give in to such fears, we need to ask what the implications of Determinism really are. If we do not have free will, are we still responsible moral agents? Does ethics lose its point?

Robots, Fatalism, and Deliberation. We can set aside the idea that if we lack free will we are "mere robots." We are nothing like robots. We have thoughts, intentions, and emotions. We experience happiness and unhappiness. We love our children and, if we are lucky, they love us back. We take pleasure in going to parties, playing darts, and listening to music. Robots can do none of this. Our capacity for these experiences and activities does not depend on our having free will. Even if our behavior is determined, all of this is still true.

Another way we differ from robots is that we often have *reasons* for what we do, and this will still be so even if we lack free will. As long as our beliefs and desires can guide our behavior, we will be able to act rationally. We will still be pursuing our own goals, just as before. Of course, the sense in which our goals are "our own" would change. We could no longer think of them as something that we freely choose. Instead, we would see them as goals that we have as a result of our makeup, our brain activity, and the influence of our environment. But what of that? Our goals are still our goals, and we still care about them.

It is sometimes suggested that the denial of free will would lead to a fatalistic attitude about the future: There would be no point in striving to change things. But clearly, this does not follow. The future depends on what we do, and if we want a certain sort of future, we have good reason to do what is needed to bring it about. Suppose you want sick children in Niger to get medical care, and so you contribute to humanitarian efforts. You help change the future. And there is certainly a point to it—without the help, the children will be worse off. Once again, the presence or absence of free will makes no difference.

Could we deliberate about what to do if we did not believe we had free will? Some philosophers have argued that, if we believe we are not free, "deliberating" makes no sense. After all, deliberating means trying to decide, and the effort to decide seems to presuppose that we could do different things. This reasoning sounds plausible. But what do we actually do when we deliberate? Mainly, we think about what we want and about how different actions would lead to different outcomes. We think about the children in Niger, what it's like to be sick and helpless, how our money could supply their needs, and so on; and we might also think about other things we could use our money for. Nothing in all that presupposes freedom.

Therefore, the denial of free will does not mean the end of ethics. We may still regard some things as good and others as bad—even if no one has free will, it is still better for the children in Niger not to die. We may still regard actions as better or worse depending on their consequences—contributing to humanitarian efforts is a good thing, even if we lack free will. And we can still think about all this in deciding what to do.

Evaluating People as Good or Bad. Can we continue to regard *people* as good or bad if they do not have free will? In a sense, we certainly can. Even without free will, people will still have virtues and vices. They will still be brave or cowardly, kind or cruel, generous or greedy. A murderer will still be a murderer, and a murderer will still be a bad thing to be. Of course, it may be possible to explain someone's misdeeds as the result of his genes, his history, or the chemistry of his brain. This may lead us to see him as unlucky. But that doesn't mean he is not bad. We need to distinguish *whether* someone is bad from *how he came to be* bad. A causal account of someone's character doesn't imply he isn't bad. It merely explains how he got to be that way.

Consider again Eric Rudolph, whose terrorist bombing spree in the 1990s killed two people and injured over 100 others. Rudolph's life story provides ample evidence that he is not responsible for having turned out as he did. Knowing his background, we may regard him as unlucky to have had his unfortunate history. As the old saying has it, there but for the grace of God go I. Yet we may still think of Rudolph as a bad man, because he is, after all, a murderer. He deliberately set out to harm innocent people. Now, however, we have a better understanding of what made him that way.

Responsibility. But, it may be protested, if people do not have free will, then they are not *responsible* for what they do. So how can we say that Eric Rudolph, or anyone else for that matter, is really bad?

It is natural to assume that, if we do not have free will, then we are not responsible. Philosophers disagree about whether this is a disturbing conclusion or an enlightened idea. Bertrand Russell (1872–1970) took the latter view. He wrote:

> No man treats a motorcar as foolishly as he treats another human being. When the car will not go, he does not attribute its annoying behavior to sin; he does not say, "You are a wicked motorcar, and I shall not give you any more

petrol until you go." He attempts to find out what is wrong
and to set it right.

Similarly, Russell says, when a person misbehaves we should try
to figure out why and deal with that. There is surely something
to this idea, especially when we think about the criminal law
and the social causes of crime.

Is responsibility compatible with Determinism? Let's see if
we can develop an account of responsibility that goes along
with Determinism. Being responsible means, at least, that you
may be held accountable for what you do—you may be blamed
when you behave badly and praised when you behave well. So,
if you are a responsible being, there must be some conditions
under which you are *blameworthy* for having done something.
What would those conditions be? At a minimum there are three
such conditions: (a) You must have done the act in question,
(b) the act must in some sense have been wrong, and (c) you
must have no excuse for having done it.

The notion of an excuse is crucial. Excuses are facts that
get you off the hook when you have done something bad. It was
an accident, you may say, or you didn't know what you were
doing, or you were forced to do it. It is not possible to give a
complete list of excuses, but here are some common ones:

- *Mistake.* For example, when you left my apartment,
  you took my umbrella by mistake—you thought it was
  yours. If you had taken my umbrella intentionally, you
  would be blameworthy.
- *Accident.* You were driving safely, taking every sensible
  precaution, when the child darted in front of the car,
  and you hit her. If you had been trying to hit her, or if
  you had been driving carelessly, you could be blamed.
- *Coercion.* You were forced to open the safe because the
  robbers threatened you. If you had opened it voluntar-
  ily, you could be blamed.
- *Ignorance.* You gave your boyfriend poison because the
  bottle was mislabeled. If you had known it was poison,
  you'd be a murderer.
- *Insanity.* You are suffering from Capgras syndrome,
  a rare delusional disorder that makes people believe
  someone known to them—usually a friend or relative—
  has been replaced by an imposter. So your behavior is

not your fault. There are many such disorders, and they are generally believed to be caused by damage to specific parts of the brain.

The logic of praise is similar to the logic of blame. Being praiseworthy for an action requires that (a) you did it, (b) it was a good thing to do, and (c) there are no conditions present analogous to excuses. It is curious that there is no name for these analogous conditions. We have a word, "excuses," for the conditions that make blame inappropriate; but we have no word for the comparable conditions that make praise inappropriate. Yet, clearly, similar conditions function in similar ways. If you do something splendid but do it merely by accident or from ignorance, you do not merit praise as you would if you had done it knowingly. Perhaps there is no general word for these conditions because people do not ordinarily try to avoid being praised. We might call them "credit-eliminating conditions."

According to this account of responsibility, people are responsible for what they do if there are no excusing conditions or credit-eliminating conditions present. Then, if they behave well they merit praise, while if they behave badly they merit blame. Nothing in this account conflicts with the assumption of Determinism. Compatibilists may accept this theory, not just as an account of responsibility, but as an account of freedom: you act freely when you act in the absence of excuses and credit-eliminating conditions. What makes people responsible can also be seen as what makes them free.

Is Something Still Missing? If we lack free will, there is still a sense in which we can be good or bad. Our actions can still have good or bad consequences, and we can still lack any of the standard excuses for doing what we do. Something feels missing, however, from this picture of agent assessment. Without free will people can be evaluated only as we now evaluate dogs. Some dogs are gentle and sweet; others are mean and vicious. In this vein we do speak of "good dogs" and "bad dogs." However, we normally think of human beings as capable of a higher goodness—a *moral* goodness. People, we believe, can freely create value. They can freely choose to do what's right or to do what's wrong. Dogs can't.

Now consider the notion of responsibility. If you're training a puppy to be a good companion, you treat her as if she were responsible: you punish her for behaving badly, and you reward her for behaving well. Moreover, as part of the training, you would recognize some excuses on her behalf (she can't be expected to resist eating meat that has been left out too temptingly), and you would reject other alleged excuses (she *can* resist the urge not to beg for meat at the table). However, none of us would say that dogs are "really" responsible for what they do; rather, we would say that sometimes we treat dogs *as if they were responsible,* based on the advantages of doing so, even though we know they're not responsible. If human beings lack free will, shouldn't we say the same about us—shouldn't we say people are not really responsible for what they do, even though it is useful to treat them as though they were? People could be "really responsible" only if they had free will.

A related point is that, without free will, it would be odd to say that someone "ought" to have behaved differently than he did behave. After all, this would imply that *he should have done something that was impossible for him to do.* For example, suppose that a member of the president's inner circle lies at a congressional hearing. If there is no free will, then the laws of nature compelled him to lie—he could not have done otherwise. To say that he "ought" to have been truthful would thus violate the age-old principle *ought implies can.* This is the principle that if you ought to do something, then it must be true that you can do it. On this principle, to say, "The government official should have told the truth" would make no more sense than to say, "The government official should have jumped over the moon." He couldn't have jumped over the moon, so he can't have been morally obligated to do so. And similarly for telling the truth.

Those who reject free will, it seems, must also reject the principle of "ought implies can." For them, to say that the official "ought to have told the truth" means something like "it would have been good if he had told the truth, supposing that were possible." But we don't want to say that the official ought to have jumped over the moon, even if such a leap would be a fine thing. Thus, those who deny free will might suggest that we apply the word "ought" only to the types of behavior we might influence—our condemnation might help convince the next official not to lie (by affecting his brain chemistry in the right way), but it could never cause anyone to jump over the moon. In this way moral language will be useful, and our ordinary practices of praise and blame can be retained. However, the whole business of praise and blame now sounds more like manipulation than the recognition of a deep underlying moral truth.

Thus, a belief in free will seems necessary to retain the commonsense picture of moral agency. This is not to say, however, that common sense is correct.

CHAPTER 10

*O*ur Knowledge
of the World around Us

In some remote corner of the universe, poured out and glittering in innumerable solar systems, there once was a star on which clever animals invented knowledge. That was the haughtiest and most mendacious minute of "world history"—and yet only a minute. After nature had drawn a few breaths the star grew cold, and the clever animals had to die.

—FRIEDRICH NIETZSCHE,
ON TRUTH AND LIE IN AN EXTRA-MORAL SENSE (1873)

10.1. Vats and Demons

A human brain has inputs and outputs. The inputs are signals from the person's eyes and ears and the rest of the nervous system. The brain receives the inputs and processes the information. Then it sends signals—the outputs—to various parts of the body, which move, breathe, and do other things as a result.

But suppose a scientist removes someone's brain and keeps it alive in a vat of nutrients. The scientist hooks up the brain to a computer that supplies the same inputs that would ordinarily come from the eyes and ears. The computer does its job so well that the brain can't tell the difference. The brain processes the signals in the same way it previously processed signals from the eyes and ears, and then it produces the same outputs, which are transmitted back to the computer. The computer returns new inputs, and so on.

If the computer does its job perfectly, the person whose brain is in the vat will continue to have the same experiences as before. From his point of view, nothing will have changed. Life will go on. He will meet his friends, go to work, have dinner, and watch TV. Or at least he will believe he is doing those things. None of it will actually be happening. His life will be an illusion created by the computer.

Now suppose it is suggested that you are that person—you are a brain in a vat, and your "life" is only an illusion. The suggestion seems absurd, but how could you prove it wrong? There seems to be nothing you could do that would prove your life is real. After all, every experience you have, including your attempts to prove you are not a brain in a vat, could be supplied by the computer. You might protest that the whole story is technologically impossible—brains cannot be kept alive in vats, and no computer can do what we are describing. But perhaps that is true only in the dream world you are experiencing. In the real world outside your vat, such computers do exist.

The Matrix (1999), a gripping movie starring Keanu Reeves, exploits this possibility. In the movie people's brains are not removed, but their bodies are connected to a giant computer that achieves the same effect. The people in the Matrix are made to think that they live in a physical world of buildings and weather and cars, but in fact that world exists only in their minds. Some other good movies, such as *The Thirteenth Floor* (1999) and *Total Recall* (1990), exploit similar themes.

Long before there were motion pictures and digital computers, René Descartes (1596–1650) dreamed up a similar scenario. Rather than imagining brains in vats, Descartes imagined that a powerful "evil spirit" was intent upon deceiving him:

> I will therefore suppose that, not a true God, who is very good and who is the supreme source of truth, but a certain evil spirit, not less clever and deceitful than powerful, has bent all his efforts to deceiving me.

If such an Evil Demon tried to deceive us, what would happen? Presumably, we would acquire false beliefs about everything. We would think that $3 + 3 = 5$, and that belief would seem as certain as $3 + 2 = 5$ now does to us. We might be sure about everything, yet right about nothing. And how could we possibly figure out what was really going on? Every thought we might have could be manipulated by the Demon.

The problem is not merely to say how can we *know for sure* that there is no Demon, and that we're not brains in vats; the problem is how we can offer any evidence at all against these scenarios. Any alleged evidence we produce might just as easily be offered by a brain in a vat; and any evidence that seems convincing to us might seem so only because the Evil Demon has tricked us into believing it.

We'll return to these ideas later. Now consider another outrageous possibility, which some philosophers believe describes the real world.

10.2. Idealism

When you look at the tree outside the window, what exactly do you see? One answer is that you see a patchwork of colors, mainly shades of brown and green. If you move your head, the pattern shifts slightly. Close your eyes, and it disappears altogether. The tree is still there, of course, but the thing you were experiencing—the splash of colors—will vanish. It will reappear when you open your eyes again.

The seventeenth-century philosophers called this pattern of colors an *idea* in your mind. In the twentieth century the terms *sense-datum* and *qualia* were popular. But whatever term is used, the point is that what you literally see is not the tree itself. The object of your experience is a representation in your mind. The mental representation changes when you look at the tree from different angles. When you close your eyes, it disappears. But the tree, presumably, remains the same. A color-blind person might have a different experience when looking at the tree—rather than green and brown, she might see shades of purple.

But now a startling possibility arises. If we are aware only of our own ideas, why do we need "physical objects" as part of our worldview at all? What do they add? We can never experience them, and if we say they cause our experiences, there is no way to verify it. For all we can know, *the only things that really exist are our minds and their ideas*. The physical world is an unnecessary metaphysical supposition, so we might as well forget about it.

This conclusion was embraced by George Berkeley (1685–1753), an eccentric but brilliant Irish bishop. "I suspect that [the man in Ireland] is one of those people who seek to become famous by their paradoxes," Leibniz said of him. Berkeley opposed much of the science of his day, including Newton's great contributions, because of its materialist underpinnings.

But his philosophical writings have a vigor and incisiveness that have earned them a permanent place in the history of the subject. The theory that reality is constituted entirely of minds and their ideas is called "Berkelian Idealism" in his honor—if it is an honor. Berkeley's summation of this view and of the reasons for it is admirably clear:

> But, though it were possible that solid, figured, movable substances may exist without the mind, corresponding to the ideas we have of bodies, yet how is it possible for us to know this? Either we must know it by sense or by reason. As for our senses, by them we have the knowledge only of our sensations, ideas, or those things that are immediately perceived by sense, call them what you will; but they do not inform us that things exist without the mind, or unperceived, [that resemble] those which are perceived. This the materialists themselves acknowledge. It remains therefore that if we have any knowledge at all of external things, it must be by reason, inferring their existence from what is immediately perceived by sense. But what reason can induce us to believe the existence of bodies without the mind, from what we perceive, since the very patrons of matter themselves do not pretend there is any necessary connection [between material bodies] and our ideas? . . .
>
> In short, if there were external bodies, it is impossible we should ever come to know it; and if there were not, we might have the very same reasons to think there were that we have now.

Idealism strikes most of us as absurd because it denies that physical objects exist. But aside from insulting the view, what can we say against it? A number of objections come to mind. When I look outside my window, why do I always experience the same splash of colors? You and I can say, "Because you're always looking at the same tree." What can an idealist say? He doesn't believe there is a tree. Or, when you and I both look out my window, why do we both see the same kind of thing? Again, we can say it's because we're seeing the same tree; but the idealist must call it a coincidence. And again: When I start the dishwasher and later come back to unload it, it appears as though something has been going on in my absence—the dishes have been getting cleaned. But what can Berkeley say? On his view there is no dishwasher, and there are no dishes. The objections to Idealism all boil down to the same thing: Our experiences suggest that there is a world independent of us—a world that affects different people similarly, that affects the same person similarly at different times, and that keeps going when we're asleep.

Bishop Berkeley's response to these objections was to appeal to God. God is responsible for ordering our ideas so that we can make sense of the world. When we both are looking through the same window, God makes sure we have the same experiences. And when I come back to unload the dishes, God makes sure that the dishes look clean. In fact, God saw them being cleaned—even when no one is looking at the tree or the dishes, they still exist as ideas in God's mind. God is always perceiving everything.

If in response, the "materialist" challenges Berkeley to prove that God exists, Berkeley might offer some of the traditional arguments for God's existence. Or he might say, "To make sense of my theory, I have proposed we accept the existence of one thing in addition to minds and ideas—namely, God. However, believers in an independent, physical reality are proposing that we accept the existence of countless additional things—namely, every single physical object in the universe."

10.3. What Evidence for These Views Might Be Like

Despite Berkeley's arguments, most people find Idealism to be unbelievable. And nobody has ever believed in Descartes' Evil Demon or in the brain-in-a-vat scenario. However, it is conceivable that these views might turn out to be true.

Suppose that, when you finish reading this paragraph, there is a sudden discontinuity in your experience. In an eye blink, you find that you are in a hospital bed. Across the room is a mirror, and in the mirror you see an unfamiliar person with bandages on his (or her) head. You are feeling thoroughly confused and panicky, when a doctor comes in and explains what is going on. She says that your brain was just removed from a vat, where it had been connected to a computer for many years, and reinstalled in your head. You are given a tour of the facility, where you see other brains still connected by wires to the colossal computer. Then, leaving the hospital, you find that you are in a city that you have never heard of and that your "hometown," in which you believed you had been living, does not exist on any map. And so on. If you had those experiences, it would be reasonable for you to conclude that you had been a brain in a vat.

Or instead, suppose that, after you finish reading this paragraph, the world begins to tremble and everything around you dissolves—all the buildings, trees, and even the ground melts away, leaving nothing but a white-tinged background. Other than being confused, you feel no discomfort. Then it is all replaced by a different, strange-looking environment, which in turn disappears, to be replaced by still another environment. After this happens a few times, you hear a booming voice, coming from everywhere at once. The voice identifies itself as God, and it explains that he has been giving you a demonstration of the way in which he channels perceptions into your mind. There are no "physical objects," he explains; they are unnecessary— why should he create physical objects to cause you to have experiences when he can supply you with the experiences directly? If all this happened, it would be reasonable for you to believe in Idealism. And if the booming voice had instead described a battle in which he had triumphed over the Evil Demon, then, given enough detail, it could be reasonable for you to accept the existence of Descartes' powerful deceiver.

If any of these things happened, you would not be forced to change your worldview. Instead, you could conclude that you had gone crazy. But it would at least be clear that you possessed evidence for Idealism, or for the Evil Demon, or the brain-in-a-vat hypothesis. Of course, as things stand, we have no such evidence. However, we have not yet offered any reason to *reject* these crazy ideas, either. Can we come up with any?

10.4. Descartes' Theological Response

Descartes was the first person to consider this question. He lived in the early seventeenth century, when modern science was very young. Descartes was excited about the development of science, and he wondered whether scientific knowledge had secure foundations. In fact, Descartes wondered if *any* of our beliefs were on firm footing, since science is just the rigorous application of common sense to the study of the empirical world.

For our knowledge to be secure, Descartes thought, it must ultimately rest on foundations that cannot be doubted.

Thus, Descartes hoped to find an absolutely certain ground for human knowledge. And he thought he did find such a ground, in the following chain of reasoning:

(1) What can I know for sure? If I seem to see a fireplace in front of me, or even if I believe $2 + 3 = 5$, I can't be sure of these things because an evil spirit might be controlling my thoughts. But, Descartes says, there is one thing that I do know with absolute certainty: *I know that I am now having certain thoughts and experiences.* Even if it is nothing but an illusion, I know that I am having the *experience* "fireplace in front of me." I cannot be wrong about that. Similarly, even if an evil spirit is deceiving me, I still know that I am having the *thought* "$3 + 2 = 5$." I know my own thoughts and experiences, and you know your own thoughts and experiences. That's the one thing we can't be wrong about.

(2) If it is certain that we have thoughts and experiences, then it is certain that we exist. After all, if we did not exist, we could not be having those thoughts. Descartes expresses this inference as "I think, therefore I am"—or, in the Latin version, *Cogito, ergo sum*— one of the most famous propositions in the history of thought.

(3) Among our thoughts is one that stands out, namely, the idea of God. Our other ideas, such as the idea of a fireplace, are ideas of things that might not exist in reality. But the idea of God is different, because it is the idea of a perfect being, and so it is the idea of something that must exist in reality. Why? Because not existing in reality is incompatible with being perfect. Therefore, God must exist. (This is the Ontological Argument, which we have seen before, in chapter 2.)

(4) We have now established that we exist, along with our thoughts and experiences, and that God, a perfect being, also exists. But God, if he is perfect, cannot be a deceiver. It follows that God could not have made us so that we would be systematically deceived about what the world is like. A perfect, truthful God could not have endowed us with senses and powers of reasoning

that would inevitably lead us to believe all sorts of things, unless those things were true.

(5) It follows, then, that our senses and our powers of reasoning are reliable sources of knowledge about the world around us.

This argument leaves Descartes with a residual problem: If our faculties were designed and made by a perfectly good creator, why do we sometimes make mistakes? Descartes' answer is a variant on a familiar theme from the discussion of evil—free will. Error, he says, is a result of human action, not divine action. When we make mistakes, it is because we employ our faculties carelessly—or because other humans set out to deceive us.

Descartes' argument provides obvious responses to the hypothetical scenarios we've been entertaining. If there is a perfect God, as it says in step (3), then there is no Evil Demon (or, if there is one, his power to deceive us is kept in check by God). And if, as it says in step (5), our senses and powers of reasoning are reliable, then Idealism should be false, since we so naturally believe that objects exist independently from us. If Idealism were true, then God would be a deceiver, which he isn't. Finally, the brain-in-a-vat hypothesis should at least be unlikely in Descartes' world, since one would hope that a perfect being might rescue us from a life of perpetual illusion.

Is Descartes' argument sound? Descartes' reasoning has been analyzed endlessly for the last three-and-a-half centuries. Today in North America there are probably a dozen graduate students writing dissertations about it. One problem is that the Ontological Argument is dubious. Another is that, in doing all this reasoning, Descartes is using the same rational powers the argument is intended to validate. Thus, his procedure seems to be circular: He is reasoning his way to the conclusion that reasoning can be trusted. Essentially, his argument goes like this: How do we know that reasoning can be trusted? Because God has made our powers of reasoning, and God is not a deceiver. How do we know that? Because we have a chain of reasoning to prove it. In the philosophical literature this is known as "the Cartesian Circle." Because of these problems, nobody now thinks that Descartes provided an absolutely certain basis for human knowledge. That goal, it is widely thought, is too ambitious. Complete certainty is beyond human powers.

Even if his argument was faulty, Descartes made a number of lasting contributions. One is that he clearly identified the problem. Another is that he pointed out, correctly, that a theological perspective provides one way to solve it. The theological solution is that if we combine the evidence of our senses with the thought that God has given us our senses as a way of knowing the world, then we can be sure that our senses reliably provide knowledge of the world around us.

Indeed, we might take the upshot of Descartes' work to be a challenge: If we do *not* assume a religious perspective, how can the problem be solved? It is a commonplace that religion might shed light on such matters as the origin of the world, death, and morality. Surprisingly, Descartes shows that, for those who take such a perspective, it might also help explain the basis of empirical knowledge.

10.5. Direct vs. Indirect Realism

We still haven't solved our central problem: We haven't explained why a belief in physical matter is more reasonable than a belief in Idealism, nor have we warded off Descartes' deceiving Demon or slam-dunked the brain-in-a-vat scenario. Admittedly, our problem has an air of unreality about it. You might think it looks like a problem conjured up by people with too much time on their hands. If so, many philosophers agree with you. On their view the problem arises from a mistake.

So far, our discussion has assumed a certain picture of how sense-perception works. The picture is this:

> When we look at an object, we do not see the object itself. Instead, we are aware of an "experience," or an "idea in our minds," or a "sense-datum," or a "mental representation," or some such. Then we must infer something about the world outside us from these experiences. The problem is to explain how this inference is justified, given the existence of rival hypotheses.

But, it is said, this is all very misleading. Once the "problem" is formulated in this way, the mistake has already been made.

The mistake is saying that when we look at an object such as a tree we see only some sort of mental representation. We do not. Instead, *we see the tree.* We see a physical object that exists outside us. We do not "infer" that the tree exists. We see it in a direct, unmediated way. So the correct answer to the question of how we know there is a tree outside the window is simple: We see it. Thus, common sense answers Idealism.

Seeing—along with hearing, touching, and the other senses—is a way of getting information about the world around us. But it is not a two-step process, in which we first get information about "sense-data" and then move from that to information about the tree. Instead, it is a one-step process: We see the tree. No further justification is required for saying we know the tree is there. The brain-in-a-vat and the Evil Demon hypotheses cannot be refuted, but under normal circumstances we have good reason to reject them—our direct access to the reality they deny.

Of course, we may sometimes be mistaken, but this fact poses no special problem. We discover our mistakes in the same way we learn everything else, by using our senses and our intelligence. I think I see a tree—is it an illusion? I find out by looking more closely, or by trying to touch it, or by asking someone else to check, or by considering whether I have been drinking too much. If I think I might be suffering a hallucination but at the moment have no way to check, I may simply suspend judgment. Under normal circumstances, however, I know I see a tree.

This view is known as Direct Realism. It is contrasted with Indirect Realism, which holds that our immediate object of perception is something mental—our idea of a tree—whereas we are only indirectly aware of the tree itself. Direct Realism appeals to common sense and seems to provide a straightforward answer to the science-fiction scenarios. Such eminent figures as Ludwig Wittgenstein (1889–1951) and J. L. Austin (1911–1960) have defended it. But Direct Realism is ultimately unsatisfying, for two reasons.

First, Direct Realism doesn't actually help us solve problems like the Brain in the Vat. We want to be given evidence that we're not brains in vats; we want a reason to believe that we *are* in touch with an external reality. Direct Realism, however, merely asserts that we're in touch with such a reality, and since we are, it allows us to say that we know we are. As Bertrand Russell might have said, this approach to the problem has all the advantages of theft over honest toil.

Second, Direct Realism does not fit well with what we know about how the brain processes information. "Seeing" a tree is not a simple matter at all. It is the result of neurological processes that have a complicated structure, and we should want a theory of perception that connects with our scientific understanding of how this processing works.

10.6. Vision and the Brain

The German philosopher Immanuel Kant (1724–1804) is famous for insisting that perception is not a passive process. The mind does not simply record what passes before it; instead, the mind actively interprets experience according to certain built-in principles. Therefore, what we think of as "simple" perception is actually the result of a complicated interpretation of the sensory data. Kant's detailed account of how this works is no longer widely accepted. However, his basic thought is confirmed by current research.

Psychologist Steven Pinker writes:

> When [organisms] apprehend the world by sight, they have to use the splash of light reflected off its objects, projected as a two-dimensional kaleidoscope of throbbing, heaving streaks on each retina. The brain somehow analyzes the moving collages and arrives at an impressively accurate sense of the objects out there that gave rise to them.

How does the brain do this? There is a great deal of ongoing research in this area, and no one pretends to have the final answer. But one leading idea is that the brain makes a series of assumptions about how the "throbbing, heaving streaks" are to be interpreted. Thus, what we see is determined by these assumptions as well as by the streaks. Here are four of those assumptions:

1. Sharp lines are interpreted as boundaries (edges), while enclosed areas of one color are taken to be surfaces.
2. Objects have the simplest shapes consistent with the pattern of light on the retina. Thus, a skinny rectangle is more likely to be a stick than a penny viewed edgewise.
3. Surfaces are assumed to be evenly textured. Gradual changes in surface coloration are therefore interpreted as due to lighting and perspective. For example, if you see a surface covered with rows of dots, and if the dots in

succeeding rows seem to be closer and closer together, your brain will interpret this as an effect of perspective. It will "see" the dots as evenly spaced. Likewise, if the surface grows gradually darker from one side to the other, the surface will be perceived as evenly colored, with the shading interpreted as an effect of the lighting.

4. "Objects have regular, compact silhouettes, so if Object A has a bite taken out that is filled by Object B, A is behind B; accidents don't happen in which a bulge in B fits flush into the bite of A." Think of a suitcase with a bowl in front of it, so that you can't see the corner of the suitcase. You don't assume that the corner of the suitcase is missing and that the bowl fits neatly into the vacant space. Instead, you assume that the bowl is in front of the suitcase, blocking your view.

These assumptions are what philosophers call *defeasible*— they are correctable in light of further experience. Thus, we might move the bowl and discover that the suitcase really does have a missing corner. Again, if the sticklike object is rotated, it could turn out to be a penny.

A further problem is why we do not perceive the world simply as a montage of two-dimensional surfaces. We perceive the world as a collection of three-dimensional *objects*. How do we manage that? Psychologist Irving Biederman argues that the brain interprets information from the eyes using a stock of 24 basic three-dimensional shapes, which he calls "geons." Biederman suggests that the geons are the brain's inbuilt device for constructing objects from the data of experience. The geons include such basic units as a sphere, a cube, a cylinder, and a bent tube; and all objects are said to be constructed by combining these basic units. (This will come as no surprise to art students, who traditionally are taught to draw and shade such standard "solids" as a preliminary to tackling more complicated objects.) A bent tube on top of a box is a suitcase. A bent tube on top of a cylinder is a pail. A bent tube on the side of a cylinder is a cup. And so on. Kant spoke of the mind imposing its forms on experience; according to Biederman, geons are some of the forms.

Color, one of the last elements to be added by the brain, can make a huge difference to our emotions. Neurologist Oliver Sacks has studied what happens to people who suffer brain damage that makes them completely colorblind, so that they see only whites, blacks, and greys. For some of these people, vision is not like watching black-and-white TV—rather, something important in addition to the colors is missing. One of Sacks's patients, Jonathan I., was a painter who became colorblind after a car accident. His eyes weren't damaged, but the part of his brain that constructs color was. According to Sacks, Jonathan I. found his new world to be alien, empty, and dead. He avoided other people, who seemed to him "like animated grey statues," and he found food to be disgusting—even when he closed his eyes, the mental image of a tomato looked as black as its appearance.

Finally, we have two eyes that view the world from slightly different angles, and the brain has a way of combining the information from them to tell us how far away objects are. (With only one eye, the photon striking it could come from any point on a straight line stretching out to infinity—there would be no easy way to judge where on this line the signal originated.) To us, it seems obvious that perceiving depth is the purpose of binocular vision. However, this is a recent discovery. Until the nineteenth century it was thought that having two eyes is simply a by-product of the fact that our bodies are symmetrical; or, it was thought, perhaps the second eye is simply a spare in case something happens to the first one.

We see a world of physical objects, then, because the brain makes all these assumptions (and more) in interpreting the signals from our eyes. Are these assumptions arbitrary? Why do we make precisely these assumptions, rather than different ones? The answer is that the human brain is the product of evolution. We have inherited the ways of processing information that contributed to the survival of our ancestors, who needed to find food, avoid predators, interact with members of their own species, and otherwise move safely through the world. Thus, we have evolved a perceptual system that is useful but also full of gaps. We are blind to most of the electromagnetic spectrum. We automatically notice some features of the environment but ignore others. And we are good at distinguishing individual people but bad at distinguishing individual members of other species. It is easy to imagine how we might perceive the world differently if our brains were constructed differently. But it is unlikely that alternative ways of perceiving would serve us much better.

10.7. The Natural Theory

"Seeing a tree" seems for all the world like a simple thing. You turn toward the tree and open your eyes, and there it is. But we know it is not simple at all. A great deal of processing goes on behind the scenes. We might say that a perception consists of two parts: first, the raw data that come from the senses, and second, the assumptions that we make in interpreting the data. These assumptions, taken together, form a theory about what the world is like.

Our commonsense view of how perception works is part of such a theory, which we might call—with obvious bias—the Natural Theory. The gist of it is this:

> *The Natural Theory:* We have experiences such as "seeing the tree" because our bodies, including our eyes and ears, interact with a physical world. The physical world exists independent of us—that is, it would exist even if we did not, and it continues to exist even when we are not observing it. The physical world impinges on our senses, causing us to have experiences that represent, more or less accurately, how things are. The experiences, in turn, cause us to have true beliefs about the tree.

The Natural Theory is a rival of other theories, such as Idealism and Direct Realism. Basically, it combines Indirect Realism with a dose of common sense.

Part of its "dose of common sense" is the claim that we interact with a physical world. In claiming this, the Natural Theory assumes that Idealism is wrong, since Idealism claims that there is no physical world. Also, the Natural Theory follows common sense in saying that the process of perception ultimately results in true beliefs. In saying this, the theory assumes that we're not brains in vats and that we're not systematically deceived by a Demon, since brains in vats and those who are duped mostly get things wrong. However, these are mere assumptions—the Natural Theory offers no argument against these bizarre possibilities. What, then, has become of our attempt to offer reasons on this score? It has failed.

CHAPTER 11

*E*thics and Objectivity

There are no objective values.
—J. L. MACKIE, *ETHICS: INVENTING RIGHT AND WRONG* (1977)

11.1. Thrasymachus's Challenge

Thrasymachus has the misfortune of being remembered through the eyes of someone who despised him. He was a Sophist, one of the professional teachers who flourished in Athens during the time of Socrates. Unlike Socrates the Sophists charged a fee for their instruction, and Plato is quick to insinuate that they liked money more than truth. Plato is especially hard on Thrasymachus, who is introduced in the *Republic* like this:

> While we had been talking [says Socrates] Thrasymachus had often tried to interrupt, but had been prevented by those sitting near him, who wanted to hear the argument concluded; but when we paused, he was no longer able to contain himself and gathered himself together and sprang on us like a wild beast, as if he wanted to tear us in pieces. Polemarchus and I were scared stiff, as Thrasymachus burst out and said, "What is all this nonsense, Socrates?"

The "nonsense" was a discussion of the nature of justice. Thrasymachus was impatient because Socrates and his friends were assuming that justice is something real and important. Thrasymachus denied this. According to him, people believe in right and wrong only because they are taught to obey the rules of their society. These rules, however, are merely human contrivances. Thrasymachus added that the ethical code of a society will reflect the interests of its ruling classes, so when ordinary people think they must "do the right thing," they are just being chumps.

Thrasymachus challenged Socrates to prove that ethics has an objective basis. Of course, we would like to believe it does. We would like to think that some things really are good and others really are bad, independent of our attitudes and social conventions. But how can this be shown? In the ancient world the idea that ethics is just a matter of opinion was commonplace; with the rise of modern science, skepticism about ethics became even more attractive. Modern science sees the world as a cold, indifferent place that cares nothing for us or our projects; the universe is a realm of facts that know nothing of right or wrong. As David Hume (1711–1776) put it, "The life of a man is of no greater importance to the universe than that of an oyster." Thus, it seems natural to conclude that ethics can be nothing but a human invention.

One way of meeting Thrasymachus's challenge might be to introduce religious notions. If the universe was created by God, according to a divine plan, and if God issues commands about how we should live, we might find in this an objective basis for our judgments of right and wrong. But suppose we set this possibility aside. Is there any way to defend the objectivity of ethics without invoking religious considerations? We will see that there is a way. The arguments for ethical skepticism are not as powerful as they appear.

11.2. Is Ethics Just Social Convention?

The idea that ethics is nothing more than social convention has always appealed to educated people. Different cultures have different moral codes, it is said, and it is merely naive to think that there is one universal standard that applies in all places and times. Examples are easy to come by. In Islamic countries men may have more than one wife. In medieval Europe lending money for interest was considered a sin. The native peoples of northern Greenland would sometimes abandon old people to die in the snow. Considering such examples, anthropologists have long agreed with Herodotus that "Custom is king o'er all."

Today the idea that morality is a social product is attractive for an additional reason. Multiculturalism is currently an important issue, especially in the United States. Given the dominant position of the United States in the world, it is said, and the way American actions affect other peoples, it is incumbent upon Americans to respect and appreciate the differences between cultures. In particular, we must avoid the arrogant assumption that our ways are "right" and that the customs of other peoples are inferior. This means, in part, that we should refrain from making moral judgments about other cultures. We should adopt a policy of live and let live.

On the surface, this attitude seems enlightened. Tolerance is important, and many cultural practices obviously involve nothing more than social custom—standards of dress, food, domestic arrangements, and so on.

But fundamental matters of justice are different. When we consider such examples as slavery, racism, and the abuse of women, it no longer seems enlightened to give a shrug and say, "They have their customs and we have ours." Consider these two examples.

In a Pakistani village a 12-year-old boy was accused of being romantically involved with a 22-year-old woman of a higher social class. He denied it, but the tribal elders did not believe him. As punishment they decreed that the boy's teenage sister—who had done nothing wrong—should be publicly raped. Her name is Mukhtar Mai. Four men carried out the sentence while the village watched. Observers said there was nothing unusual in this, but with so many foreigners in the region, the incident was noticed and reported in *Newsweek*. This was in 2002.

In the same year, in Northern Nigeria, a religious court sentenced an unwed mother named Amina Lawal to be stoned to death for having had sex out of wedlock. When the verdict was read, the crowded courtroom shouted out their approval. The judge said that the sentence should be carried out as soon as the baby was big enough not to need breast-feeding. The woman identified the father, but he denied the accusation, and no charges were brought against him. This was only one in a series of such sentences imposed there. Responding to international pressure, the Nigerian government announced that it would not enforce the sentence against Amina Lawal, and in 2004 a Nigerian court overturned her sentence and set her free.

The rape of Mukhtar Mai seems to have been regarded as a matter of tribal honor. Her brother was allegedly romancing a woman from a different tribe, and the elders of her tribe demanded justice. The stonings in Nigeria, on the other hand, are the application of the Islamic law of Sharia, which has been adopted by 12 of Nigeria's 36 states. Both actions seem horrible. Our instincts are to condemn them. But are we *justified* in saying the rape and the stonings are wrong? Two thoughts stand in the way of this natural response. Let us consider them one at a time.

First, there is the idea that *we should respect the differences between cultures*. No matter how questionable the practices of another society may seem to us, we must acknowledge that people in those cultures have a right to follow their own traditions. (And, it will be added, our traditions may seem equally questionable to them.) Is this correct? As we have noted, this thought is appealing. But when we analyze it, it falls apart.

Respecting a culture does not mean regarding everything in it as acceptable. You might think that a culture has a wonderful history and has produced great art. You might think that its leading figures are noble and admirable. You might think that your own culture has much to learn from it. Still, this does not mean that you must regard it as perfect. It can also contain elements that are terrible. Most of us take just this attitude toward our own society—if you are an American, you probably think that America is a great country but that some aspects of American life are regrettable. Why should you not think the same about Pakistan or Nigeria? If you did, you would be agreeing with many Pakistanis and Nigerians.

Moreover, it is a mistake to think of the world as a collection of discrete, unified cultures that exist in isolation from one another. Cultures overlap and interact. In the United States there are cultural differences between Irish Catholics, Italian Americans, Southern Baptists, African Americans in Los Angeles, African Americans in Mississippi, and Hasidic Jews in Brooklyn. Oklahomans who happily execute criminals are quite different, culturally, from the Amish in Pennsylvania. In some ways we think that "live and let live" is the best policy, but no one takes this to mean that you should have no opinion about what happens in another part of the country.

Similarly, in both Pakistan and Nigeria, rival groups coexist. When the Pakistani girl was raped, authorities in the Pakistani government took action against the local tribal leaders who had ordered it. Which group—the local leaders or the national government—sets the standards that we must respect? There is no clear-cut answer. Lacking an answer, the idea that we must "respect the values of that culture" is empty.

This also raises the critical question of who speaks for a culture. Is it the priests? The politicians? The women? The slaves? Opinions within a society are rarely uniform. If we say, for example, that slavery was approved in ancient Greece, we are referring to the opinions of the slave-owners. The slaves themselves might have had a different idea. Why should we take the view of the slave-owners to be more worthy of respect than that of the slaves? Similarly, when Mukhtar Mai was raped, her father and uncle, who were forced to watch, did not think it was right.

Finally, we should notice a purely logical point. Some people think that ethical relativism *follows from* the fact that cultures have different standards. That is, they think this inference is valid:

(1) Different cultures have different moral codes.

(2) Therefore, there is no such thing as objective right and wrong. Where ethics is concerned, the standards of the different societies are all that exist.

But this is a mistake. It does not follow from the fact that people disagree about something, that there is no truth about it. When we consider certain matters, this is obvious. Cultures may disagree about the Milky Way—some think it is a galaxy, others think it is a river in the sky—but it does not follow that there is no objective fact about what the Milky Way is. The same goes for ethics. The explanation of why cultures disagree about an ethical issue might be that one of them is mistaken. It is easy to overlook this if we think only of such examples as standards of dress, marriage practices, and the like. Those may indeed be nothing but matters of local custom. But it does not follow that *all* practices are mere matters of local custom. Rape, slavery, and stoning might be different.

The upshot of all this is that, while we should be respectful of other cultures, this provides no reason why we must always refrain from making judgments about what they do. We can be tolerant and respectful and yet think that other cultures are not perfect. There is, however, a second reason why it may seem that being judgmental is inappropriate.

The second troublesome thought is that *all standards of judgment are culture-relative.* If we say that the rape of Mukhtar Mai was wrong, we seem to be using *our* standards to judge *their* practices. From our point of view, the rape was wrong, but who is to say that our point of view is correct? We can say that the tribal leaders are wrong, but they can equally well say that we are wrong. So it's a standoff, and there seems to be no way to get beyond the mutual finger-pointing.

This second argument can be spelled out more explicitly like this:

(1) If we are to be justified in saying that the practices of another society are wrong, then there must be some standard of right and wrong, to which we can appeal, that is not simply derived from our own culture. The standard to which we appeal must be culture-neutral.

(2) But there are no culture-neutral moral standards. All standards are relative to some society or other.

(3) Therefore, we cannot be justified in saying that the practices of another society are wrong.

Is this correct? It looks plausible, but in fact there *is* a culture-neutral standard of right and wrong, and it is not hard to say what it is. After all, the reason we object to the rape and the stoning is not that they are "contrary to American values." Nor is our objection that these practices are somehow bad for *us.* The reason we object is that Mukhtar Mai and Amina Lawal are being harmed—the social practices at issue are bad, not for us, but for them. Thus, the culture-neutral standard is *whether the social practice in question is beneficial or harmful to the people who are affected by it.* Good social practices benefit people; bad social practices harm people.

This criterion is culture-neutral in every relevant sense. First, it does not play favorites between cultures. It may be applied equally to all societies, including our own. Second, the source of the principle does not lie within one particular culture. Rather, every culture values the welfare of its people. It is a value that must be embraced, at least to some extent, if a culture is to exist. It is a precondition of culture rather than a contingent norm arising out of it. And so, the suggestion that a social practice harms people can never be dismissed as an alien standard "brought in from the outside" to judge a culture's doings.

11.3. Ethics and Science

Several things might make us skeptical about ethics. Reflecting on the differences between cultures is one of them. Another is that ethics seems so different from science. Science provides our paradigm of objectivity, and ethics seems to fall short of science in various ways. So how can ethics be objective? Here are three arguments along these lines against the objectivity of ethics.

The Argument from Disagreement. It is troubling that ethical disagreement seems to be so widespread and persistent. If ethics were a matter of objective truth, shouldn't we expect greater consensus? Yet it seems that in matters of ethics people disagree about everything. They clash over abortion, capital punishment, gun control, euthanasia, the environment, and the moral status of animals. They disagree about sex, drug use, and whether we have a duty to help needy children in foreign countries. The list could go on. In science, however, there appears to be widespread agreement on all essential points. The natural conclusion is that ethics, unlike science, is a mere matter of opinion. We may summarize this argument like this:

(1) In ethics there is widespread and persistent disagreement.

(2) The best explanation of this situation is that there is no objective truth in ethics.

(3) Therefore, we may conclude, at least tentatively, that there is no objective truth in ethics.

Is this correct? We may begin by observing that ethics is more like science than you might think. There is a tremendous amount of agreement about ethics. All thoughtful people agree that murder, rape, and theft are wrong. All agree that we should tell the truth and keep our promises. Everyone acknowledges that kidnapping and extortion are outrageous and that racism is abhorrent. This list, also, could go on. If it is said that some people do not agree with these judgments—racists and thieves, for example—it can be replied that some people disagree with the findings of science—flat-earthers and psychics, for example. The situation in ethics is the same as in science: The vast majority of people agree—while some dissenters are ignored, for good reason. In fact, there may be more dissenters in science than in ethics, if you count religious fundamentalists who reject Darwinism.

In ethics, then, there is massive agreement about fundamental matters. But there is also disagreement about abortion, capital punishment, and the other issues mentioned above. What are we to make of this? We might notice, first, that from a social point of view most of the issues we disagree about are less important than the matters we agree on. No matter how much passion is generated by the debate over affirmative action, affirmative action is a less significant issue than murder, truth telling, or promise keeping. It is less significant in that societies can function with a variety of policies on affirmative action. But social living would be impossible without a prohibition on murder. Likewise, society would be impossible without requirements that people speak the truth and keep their bargains. To see this, try to imagine what it would be like to live in a society in which those rules were not accepted. What would happen if people could kill one another at will? Or suppose there was no presumption that people would speak the truth? Or suppose you could not rely on others to do as they promised? In these circumstances society would fall apart.

We might also notice that many of the disputed issues are *harder* than the matters about which we agree. To decide the question of abortion, we would have to come to some rational understanding of why human life is valuable: What is it about people that makes it wrong to kill them? Why is it worse to kill a human than to kill an animal (if it is worse)? Then we would have to figure out when, in the course of human development, we acquire whatever properties make our lives valuable. Moreover, we would have to determine the moral importance of potentiality: What is the significance of the fact that an individual who is not yet a full human person can nonetheless develop into one? All this is hard enough, but to make things worse, it is not obvious that these are even the right questions to ask. It is no wonder that people disagree. In such cases the difficulty of the issues, not the absence of "truth," may be the best explanation of why people cannot agree.

A similar pattern of agreement and disagreement exists in science. All scientists agree about a large central core of accepted truth. Yet there is also a host of disputed issues. As everyone knows who reads the science section of *The New York Times*, scientists disagree about the relation between quantum theory and classical relativity, the prospects for string theory, what is really shown by the famous experiments on infant cognition, and the path that evolution has taken. This list, too, could go on. So, contrary to superficial impressions, there does not appear to be any fundamental difference between ethics and science in terms of the amount of disagreement that exists. Both are characterized by broad agreement alongside some disagreement.

The Argument from Lack of Proof. A second difference between science and ethics seems to be that, in science, there are ways of resolving disagreements rationally. While scientists may disagree about some things, they nevertheless agree on how to go about resolving their disputes. They make observations and perform experiments and eventually reach agreement. This means that in science disagreement is only temporary. Scientists look forward to resolving their disagreements, and they know how to do it. But ethical disagreement seems different. In ethics disagreement is endless, because no one can prove who is right and who is wrong. No one even knows how to prove anything.

The argument may be summarized like this:

(1) If there were any such thing as objective truth in ethics, it should be possible to prove which ethical opinions are true.

(2) But it is not possible to prove an ethical opinion to be true.

(3) Therefore, there is no such thing as objective truth in ethics.

Is this correct? It certainly sounds plausible. Anyone who has tried to persuade someone else about an ethical matter will know the frustration it involves. A pacifist, for example, will not be persuaded that violence is sometimes necessary, no matter what reasons are offered. Or, to look at the same example from the opposite side, a defender of violence will not be persuaded to change his mind no matter how often he is told that violence only begets more violence.

If we turn to simpler examples, however, things look very different. Suppose the issue is whether a certain doctor is unethical. I say that Dr. Jones behaves shamefully, and you are surprised to hear it because you think she's a fine doctor. So I point out several things:

- Dr. Jones owns stock in a local drug company she helped found, and she prescribes that company's drugs for all her patients, even if the drugs are of questionable value.
- She drinks heavily, and she sometimes treats patients while under the influence.
- She won't listen to the advice of other physicians, and she becomes angry when her patients want a second opinion.
- She doesn't read medical journals or otherwise try to keep up with current medical knowledge.

Suppose all this is true. Isn't this good evidence that she is unethical? Doesn't this *prove* that she is unethical? Suppose, further, that little could be said on the other side, in her defense. Doesn't this settle the matter? What more in the way of proof could anyone want?

Other examples come easily to mind. The proof that Mr. Smith is a bad man is that he is a habitual liar who is frequently cruel. The proof that Mr. Brown is an unethical poker player is that he cheats. The proof that Professor Adams should not have given the midterm on Tuesday is that she announced it would be given on Wednesday. In each case, of course, further facts may need to be considered. But the point is that such judgments are not merely "subjective." Facts may be given in their support, and these facts, taken together, may add up to a decisive case.

Proofs in ethics may be different, in some ways, from proofs in science. But that does not mean that the ethical proofs are somehow deficient. Ethical proofs consist in giving reasons to support the moral conclusions. If the reasons are sufficiently powerful and there are no opposing considerations of equal weight, then the case is made.

This may seem too quick. If the idea that ethical judgments can be proven is so obvious, you may ask, why was the

contrary idea so plausible in the first place? Why is it so intuitively appealing to think that there are no ethical proofs? There
are at least three reasons.

First, when we think philosophically about ethics, we do
not think much about the simple matters. The very fact that
they are so obvious makes them boring, so we tend to ignore
them. We are attracted instead to the harder issues, such as
pacifism, abortion, affirmative action, and the rest. They are
more interesting. But this is what leads us astray. If we think
only about the harder issues, we may naturally conclude that
there are no proofs in ethics, because no one seems to have a
knockdown proof of his or her views about pacifism or abortion. We might overlook the fact that, on the more humdrum
issues, proofs are easily available. In the same way, if we concen-
trated only on the most controversial issues in science, we
might conclude that scientists can't prove anything.

Second, there are often good reasons on both sides of a
moral issue, and this leads people to despair about ever reaching definite conclusions. If I say that Smith is a bad man because he is frequently cruel, someone may reply that he is also
a hard worker for some good causes. The first fact counts
against him, but the second is in his favor. Doesn't this make it
impossible to conclude that he is a good man or a bad man?

But this feature of moral thinking should not make us despair. Moral thinking requires taking all the facts into account
and weighing them against one another. Where Smith is concerned, the right conclusion might be that he is on the whole
a bad man, even though he has some good points. Or the right
conclusion might be simply that he is good in some ways and
bad in others. It just depends on what the facts are. The difficult issues are all like this; there is much to be said on both
sides.

This simple point is often overlooked. In the heat of the
debate over capital punishment, or any other such matter, it is
common for people on one side to deny that there are any
good points on the other side. To win the debate, they feel they
must concede nothing to their opponents. This, of course,
means that the debate will go on endlessly. If we proceed under
this assumption—if we assume that no case can be made unless
all the relevant reasons favor only one side—then it will be rare
that anyone can prove anything. Reality is messy. But this is no

bar to reaching reasonable conclusions. We need only to make our conclusions suitably modest.

Finally, it is easy to confuse two things that should be kept separate: *proving an opinion to be true* and *persuading someone to accept your proof.* The first is a matter of sound reasoning; the second is a psychological process that involves more than reasoning. Someone may not accept a perfectly good argument because he is stubborn, or prejudiced, or simply uninterested in finding the truth. It does not follow that the argument itself is defective. A Klansman or a neo-Nazi may not listen to good arguments about racism, but that says something about them, not the arguments. And there is a more general reason why people might resist listening to reason when morals are at issue. Accepting a moral argument often means that we must change our behavior. People may not want to do that. So, not surprisingly, they will sometimes turn a deaf ear.

The Metaphysical Argument.   There is one further argument to consider, namely, the idea that ethics cannot be objective because "values" do not exist as part of the objective world.

If we take an inventory of the world, noting all the things that exist, we can make a very long list, mentioning rocks, rivers, mountains, plants, and animals. We would find buildings, deserts, caves, iron, and air. Looking up, we would see stars, comets, clouds, and galaxies. Of course, we could never complete such a list. Life is too short, there are too many things in the universe, and we are too ignorant. But we think we know, at least roughly, the *kinds* of things that exist. There are physical objects, made of atoms, that obey the laws of physics, chemistry, and biology; and there are conscious beings, such as ourselves, which may or may not be just another type of physical object. A complete inventory would just be a longer list of the same kinds of things, or so we assume.

But where, among all these things, are *values?* The answer, it seems, is nowhere. Values do not exist, at least not in the same way as rocks and rivers. Considered apart from human feelings and interests, the world appears to contain no values whatever. David Hume made this point clearly:

> Take any action allow'd to be vicious: Willful murder, for instance. Examine it in all lights, and see if you can find that matter of fact, or real existence, which you call *vice.* In

> which-ever way you take it, you find only certain passions, motives, volitions and thoughts. There is no other matter of fact in the case. The vice entirely escapes you, as long as you consider the object. You never can find it, till you turn your reflection into your own breast, and find a sentiment of disapprobation, which arises in you, towards this action. Here is a matter of fact; but 'tis the object of feeling, not of reason.

Of course, there may be other conscious beings who also have feelings and interests—nonhuman animals, for example, and possibly the inhabitants of other planets. But they will be in the same position that we are in. They will find no values in the world around them. Only their "passions, motives, volitions, and thoughts" will give rise to values for them.

Other philosophers have taken up this theme. Friedrich Nietzsche (1844–1900) was a troubled figure who, for much of his life, had no real home. He moved around Europe, writing book after book but being largely ignored. He was insane for the last 11 years of his life. After his death his fame grew; but he was embraced by the Nazis, who wrongly took him to be a nationalist and anti-Semite like themselves. Later he was rescued from this misunderstanding, and today he is one of the most frequently cited modern thinkers.

Like Hume, Nietzsche denied that there are moral facts. "There are no moral phenomena at all," he wrote, "but only moral interpretations of phenomena." The right way to think about ethics, therefore, is not to focus on *morality*, as though it were one unified thing, but to study *moralities*, the historically contingent systems of values that have been created by different peoples at different times. Nietzsche himself devoted considerable space to analyzing the dominant morality of Western culture, which he called "slave morality." He held slave morality in contempt because it glorifies such human qualities as meekness, self-denial, and obedience. This outlook, he said, is unworthy of noble men, and he advocated replacing it with an ethic that emphasizes assertiveness and mastery.

This is the "Metaphysical Argument": *Ethical opinions cannot be objectively true or false because there is no moral reality that they may match or fail to match.* This is the deep way in which ethics differs from science. Science describes a reality that exists independent of observers. If sentient beings ceased to exist, the world would be otherwise unchanged—it would still be there, and it would still be just as science describes it. But if there were no sentient beings, there would be no moral dimension to reality at all. We may summarize the argument like this:

(1) There are objective truths in science because there is an objective reality—the physical world—which science describes.

(2) But there is no moral reality comparable to the reality of the physical world. There is nothing "there" for ethics to describe.

(3) Therefore, there are no objective truths in ethics.

Once again we may ask, Is this correct? It is true, I think, that there is no moral reality comparable to the reality of the physical world. However, it does not follow from this that there can be no objective truths in ethics. There may be a different way in which ethics has an objective basis.

An inquiry might be objective in two ways:

1. An inquiry may be objective because there is an independent reality that it describes correctly or incorrectly. Science is objective in this sense.

2. An inquiry may be objective because there are reliable methods of reasoning that determine truth and falsity in its domain. Mathematics is objective in this sense. Mathematical results are objective because they are provable by the relevant kinds of arguments.

Ethics is objective in the second sense. We do not discover whether an ethical opinion is true by comparing it to some sort of "moral reality." You only have to try to imagine what this would be like to realize what a silly notion it is. Instead, we discover what is right by examining the reasons, or arguments, that can be given on both sides of an issue—the right thing to do is whatever there are the best reasons for doing. It is enough that we can identify and evaluate reasons for and against ethical judgments and come to rational conclusions.

11.4. The Importance of Human Interests

The preceding discussion should have dispelled most of our doubts about the objectivity of ethics, but not all of them. Some nagging doubts might remain, for good reason. We have not yet gotten to the bottom of things. We need now to look a little deeper into the nature of ethical reasoning.

Every inquiry, whether in science, mathematics, or ethics, involves reasoning: We gather data, marshal arguments, and draw conclusions. But reasoning cannot go on forever. If I tell you that A is true, and you want to know why, I may cite B as my reason. If you call B into question, I may justify B by appealing to C. And so on. But at some point we come to the end of the line. Every chain of reasoning must terminate somewhere. This means that every chain of reasoning ultimately appeals to some consideration that is not itself justified but is simply taken for granted.

Scientific reasoning terminates when we reach simple facts about the physical world. We know, for example, that the galaxies are moving apart. How do we know this? Because of facts about the light that reaches the earth—in particular, facts about the red shift in the spectrum. How do we know what the red shift means? Because of many past observations and experiments. This example is greatly simplified, but when we reach the simplest observed facts, we have reached the bedrock on which everything else rests. Mathematical reasoning is somewhat different in that it does not appeal to facts about the physical world. Instead, it relies on axioms, which may be taken as self-evidently true or may simply be assumed for the purposes of the argument.

Where do ethical arguments terminate? To what do they ultimately appeal? Let us look more closely at one of our previous examples. Smith is a bad man because, among other things, he is a habitual liar. This is a good reason for judging him to be morally deficient, we said, and so this fact forms part of a "proof" that he behaves unethically. But why does this count against him? Why is it bad to lie? It is easy to explain.

Lying is bad for several reasons. First, it is harmful to people. If I lie to you, and you believe me, you acquire a false belief. This can cause things to go wrong for you in various ways. Suppose you ask me when the concert starts, and I tell you 10:00 although I know it really begins at 7:30. You arrive at 9:45 only to find that you've missed out. Multiply this many times over, and you will see why it is important that people tell you the truth. Second, lying is a violation of trust. When you believe me without checking on what I say, you are trusting me, so if I lie to you,

I am causing you harm in a special way, by taking advantage of your trust. That is why being given the lie is experienced as such a personal affront. Finally, we may point out that the rule against lying is a fundamental social rule, in the sense that no society could exist without it. If there is no presumption that people will speak truthfully to one another, then communication could not take place; without communication between its members, society could not exist.

Thus, the judgment that lying is wrong is not arbitrary. It has good reasons behind it that reach fairly deep. Suppose, though, you pushed further and wanted to know why it matters that people are harmed, or that trust is violated, or that society exists. We could say a little more. We could point out that people are *worse off* when they are harmed or when they cannot trust others. We could point out that we would all be much worse off if we could not live with other people in peaceable, cooperative societies. But you persist: Why does it matter if people are worse off? Here we come to the end of the line. Ethical reasoning terminates in considerations about people being better or worse off—or, perhaps, in considerations about what makes all sensitive beings better or worse off—just as scientific reasoning terminates in the appeal to observations of simple physical facts.

Some people think that this vindicates the use of the word "subjective" to describe ethics—ethics is subjective in the sense that it is ultimately about what makes people better or worse off. I would not use the word like that, but of course, others are free to use the word as they see fit. The important thing is to be clear about what follows from our choice of terminology. If, in saying that ethics is subjective, we mean only that it is ultimately about what makes people better or worse off, it does not follow that ethics is arbitrary. Nor does it follow that people are free to accept whatever ethical judgments they like, or that one person's opinions are as good as another's. Ethics remains a matter of following reason, and it will still be objectively true that ethics requires some things and forbids others. Ethical judgments can still be correct or incorrect. In these ways the objectivity of ethics is secure.

CHAPTER 12

Why Should We Be Moral?

Let it be allowed, though virtue or moral rectitude does indeed consist in affection to and pursuit of what is right and good, as such; yet, that when we sit down in a cool hour, we can neither justify to ourselves this or any other pursuit, till we are convinced that it will be for our happiness, or at least not contrary to it.

—JOSEPH BUTLER,
FIFTEEN SERMONS PREACHED AT THE ROLLS CHAPEL (1726)

12.1. The Ring of Gyges

An ancient legend tells the story of Gyges, a poor shepherd who found a magic ring in a fissure opened by an earthquake. Gyges discovered that when he twisted the ring on his finger, he would become invisible. This allowed him to do what other people can only dream of: He could go anywhere and do anything he pleased, without fear of detection. He used the power of the ring to enrich himself, taking what he wanted and killing anyone who got in his way. Eventually, he invaded the royal palace, where he seduced the queen, murdered the king, and seized the throne. He ended up king of all the land.

Glaucon tells this story in Book I of Plato's *Republic*. Despite the fanciful nature of the tale, Gyges was a real person, the king of an ancient city called Sardis, in what is now Turkey. Herodotus also gives an account of how Gyges came to power. According to Herodotus, Gyges started out as a servant of King Candaules, "a man who was in love with his own wife." (Apparently, Herodotus thought this was unusual.) One day Candaules was bragging to Gyges about how beautiful his wife was, and to prove the point, he decided that Gyges should see her naked. Gyges protested, but the king ordered him to hide in the queen's bedchamber and watch her disrobe. Gyges reluctantly did so. As fate would have it, the queen caught him, and she told Gyges that he would be put to death unless he killed Candaules and married her, in which case it would be acceptable that he saw her naked. So, as in Glaucon's version of the story, Gyges murdered Candaules and became king himself.

Glaucon tells the story of Gyges to illustrate how immoral behavior can sometimes be to one's advantage. If Gyges had remained virtuous, he would have remained poor. By breaking the moral rules, he became rich and powerful. Considering this, why should Gyges care about morality? For that matter, why should any of us bother with morality if it doesn't serve our own needs? Why should you tell the truth, if lying is more convenient? Why should you give money to charity, when you can spend it on yourself? Morality places restrictions on us that we may not like. So why shouldn't we just forget about it? Glaucon adds that, in his opinion, all of us would behave like Gyges, if we thought we could get away with it.

In what follows we will take up the question of why we should be moral. But first, we need to understand the question. It is not a request for a justification of moral behavior. If that were all it demanded, the answer would be easy. We could easily say why Gyges shouldn't have robbed and murdered his way to the throne. Robbery is taking things that do not belong to you, and murder inflicts a terrible harm on victims who do not deserve it. Similarly, it is easy to explain why we should be truthful or why we should give money to help the needy. Lying harms people, and hungry people need food more than people like us need new carpets or nice clothes. Of course, these reasons may need to be spelled out more fully, but it is obvious how the elaboration would go.

Such reasons, however, only determine what is right, and that is not the issue. Glaucon's challenge arises after the moral reasoning has all been done. We may grant that it is morally right to respect people's lives and property. We may concede that it is right to tell the truth and help people. Glaucon's question is *why we should care about doing what is right*. Why shouldn't we just shrug it off and go on living as we please?

To answer this question, we must show that living morally is in our own interests, and that is not an easy thing to do. On the surface it looks like ethics is more of an impediment than a help where one's self-interest is concerned. Of course, it may be a good thing for you if *other people* live ethically, for then they will respect your rights and be helpful to you. But if *you* are bound by moral constraints, that is another matter, for morality may sometimes tell you not to further your own agenda.

Can it be shown that, contrary to appearances, accepting moral constraints really is in one's self-interest? We might be able to meet Glaucon's challenge, and we might not. It all depends on what we take morality to be and what we think is the source of moral requirements.

12.2. Ethics and Religion

One familiar idea is that right living consists in obedience to God's commands. On this conception God has set out the rules we must obey, and he will reward those who keep his commandments and punish those who do not.

If this were true, we could answer Glaucon's challenge as follows: We should be moral because otherwise God will punish us. Even if, like Gyges, we had the power of invisibility, we would still be subject to divine retribution, and so, ultimately, we could not get away with doing whatever we wanted. In one familiar scenario the righteous will spend eternity in heaven while the wicked will go to hell. Thus, any benefit you might gain from wrongdoing will be only temporary. In the long run virtue pays.

That response, however, is not clear-cut. On the familiar scenario God does not reward individuals in proportion to their virtue. Rather, God sorts everyone into just two groups: the heaven-bound and the hell-bound. In the end the saints and those who barely scrape by wind up going to the same heavenly paradise. Thus, it might be to your advantage to do just enough to get into heaven, but no more. And so you can ask: Why should I be moral, when a little immorality will benefit me on earth without spoiling my chances of getting into heaven?

On these assumptions Glaucon's challenge can be partly answered: Even if we can get away with some immorality, we shouldn't risk hellfire by robbing and murdering our way to the throne. In fact, much more virtue than that might be called for. In examining our own lives, we can never be too sure as to what God might be thinking. You never know when one more selfish act might tip the scales. Thus, we should probably be as good as we can be, to increase our chances of eternal bliss.

We may distinguish between (a) the Divine Command Theory as a general account of ethics and (b) the claim that God rewards virtue. Let us take a brief look at the general theory.

The Divine Command Theory says that *an action's being morally right* is the same thing as *the action's being commanded by God*. We may notice, to begin with, that if we took this seriously there would be enormous practical difficulties. How are we supposed to know what God commands? There are, of course, people who claim to have spoken with God and who offer to pass on his instructions to the rest of us. But why should we trust them? Hearing voices can be a sign of schizophrenia, and anyway these people might be lying. They might be saying they've spoken to God merely to get attention or to persuade their followers to send them money.

Others, more modestly, rely on Scripture or Church tradition for guidance. Those sources are notoriously ambiguous. They give vague and sometimes contradictory instructions. So, when people consult these authorities, they typically rely on their own judgment to sort out what seems acceptable. In reading Scripture, they pay attention to whatever supports the moral views they favor and disregard the rest. For example, they may cite the passage in Leviticus that condemns homosexuality while ignoring the passage that requires you to wash your clothes if you touch anything a menstruating woman has sat upon.

But these are just practical difficulties. It may still seem plausible that God's commands provide the ultimate basis for ethics: God's saying that something is wrong is what *makes it* wrong. Many religious people seem to think that it would be sacrilegious not to accept some such view as this. It is an old thought. Socrates was familiar with this idea, and he did not believe it.

In the *Euthyphro* Socrates considers whether "right" can be the same as "what the gods command." Socrates accepted that the gods exist and that they may issue instructions. But he showed that this cannot be the ultimate basis of ethics. As he said, we need to distinguish two possibilities: Either the gods have good reasons for the instructions they give, or they do not.

If they do not, then their commands are arbitrary—the gods are like petty tyrants who demand that we do this and that even though there is no good reason for it. This is an impious view that religious people will not want to accept. On the other hand, if the gods do have good reasons for their instructions, then there must be a standard of rightness independent of their commands—namely, the standard to which they themselves refer in deciding what to require of us.

It follows, then, that even if one accepts a religious picture of the world, the rightness or wrongness of actions cannot be understood merely in terms of their conformity to divine commands. We may always ask why the gods command what they do, and the answer to that question will reveal why right actions are right and why wrong actions are wrong.

The same is true of sacred texts. Nothing can be morally right or wrong simply because an authority says so, not even an authority as esteemed as the Bible. If the precepts in the text are not arbitrary, then there must be some reason for them. For example, the Bible says we should not lie about our neighbors—we should not "bear false witness" against them. Is this an arbitrary rule that God imposes on us for no reason? On the contrary, it is easy to see why this rule makes sense. Lying causes harm and violates the trust that others have in us, and lying about our neighbors is insulting to them and harms them unjustly. If you want to know why lying is wrong, those are the reasons. Similarly, we may ask why homosexuality is condemned. Are there comparably good reasons for this pronouncement? If so, then those reasons will give the real explanation of why homosexuality is wrong. The other side of the coin is that, if no such reasons exist, then the biblical condemnation is unjustified.

These problems make the Divine Command Theory an implausible account of ethics, but they do not refute the separate idea that, if God punishes wrongdoing, then we have good, self-interested reasons to act rightly. The latter idea so impressed Immanuel Kant (1724–1804), the great German philosopher, that he made it into an argument for the existence of God. Kant reasoned that if God does not exist, the universe is morally incomplete, because virtue will go unrewarded and wickedness will be unpunished. This thought was intolerable to him, so he concluded that God must exist. Even great philosophers, it seems, can indulge in wishful thinking.

12.3. The Social Contract

So far, we have been assuming that God exists. But what if there is no God—what becomes of ethics? This has been one of the main questions of philosophy from the seventeenth century on. In the modern period there has been a rough consensus that ethics must be understood as a human phenomenon—as the product of human needs, interests, and desires—and nothing else.

Thomas Hobbes (1588–1679) was the first important modern thinker to provide a secular, naturalistic basis for ethics. Hobbes, who earned his living as a tutor and secretary to aristocratic families, was a monarchist and a materialist, both of which sometimes got him into trouble. His *Leviathan,* published when he was 63, is the greatest work of modern political philosophy.

Hobbes assumed that "good" and "bad" are names we give to the things we like or dislike. Thus, when you and I like different things, we may regard different things as good or bad. However, Hobbes said, in our fundamental psychological makeup we are all very much alike. We are all basically self-interested creatures who want to live and to live as well as possible. This is the key to understanding ethics. Ethics arises when people realize *what they must do* to live well.

Hobbes points out that each of us is enormously better off living in a cooperative society than if we tried to make it on our own. The benefits of social living go far beyond companionship. Social cooperation makes possible schools, hospitals, and highways; houses with electricity and central heating; airplanes and cell phones; newspapers and books; movies, opera, and football; science and agriculture. Without social cooperation we would lose all of this. Therefore, it is to the advantage of each of us to establish and maintain a cooperative society.

But it turns out that a mutually cooperative society can exist only if we adopt certain rules of behavior—rules that require telling the truth, keeping our promises, respecting one another's lives and property, and so on:

- If people couldn't be relied upon to tell the truth, then no one would care what anyone else said. Communication would be impossible. And without communication society would collapse.

- Without the requirement that people keep their promises, there could be no division of labor—workers could not count on getting paid, retailers could not rely on their agreements with suppliers, and so on— and the economy would collapse. There could be no business, no building, no agriculture, no medicine.
- Without assurances against assault, murder, and theft, no one could feel secure. Everyone would have to be constantly on guard, and social cooperation would be impossible.

Thus, to obtain the benefits of social living, we must strike a bargain with one another, with each of us agreeing to obey these rules, provided others do likewise. This "social contract" is the basis of morality. Thus, morality may be understood as *the set of rules that rational people will agree to obey, for their mutual benefit, provided that other people will obey them as well.*

Why the Social Contract Theory Is Attractive. This way of thinking about morality has a number of appealing features. First, it takes the mystery out of ethics and makes it a practical, down-to-earth business. Living morally is not a matter of blind obedience to the mysterious dictates of a supernatural being, nor is it a matter of fidelity to lofty but pointless abstract rules. Instead, it is a matter of doing what it takes to make social living possible.

Second, the social contract approach gives us a sensible and mature way of determining what our ethical duties really are. When "morality" is mentioned, the first thing that pops into many people's minds is an attempt to restrict their sex lives. It is unfortunate that the term "morals" has come to suggest this. The whole purpose of having a system of morality, according to the Social Contract Theory, is to allow people to live their lives in a setting of social cooperation. Its purpose is *not* to tell people what kinds of lives they should live, within that setting. Therefore, an ethic based on the social contract would have little interest in what people do in their bedrooms.

Third, the Social Contract Theory assumes relatively little about human nature. It treats human beings as self-interested and does not assume that they are naturally altruistic, to even the slightest degree. One of the theory's charms is that it can say we ought to *behave* altruistically in various ways, without assuming that we *are* naturally altruistic. We want to live as well as possible, and moral obligations are created as we band together with other people to form the cooperative societies needed to achieve this fundamentally self-interested goal.

Finally, the Social Contract Theory gives a plausible answer to Glaucon's question. If there is no God to punish us, why should we bother to do what is right, especially when it is not to our advantage? The answer is that it *is* to our advantage to live in a society in which people behave morally. Thus, it is rational for us to accept moral restrictions on our conduct as part of a bargain we make with other people. We benefit directly from their ethical conduct, and our own compliance with the rules is the price we must pay to secure their compliance. There is, however, a problem with this explanation.

The Problem of the Free Rider. Schemes of social cooperation always face the "free rider" problem. A free rider is someone who benefits from a cooperative arrangement without contributing to it. Suppose the home owners in my neighborhood chip in to pay for a streetlight. I will benefit from the light as much as anyone else, and I want the light. But I refuse to pay, knowing that they will go ahead without me. They do. The light is put up, and I get to use it for free. That makes me a free rider.

If ethics is essentially a scheme of social cooperation, there will be free riders—individuals who benefit from living in a society governed by ethical norms but who do not respect those norms themselves. Glaucon's challenge may therefore be reformulated: Why not be a free rider? Each of us now lives in a stable society in which people generally obey the social rules, so we already enjoy the benefits of social living. If everyone stopped obeying the rules, society would collapse. We don't want that to happen. So we have good reason to encourage others to obey the rules and to pretend to obey them ourselves. But, you might ask, why shouldn't you secretly break the rules when you need to, if you can get away with it?

The free-rider problem for ethics can be solved, but only partially. The partial solution goes like this: Each of us has good reason not only to encourage others to obey the social rules but also to make it as hard as possible for them to break those rules.

Take the rule against murder, for example. You don't want merely to encourage others not to murder you. In addition, you want a situation in which *no one can get away with* murdering you. Each of us is in this position. Each of us has good reason to support the creation and maintenance of a social system in which other people could not murder us. To accomplish this, we establish laws and other methods of enforcement. But in doing so we create a situation in which *we* cannot get away with murder, either.

I said that this is a "partial" solution, for two reasons. First, we use the power of the law to enforce the rules against murder, theft, and other grave offenses, but not all social rules are suitable for legal enforcement. Rules of ordinary decency must be enforced in "the court of public opinion" rather than in the court of law. The penalty for lying, for example, is only that people will be mad at you and you will get a bad reputation. Of course, this may be harmful to you. However, such informal mechanisms are less effective than the law.

Second, no mechanisms, formal or informal, are going to be perfect. It is easy to get away with the occasional lie. One might even get away with the occasional murder. Glaucon's challenge remains in a new form: Why should you obey the moral rules when you think you can get away with breaking them?

12.4. Morality and Benevolence

The Social Contract Theory does not assume that people are altruistic. Each person can be motivated to enter the agreement to obey the social rules out of simple self-interest. However, people are not entirely selfish. Human beings have at least some benevolent feelings, if only for their family and friends. We have evolved as social creatures just as surely as we have evolved as creatures with lungs. Caring for our kin and members of our local group is as natural for us as breathing.

If humans do have some degree of natural altruism, does this have any significance for ethics? David Hume thought so. Hume agreed with Hobbes that our moral opinions are expressions of our feelings, but he did not agree that our feelings are merely self-centered. He believed that we also have "*social* sentiments"—feelings that connect us with other people and make us care about them. That is why, Hume says, we measure right and wrong by "the true interests of mankind":

> In all determinations of morality, this circumstance of public utility is ever principally in view; and wherever disputes arise, either in philosophy or common life, concerning the bounds of duty, the question cannot, by any means, be decided with greater certainty than by ascertaining, on any side, the true interests of mankind.

This view came to be known as Utilitarianism. In modern moral philosophy it is the chief alternative to the Social Contract Theory.

Utilitarianism. Utilitarians hold that one principle sums up all our moral duties. The ultimate moral principle is that *we should always try to produce the greatest possible benefit for everyone who will be affected by our action.*

This "Principle of Utility" is deceptively simple. It actually combines three ideas. First, in determining what to do, we should be guided by the consequences of our actions—we should do whatever can be reasonably expected to have the best outcome. Second, in determining which consequences are best, we should care only about the benefits and harms that would be caused—we should do whatever will cause the greatest benefits and the least significant harms. And third, the Principle of Utility assumes that each person's welfare is as important as anyone else's.

Although Hume suggested this idea, two other philosophers developed it in greater detail. Jeremy Bentham, an Englishman whose life spanned the eighteenth and nineteenth centuries, was the leader of a group that aimed to reform the laws of Britain along utilitarian lines. The Benthamites were remarkably successful in advancing such causes as prison reform and restrictions on the use of child labor. John Stuart Mill, the son of one of Bentham's original followers, gave the theory its most popular and influential defense in his book *Utilitarianism,* published in 1861.

The utilitarian movement attracted critics from the outset. It was an easy target because it ignored conventional religious notions. Morality, according to the Utilitarians, had nothing to do with obedience to God or gaining credit in heaven. Rather, the point was just to make life in this world as comfortable and as happy as possible. Thus, some critics condemned Utilitarianism as a godless doctrine. To this Mill replied:

> [T]he question depends upon what idea we have formed of the moral character of the Deity. If it be a true belief that God desires, above all things, the happiness of his creatures, and that this was his purpose in their creation, utility is not only not a godless doctrine, but more profoundly religious than any other.

Utilitarianism was also an easy target because it was (and still is) a *subversive* theory, in that it turned many traditional moral ideas upside down. Bentham argued, for example, that the purpose of the criminal justice system cannot be understood in the traditional way as "paying back" offenders for their wicked deeds—that only piles misery upon misery. Instead, the social response to crime should be threefold: to identify and deal with the causes of criminal behavior; where possible, to reform individual lawbreakers and make them into productive citizens; and to "punish" people only insofar as it is necessary to deter others from committing similar crimes. Today these are familiar ideas, but only because the utilitarian movement was so successful. Or, to take a different example: By insisting that everyone's happiness is equally important, the Utilitarians offended various elitist notions of group superiority. According to the utilitarian standard, neither race nor sex nor social class makes a difference to one's moral status. Mill himself wrote a book called *The Subjection of Women* that became a classic of the nineteenth-century suffragist movement.

Finally, Utilitarianism was controversial because it had no use for "absolute" moral rules. The Utilitarians regarded the traditional rules as "rules of thumb," useful because following them will generally be for the best. But they are not absolute— whenever breaking a rule will have better results for everyone concerned, the rule should be broken. The rule against killing, for example, might be suspended in the case of someone who is dying of a painful illness and requests a painless death. Moreover, the Utilitarians regarded some traditional rules as dubious, even as rules of thumb. Christian moralists had traditionally said that masturbation is evil, but from a utilitarian point of view, masturbation is a good thing. A more serious matter is the traditional religious condemnation of homosexuality, which has resulted in misery for countless people. Utilitarianism implies that if an activity makes people happy, without anyone being harmed, it cannot be wrong.

It is one thing to describe a moral view; it is another thing to justify it. Utilitarianism says that our moral duty is to "promote the general happiness." Why should we do that? Mill echoes Glaucon's challenge when he writes:

> I feel that I am bound not to rob or murder, betray or deceive; but why am I bound to promote the general happiness? If my own happiness lies in something else, why may I not give that the preference?

Aside from the "external sanctions" of law and public opinion, Mill saw only one possible reason for accepting this or any other moral standard. The "internal sanction" of morality must always be "a feeling in our minds." And the kind of ethic we accept, he thought, will depend on the nature of our feelings. If human beings have "social feelings," then utilitarian morality will be the natural standard for them:

> The firm foundation [of utilitarian morality] is that of the social feelings of mankind—the desire to be in unity with our fellow creatures, which is already a powerful principle in human nature, and happily one of those which tend to become stronger, even without express inculcation, from the influences of advancing civilization.

Impartiality. Utilitarianism has implications that conflict with traditional morality. Much the same could be said about the Social Contract Theory. In most of the practical matters that we have mentioned—criminal punishment, racial discrimination, women's rights, euthanasia, homosexuality—the two theories have similar implications. But there is one matter on which they differ dramatically. Utilitarians believe that we have an extensive moral duty to help other people. Social contract theorists disagree.

Suppose, for example, you are thinking of spending $1,000 for a new living room carpet. Should you do this? What are the alternatives? One alternative is to give the money to an agency such as the United Nations Children's Fund (UNICEF). Each year around 7 million children under the age of 5 die of easily preventable diseases because there isn't enough money to provide the vaccinations, vitamin-A capsules, antibiotics, and oral rehydration treatments they need. By giving the money to UNICEF and making do with your old carpet, you could provide much-needed medical care for dozens of children. From the point of view of utility—seeking the best overall outcome for everyone concerned—there is no doubt you should give the money to UNICEF. Obviously, the medicine will help the children a lot more than the new rug will help you.

The Social Contract Theory takes a different approach. If morality rests on an agreement between people—an agreement we enter into to promote our own interests—what would the agreement say about helping other people? It depends on whether those other people are in a position to help us. If they are, then we can benefit from an agreement to help each other. If not, then we have no reason to accept any restrictions on our conduct.

From this point of view, we would have no reason to accept a general duty to provide aid to children in foreign countries. Jan Narveson, a social contract theorist, writes:

> [M]orals, if they are to be rational, must amount to agreements among people—people of all kinds, each pursuing his or her own interests, which are various and do not necessarily include much concern for others. . . . But people . . . have a broad repertoire of powers including some that can make them exceedingly dangerous, as well as others that can make them very helpful. This gives us reason to agree with each other that we will refrain from harming others in the pursuit of our interests, to respect each other's property and grant extensive civil rights, but not necessarily to go very far out of our way to be very helpful to those we don't know and may not particularly care for.

Many philosophers prefer to keep things abstract, but Narveson is good about spelling out the implications in a way that leaves no room for misunderstanding:

> What about parting with the means for making your sweet little daughter's birthday party a memorable one, in order to keep a dozen strangers alive on the other side of the world? Is this something you are morally required to do? Indeed not. She may well *matter* to you more than they. This illustrates again the fact that people do *not* "count

equally" for most of us. Normal people care more about some people than others, and build their very lives around those carings.

Which view is correct? Do we have a moral duty to help strangers or not? Here is a thought experiment that might help. Suppose there are two buttons on my desk at this moment, and I can press only one of them. By pressing button A, I can provide my daughter with a memorable party; by pressing button B, I can save the lives of a dozen strangers. Is it really all right for me to press A just because I care more for my daughter? What would your "conscientious feelings" tell you? Mill believed that one's conscientious feelings—the feelings that prevail after everything has been thought through—must finally determine one's obligations. He believed that we cannot, when we are thoughtful and reflective, approve of pushing button A.

However, some contemporary Utilitarians have argued that the matter need not be left to the vicissitudes of individual feeling. Their argument goes like this: It may be true that we all care more for ourselves, our family, and our friends than we care for strangers. But we have rational capacities as well as feelings, and if we think objectively, we will realize that there are no relevant differences between ourselves and all those other people. Others, even strangers, also care about themselves, their families, and their friends, in the same way that we do. Their needs and interests are comparable to our own. In fact, *there is nothing of this general sort that makes anyone different from anyone else*—and so, no one should take his or her own interests to be more important. Peter Singer, a utilitarian philosopher, writes:

> Reason makes it possible for us to see ourselves in this way. . . . I am able to see that I am just one being among others, with interests and desires like others. I have a personal perspective on the world, from which my interests are at the front and centre of the stage, the interests of my family and friends are close behind, and the interests of strangers are pushed to the back and sides. But reason enables me to see that others have similarly subjective perspectives, and that from "the point of view of the universe," my perspective is no more privileged than theirs. Thus my ability to reason shows me the possibility of detaching myself from my own perspective, and shows me what the universe might look like if I had no personal perspective.

So, from an objective viewpoint, each of us must acknowledge that our own perspective—our own particular set of needs, interests, likes, and dislikes—is only one among many and has no special status. This means that, from a moral point of view, everyone counts equally, even strangers in foreign countries who have no ability to help us or harm us.

Conclusion. Where does this leave us with respect to Glaucon's challenge? We might reach different conclusions about what morality requires of us, depending on how we assess various moral arguments. But then Glaucon's question will remain: Why should we do what's right, if there is nothing in it for us?

As we have seen, a religious outlook that includes the threat of hellfire for the wicked could provide at least a partial answer. For those who do not believe in hell, there is the fact that we all benefit from a social arrangement in which the moral rules are acknowledged and enforced. But the ethical free-rider problem cannot be completely solved. People can always get away with a certain amount of bad behavior. Thus, at some point, after the resources of the law and social pressure have been exhausted, there is nothing left but to rely on what Mill called "the conscientious feelings of mankind."

This may seem a feeble conclusion. Yet "the conscientious feelings of mankind" are a powerful force, made stronger by education and the advancement of civilization. They should not be underestimated. Nonetheless, there are people in whom such feelings are weak. So we must concede that, if people can get away with doing wrong and genuinely don't care what their actions do to others, nothing will stop them. Reason alone will not do it. We could, of course, remind them of all the reasons why their actions would be wrong and remind them that their interests don't matter more than the interests of other people. But all that will only prove that their actions *are* wrong. To stop people from behaving badly, something more is required, namely, that they care about those reasons.

CHAPTER 13

*T*he *Meaning of Life*

Death's at the bottom of everything.
—GRAHAM GREENE, *THE THIRD MAN* (1950)

13.1. The Problem of the Point of View

In 1826 John Stuart Mill became obsessed with the thought that his life was meaningless. He was only 22 years old, and his great works were still ahead of him, but he had already begun to make a name for himself. He was a regular contributor to *The Westminster Review*, a radical journal founded by Jeremy Bentham, and he was a frequent speaker on behalf of progressive causes. "I had what might truly be called an object in life," Mill said, "to be a reformer of the world." But then he suddenly lost confidence. His work no longer seemed important. He came to believe that, even if he achieved everything he wanted, it would not make him happy. "I was in a dull state of nerves," he said, ". . . I seemed to have nothing left to live for." This condition persisted for a year while he carried on outwardly as if nothing were wrong. But inwardly the clouds grew darker. Finally, as often happens in such cases, things turned around. Reading about a boy's reaction to his father's death, Mill was moved to tears, and he found his love of life returning:

> Relieved from my ever present sense of irremediable wretchedness, I gradually found that the ordinary incidents of life could again give me some pleasure; that I could again find enjoyment, not intense, but sufficient for cheerfulness, in sunshine and sky, in books, in conversation, in public affairs; and that there was, once more, excitement, though of a moderate kind, in exerting myself

for my opinions, and for the public good. Thus the cloud gradually drew off, and I again enjoyed life.

It is tempting to understand Mill's experience as merely pathological. He was depressed, but luckily he snapped out of it. That is probably true. The question of the meaning of life comes up, as a practical problem, when people are unhappy, when they have lost their zest for living, or when things are going badly for them. Psychologists emphasize this. In his book *Psychological Symptoms*, Frank J. Bruno lists the feeling that life is meaningless as a symptom of mental illness.

But the meaning of life is a real problem that can arise even when we are not suffering from a distorted mental state. It is actually a series of problems, because different issues might be at stake depending on why the question is raised. For Mill the issue was how to be happy. A different but related issue is whether there is anything truly worth living for. We do not have to be mentally ill to wonder about such things.

At the deepest level the problem of the meaning of life results from a clash between two points of view, each of which is natural and unavoidable for us. On the one hand, each of us occupies a personal point of view from which our lives and projects are immensely important. A great many things matter to us. We care about our children, our jobs, and whether the Red Sox will win the pennant. We have desires, goals, and plans. We are distressed by the fact that we will die, and on our deathbeds we regard the prospect as a calamity.

On the other hand, we can step outside our individual points of view and look at things from an impersonal standpoint. From "the point of view of the universe," our lives have little significance. What does it matter if I raise a family, succeed in my work, or take a trip to Paris? Eventually, I will die, and everything I do will come to nothing. The whole human race will vanish one day, leaving no trace behind.

The contrast could not be greater. From your own point of view, who you are and what you do are surpassingly important. But to the universe you are nothing. What are we to make of this? As Thomas Nagel puts it, "In seeing ourselves from outside we find it difficult to take our lives seriously. This loss of conviction, and the attempt to regain it, is the problem of the meaning of life."

13.2. Happiness

The ancient philosophers had a lot to say about happiness. They assumed that "the best life" and "the happy life" are the same thing, and they generally agreed that happiness consists in a life of reason and virtue. Epicurus (341–270 B.C.) recommended plain living, so as to avoid pains and anxieties. The Stoics added that a wise man will not allow his happiness to depend on things outside of his control, such as wealth, health, good looks, or the opinions of others. We cannot control external circumstances, they said, so we should be indifferent to them, taking things as they come. Epictetus (ca. A.D. 55–135), one of the great Stoic teachers, advised his students, "Ask not that events should happen as you will, but let your will be that events should happen as they do, and you shall have peace."

Some of this may seem doubtful, but a remarkable amount of it has been confirmed by modern psychological research. Take, for example, the idea that wealth does not bring happiness. Because most of us want to be rich, we might think there would be some correlation between wealth and happiness. But there is not. Americans are three times as rich as they were 50 years ago, but there has been no increase in the number of Americans who describe themselves as "very happy." When political scientist Ronald Inglehardt compared the levels of wealth in different countries with what people in those countries say about their satisfaction with their lives, he found that people in the wealthier countries are no happier than those in the poorer countries. Sometimes it is just the opposite: Americans are four times as rich as Mexicans, but Mexicans are happier. Within single countries we find the same lack of correlation—people with more money are no happier than people with less. Whether one is impoverished, however, does matter. People suffering poverty tend to be less happy than those who have enough to get by. But for those above a certain level, additional money makes little difference. Psychologist David Myers observes that "Once beyond poverty, further economic growth does not appreciably improve human morale."

A striking confirmation of this is provided by studies of lottery winners. Lottery winners are, of course, extremely happy when they hear the good news, and their euphoria tends to last a few days. But soon they return to whatever level of happiness is normal for them. Grumpy people return to being grumpy; happy people come down from the clouds but remain happy. Lottery winners may be able to quit their jobs and buy lots of things, but their newly acquired wealth makes no long-term difference to their happiness.

Surprisingly, something similar is true of people who suffer disasters. For people who are basically happy, a calamity— even one with long-term effects—may cause a momentary drop in happiness, but soon they bounce back. One study focused on Michigan car accident victims who had suffered spinal cord injuries. Within three weeks happiness again prevailed among them. A University of Illinois study found that able-bodied students and disabled students described themselves in virtually identical terms: 49 percent of the time happy, 22 percent of the time unhappy, and 29 percent neutral. Studies of cancer patients also show no long-term difference between their emotional states before and after their diagnoses.

So what does make people happy? If not riches or health, then what? To a large extent, happiness is genetic: A study that looked at identical twins and fraternal twins found that about 80 percent of the variation in happiness among individuals is due to genes. Studies also indicate that happiness is correlated with several things in one's life. One is personal control—having control over your own life and destiny, or at least believing that you do. Having good relations with other people, especially friends and family, is also vital. Satisfying work is a third element of happiness; people who feel that they are accomplishing something worthwhile report themselves to be especially happy.

Happiness is, in a sense, self-sustaining, because happy people tend to behave in ways that keep them happy. They have higher opinions of other people and are more outgoing. Thus, they form friendships more easily. Happy people are also more optimistic. They tend to choose long-term rewards over short-term satisfactions, and because this is usually a good strategy, they benefit from it.

You might think, then, that in order to be happier you need to take control of your life, make friends, and seek out meaningful work. That may be true, but there is a catch. Paradoxically, if you value these things only as a means to happiness, they will not make you happy. Happiness cannot be sought directly. Instead, you must value friends and work in their own right. Happiness is then the welcome by-product. John Stuart Mill reported that he learned this lesson from his depression. After recovering, Mill realized:

> Those only are happy (I thought) who have their minds fixed on some object other than their own happiness; on the happiness of others, on the improvement of mankind, even on some art or pursuit, followed not as a means, but as itself an ideal end. Aiming thus at something else, they find happiness by the way. . . . Ask yourself if you are happy, and you cease to be so. The only chance is to treat, not happiness, but some end external to it, as the purpose of life.

13.3. Death

The idea that even a happy life is in some larger sense meaningless is usually supported by two thoughts. One is that we will inevitably die; the other is that the universe is indifferent to us. Let us consider these one at a time.

What attitude should we take toward our mortality? It depends, of course, on what we believe happens when we die. Some people believe they will live forever in paradise. Death, therefore, is like moving to a better address. If you believe this, you should think death is a wonderful thing, for you will be much better off after you die. Apparently, Socrates had this attitude, but most people do not.

On the other hand, death may be the permanent end of your existence. If so, your consciousness is extinguished, and that's the end of you. It is important to understand what this means. Some people assume that nonexistence is a mysterious, hard-to-imagine condition. They ask, "What is it like to be dead?" and they are perplexed. But that is a mistake. We cannot imagine what it is like to be dead because there is nothing to imagine. What your life will be like in 2110 is what it was like in 1910.

If death is the end of our existence, what attitude should we take toward this? Most of us think it is a terrible prospect. We hate the thought of dying, and we are willing to do almost anything to prolong our lives. Epicurus, however, said that we should not fear death. In a letter to one of his followers, he argued that "Death is nothing to us," because when we are dead we do not exist, and if we do not exist nothing can harm us. We will not be unhappy; we will suffer no pain: we will not be afraid, worried, or bored; we will have no wishes and no regrets. Therefore, Epicurus concluded, the wise person will not fear death. He believed that philosophical reflection can make us happier by removing our fear of death.

There is something to this. Nonetheless, it overlooks the possibility that death is bad because it is a huge deprivation—if our lives could continue, there are all sorts of good things we could enjoy. Thus, death is an evil because it puts an end to the good things of life. This seems right to me. After I die, human history will continue, but I won't get to be a part of it. I will see no more movies, read no more books, make no more friends, and take no more trips. If my wife survives me, I will not get to be with her. I will not know my grandchildren's children. New inventions will appear and new discoveries will be made about the nature of the universe, but I won't ever know what they are. New music will be composed, but I won't hear it. Perhaps we will make contact with intelligent beings from other worlds, but I won't know about it. That is why I don't want to die, and Epicurus's argument is beside the point.

But does the fact that I am going to die make my life meaningless? After all, it is said, what is the point of working, making friends, and raising a family if, in the end, we will be nothing? This thought has a certain emotional resonance, but it involves a fundamental mistake. We must distinguish the value of a thing from how long it will last. Something can be good while it lasts, even though it will not last forever. While they controlled Afghanistan, the Taliban destroyed a number of ancient monuments. It was a tragedy because those monuments were wonderful, and they were no less wonderful because they were vulnerable. A human life, too, can be a wonderful thing, even though it must end. At the very least, the mere fact that it will end does not cancel whatever value it has.

13.4. Religion and the Indifferent Universe

From the point of view of the universe, it is said, human life has no significance. W. B. Yeats (1865–1939), the great Irish poet, put the matter in chilling perspective:

> Where are now the warring kings,
> Word be-mockers?—By the Rood,
> Where are now the warring kings?

An idle word is now their glory,
By the stammering schoolboy said,
Reading some entangled story:
The kings of the old time are dead;
The wandering earth herself may be
Only a sudden flaming word,
In clanging space a moment heard,
Troubling the endless reverie.

Warring kings must die, the wandering earth is an insignificant speck, and the whole history of the human race is only a blip in time. In light of this, how can we attach any meaning to what we do?

One way to overcome this problem is to adopt a religious point of view according to which the universe is *not* indifferent to us. The great monotheistic religions—including Judaism, Christianity, and Islam—teach that the universe was created by God to provide a home for us and that our destiny is to live forever with him. Human life is not, therefore, a meaningless blip in the history of the universe. Instead, we are the central actors in the whole cosmic drama.

I will leave aside the question of whether the religious story is true, in order to ask a different question. Suppose it is true. There is no doubt that a religious perspective provides a way of understanding the meaning of life. But how, exactly, does it do this? How does the religious story help? This question turns out to be puzzling.

Perhaps our lives are meaningful because *God has a plan for us.* But it is hard to see how the intentions of an outside agent could make your life meaningful to you. Suppose your parents have a plan for you. Depending on your temperament, you might find this agreeable; but you might also find it smothering, because you want to make your own plan and live according to your own values. Indeed, to the extent that an outside force dictates the terms of your life, you might regard your life as less meaningful than it otherwise could be.

Another possibility is that our lives are meaningful because *we are the objects of God's love.* Rather than the universe being indifferent to us, the Creator of the universe cares about us very much. But again, no matter how comforting this might be, it is hard to see how it helps. If love is needed to provide meaning in our lives, most of us already have that. We have family and friends who care about us, and we care about them. If we think that our lives lack meaning despite this, how is the addition of someone else's love supposed to help?

Finally, from a religious point of view, human life is seen as a *permanent* feature of the universe rather than a passing phase. Death is overcome. But we have already considered this thought. The duration of a life is a separate issue from its meaning. Indeed, an eternal life might be meaningless if it is devoid of everything that makes life worthwhile. At the same time, a short life might be full of things that make it worth living. Mere duration, then, does not confer meaning.

The point of these remarks is not to suggest that a religious perspective cannot help us understand the meaning of life. The point is only that it does not help in these obvious ways. There must be some other element that we have not yet mentioned.

I suggest that the missing element is the religious believer's own commitment. She chooses to accept her role as God's child and adopts the way of life that goes with it. This is important, because when she embraces the religious values, they are no longer being imposed on her from the outside. Instead, they become her own. She lives a religious life "from the inside," as a matter of conviction. Her life then gets its meaning from these things that she values—God's plan for her, God's love, and the rest. But we must distinguish between two ideas:

(a) The idea that religious commitment can provide meaning for one's life

(b) The idea that religious commitment is the *only* thing that can provide meaning for one's life

The first idea can be true even if the second is not. The second claim is much stronger. Is it true?

People sometimes assume it is true when they say things like "Without God life has no meaning." But that overlooks the possibility that there are various other kinds of commitment that might give a life its meaning. One might choose the life of a scholar, an athlete, a chess master, a musician, or a businessperson. Like John Stuart Mill you might make it your object "to be a reformer of the world." Then your life would get its meaning from the values associated with those activities, just as the meaning of the religious believer's life is connected with the values she embraces.

Religion, however, does have one great advantage over these other ways of finding meaning: It solves the problem of the indifferent universe. If, like Mill, you take it as your goal to reform the world, you must still face the fact that from the point of view of the universe this is an insignificant matter. That is why it is so tempting to say that, without God, life is meaningless. At the same time, however, the religious commitment has a drawback that the other commitments do not have: Namely, it assumes that the religious story is true. We do not want to base our lives on moonshine; if the religious story is not true, we are doing just that.

13.5. The Meaning of Particular Lives

There is a difference between *life's* having a meaning and *a life's* having a meaning. If the religious story is true, human life in general has a meaning. Without religion we can only say that each life has its own particular meaning and that the meaning of our lives is up to us.

A person determines the meaning of his own particular life by embracing values that he thinks are worth living for. But what are those values? It depends to a certain extent on what sort of person one is. Perhaps there is no one kind of life that is best for everyone. Think of Socrates, St. Francis, Yogi Berra, Jonas Salk, Marilyn Monroe, Mohandas Gandhi, Ruth Graham, Bill Gates, Agatha Christie, Nelson Mandela, Mick Jagger, your next-door neighbor, and your favorite professor. Is there one kind of life that is best for all of them? They are all very different. Each may be admirable in a different way.

Despite this variety, however, it is easy to give a general list of things that anyone might find worth living for. Here are a few:

- *Satisfying personal relationships.* Nothing contributes to individual happiness as much as loving people who love you back. That is why family ties and friendships figure so prominently in most people's conception of the good life.
- *Accomplishments of which one can be proud.* Such accomplishments may or may not be related to one's job, and they need not be lucrative. Michael Jordan seemed happier winning those championships than he was

cashing his paychecks, even though he made an awful
lot of money. Not everyone can be a Michael Jordan,
but we can all make use of our talents.

- *Aesthetic appreciation.* The joy of experiencing beauty
  can come from reading books, watching *The Godfather,*
  playing over Bobby Fischer's chess games, listening to
  great music—which comes in many varieties—and
  watching a storm.
- *Enjoyable activities.* These might include playing bridge,
  eating good food, shooting baskets, having sex, climbing mountains, traveling, quilting, and acting in the
  local theater.
- *Learning.* Learning satisfies one's curiosity and helps
  one understand why things are as they are. Scientists
  may devote their lives to this, but we all benefit from
  what they do, not only because their discoveries are
  useful but because they are fascinating. Books that explain scientific findings for the layperson are among
  the most interesting published.
- *Contributing to the welfare of other people (and even to the
  welfare of animals).* Ethical living is sometimes thought
  to conflict with personal happiness, because it requires
  making sacrifices for others. But studies suggest otherwise. Happy people are generally less self-absorbed
  than unhappy people and are more involved with others. They are also more likely to help others in need,
  confirming the ancient idea of a connection between
  happiness and virtue.

This is a short list—it could easily be longer. Indeed, there are
so many good things in life that it seems incredible that anyone
would think there is nothing worth living for.

Socrates' life was a combination of such things. He had a
wife and children, and we are told that he was a faithful husband and father. His friends were devoted to him. He was a
loyal Athenian, who fought for his city in military campaigns.
He enjoyed art and athletics. But above all, Socrates was dedi-
cated to discovering the truth about the world. He lived in a
time when not much was known, but his contribution to the ex-
pansion of knowledge was immense. Through his teaching,
lines of thought were begun that are still being explored today.

And at the end of his life, he chose to die rather than go back on the values he had lived for. It is easy to understand the meaning of his life—we need only to reflect on all this.

Nonetheless, it is also easy to be skeptical. In a certain frame of mind, people are attracted to the idea that there really is nothing worth living for. They may concede that people *believe* various things are worthwhile and that this creates the illusion for them that their lives are meaningful. But it is only an illusion. A hardheaded assessment, they say, reveals that all this amounts to nothing.

Skepticism seems to be the inevitable result of viewing the world from an impersonal perspective. At the outset we distinguished the personal point of view, from which our lives are important, from the point of view of the universe, from which we are insignificant. The latter point of view is an inescapable part of our mental lives. The upshot is that, if we forgo the comforts of religion, we cannot escape the nagging thought that our lives are absurd.

Can the skeptical objection be answered? The only way to do so is to consider the various things on our list, one at a time, and explain why each of them is good. We can elaborate the ways in which personal relationships and accomplishments contribute to human happiness. We can explain the glories of Mozart and the pleasures of basketball. We can explain that humans are by nature curious, and so we naturally want to understand the world; and we are also social animals, so contributing to the welfare of others comes naturally to us.

Such reasoning may not show that our lives are "important to the universe," but it will accomplish something similar. It will show that we have objectively good reasons for living in some ways rather than others. When we step outside our personal perspectives and consider humanity from an impersonal standpoint, we still find that human beings are the kinds of creatures who can flourish and enjoy life best if they devote themselves to such things as family and friends, work, music, mountain climbing, and the rest. It would be foolish, then, for creatures like us to live in any other way.

How to Evaluate Arguments

Formulating and testing arguments is important in every subject, but it is especially critical when dealing with big abstract issues, because it is our only way to get a grip on them. A philosophical theory is only as good as the arguments in its support.

Some arguments are sound and some are not, and we need to know how to tell the difference. It would be nice if there were a simple way to do this. Unfortunately, there is not. Arguments come in many varieties, and they can go wrong in countless ways. But there are some general principles that may be kept in mind. The following are some relevant bits of advice.

1. Ask the Most Important Questions.

The word "argument" often means a quarrel, and there is a hint of acrimony in the word. Children may be taught not to quarrel because it isn't polite. In the logician's sense, however, an argument is simply a chain of reasoning designed to prove something. An argument consists of one or more premises and a conclusion. The conclusion is what we are trying to prove, and the premises are the considerations that are supposed to prove it.

Aristotle was the first person to study logic systematically. He gave this example, and teachers have been repeating it ever since:

(1) All men are mortal.

(2) Socrates is a man.

(3) Therefore, Socrates is mortal.

This example illustrates the main features of an argument: There are premises and a conclusion, and the conclusion follows logically from the premises.

The most important thing to notice is that *whether the premises are true* and *whether the conclusion follows from them* are different matters. In Aristotle's example the premises are both true, and the conclusion follows. But here is a different example in which the premises and conclusion are all true and yet the conclusion does not follow from them:

(1) Socrates was executed when he was 70.

(2) Socrates was executed in 399 B.C.

(3) Therefore, Socrates once served in the Athenian army.

And the following is an example in which the premises and conclusion are all false but the conclusion does follow from them:

(1) All the Sophists were dim-witted.

(2) Socrates was a Sophist.

(3) Therefore, Socrates was dim-witted.

What does it mean to say that the conclusion "follows from" the premises? In logic this is not just a loose expression; it is a precise technical term. It means that *it would be impossible for the premises to be true and the conclusion false at the same time.* In Aristotle's original example, it is easy to see that the conclusion follows from the premises—it would be impossible for all men to be mortal and Socrates to be a man and yet for Socrates to not be mortal.

Sometimes, whether a conclusion follows from a particular set of premises is not so obvious. Consider this argument:

(1) Different cultures have different moral codes. In some cultures polygamy is thought to be all right, while in other cultures it is thought to be wrong.

(2) Therefore, there is no such thing as objective truth in ethics. Ethics is merely a matter of opinion, which varies from society to society.

This argument is discussed in chapter 11. Many people instinctively feel that the conclusion follows from the premises, but it does not.

To mark these distinctions, logicians customarily use a bit of terminology—they distinguish *validity* from *soundness*. An argument is valid if the conclusion follows from the premises. To be sound, however, an argument must be valid *and* its premises must be true. Sound arguments are what we aim for.

One further point should be noted. The degree to which the premises support the conclusion may vary. Sometimes the premises do not absolutely prove that the conclusion is true, but they provide evidence that makes it very likely that the conclusion is true. For example:

 (1) Lola was seen kissing Frankie a few minutes before she left the party.
 (2) After the party, Lola said she had a crush on a new guy.
 (3) Therefore, Lola has a crush on Frankie.

This argument does not absolutely prove that Lola has a crush on Frankie, because she might have kissed Frankie in a game of Truth or Dare, or she might have been lying about having a crush on someone. But on this evidence, she probably has a crush on Frankie. Such evidence increases the probability that the conclusion is true.

Thus, the most important advice about evaluating arguments is this: Start by asking whether the premises are true and whether the conclusion follows from them.

2. Do Not Believe an Argument Must Be Sound Merely Because You Agree with Its Conclusion.

People often make this mistake when they see an argument that supports some idea they like, such as that God exists, or that women should have the right to an abortion, or that the government has imprisoned aliens in New Mexico. They like the conclusion, so they approve of the argument. However, a bad argument may have a true conclusion. Consider this example:

 (1) Everyone from Georgia has, at one time, been president.
 (2) Jimmy Carter is from Georgia.
 (3) Therefore, at one time Jimmy Carter was president.

The conclusion is true, but the argument is obviously unsound because its first premise is false. So you should never judge an argument by its conclusion. Whether the conclusion is true is one thing; whether the argument proves it is another.

3. If an Argument Turns Out to Be Unsound, Try to Recast It into a Better Form.

If an argument is flawed, we should try to fix it. After all, we are interested in discovering the truth. An argument might fail while suggesting a better argument that does not.

A good example of this is Socrates' argument for obeying the law, which is discussed in chapter 1. Socrates is considering whether he should drink the hemlock as ordered by the Athenian court. He gives this argument:

(1) If we do not obey the law, the state cannot exist.

(2) It would be disastrous if the state did not exist.

(3) Therefore, we must obey the law.

(4) The law has ordered me to drink the hemlock.

(5) Therefore, I must drink the hemlock.

The problem with this reasoning is that, in order for the state to exist, it is not necessary that we always obey the law. It is only necessary that we obey the law most of the time, as a general rule. So the argument as stated is unsound. That is not surprising, since it seems false that we should always obey the law in every circumstance. Yet Socrates is clearly onto something. If we want to know why we should as a general practice obey the law, this modified version of his argument seems right:

(1) If we do not in general obey the law (allowing only rare exceptions), the state cannot exist.

(2) It would be disastrous if the state did not exist, because we would all be much worse off without it.

(3) Therefore, we should in general obey the law (allowing only rare exceptions).

This version of the argument, however, does not entail that Socrates had to drink the hemlock. Unfortunately, he seems to have missed this point.

4. Be on the Alert for Common Fallacies.

Some mistakes are so common that they have been given names.
Here are a few of them.

Equivocation. Equivocation is using a word in more than one
sense. When the meaning of a word shifts midway through an
argument, the argument is ruined. Mae West joked that "Marriage is a great institution, but I'm not ready for an institution."
If we uncharitably put this in the form of an argument, we
would get:

(1) Marriage is a great institution.

(2) Mae isn't ready for an institution.

(3) Therefore, Mae isn't ready to be married.

Here the word "institution" is used in different ways, as Mae
West certainly knew.

Socrates appears to commit the fallacy of equivocation in
Book I of Plato's *Republic.* There Socrates is discussing the nature of justice with Polemarchus, who maintains that justice is
helping one's friends and harming one's enemies. Socrates
objects that it can never be right to harm anyone:

Socrates: But is it really right to harm any man?

Polemarchus: It certainly is, we ought to harm bad men who
are our enemies.

Socrates: If we harm a horse do we make it better or worse?

Polemarchus: Worse.

Socrates: Worse, that is, by the standards by which we judge
horses?

Polemarchus: Yes.

Socrates: And a dog if harmed becomes a worse dog by the
standards of canine excellence?

Polemarchus: Surely.

Socrates: But must we not then say of a man that if harmed he
becomes worse by the standards of human excellence?

Polemarchus: Certainly.

Socrates: But is not justice the standard of human excellence?

Polemarchus: It surely must be.

Socrates: Then will just men use their justice to make others
not just? Or, in short, will good men use their goodness to
make others bad?

Polemarchus: That cannot be so.

Socrates: Then since the just man is good, Polemarchus, it is not the function of the just man to harm either his friends or anyone else, but of his opposite, the unjust man.

Polemarchus: What you say is perfectly true, Socrates.

The gist of Socrates' argument is this:

(1) To harm someone is to make him worse.

(2) People are better or worse according to whether they are just or unjust.

(3) Therefore, to harm someone is to make him more unjust.

(4) It is never right to make someone more unjust.

(5) Therefore, it is never right to harm someone.

The problem is that the word "worse" is used in two senses. You can be made *worse off* in many different ways: if you get sick, if you lose all your money, if your friends turn on you, and so on. But in another sense you become *morally* worse—you become a worse person—only if you do something bad or if you undergo a change in character. Socrates' argument trades on this ambiguity. The first premise appears to be true because we have the first meaning in mind—to harm someone is to make him worse off—while the second premise appeals to the second meaning—people are morally better or worse according to whether they're just or unjust. But if we choose one meaning and stick to it, then one or the other of the premises turns out to be false.

Appeal to Authority. When people have no good arguments for their views, they will sometimes appeal to an authority to prove a point. Such appeals should always be viewed with suspicion if the point is doubtful. We may ask why the so-called authority says what it does, and if there is no good answer, then the authority's opinion may be ignored.

Often, of course, there is nothing wrong with consulting an authority to get information. If you want to know Wade Boggs' batting average for 1988, you should look it up in *The Baseball Encyclopedia.* If you want to know the source of the Nile, checking an atlas will work fine.

But, ultimately, what justifies us in believing that Wade Boggs batted .366 in 1988 is not simply that *The Baseball Encyclopedia* says so. We trust *The Baseball Encyclopedia* because we believe that somebody kept up with Boggs' hits and at-bats and then the statisticians did the required calculation. Their work justifies saying that Boggs batted .366. Similarly, we trust the atlas to tell us the source of the Nile because explorers have traveled upriver, and the atlas is based on what they found. It is their experience, not merely the atlas, that justifies saying the Nile originates in Lake Victoria.

The point is that we can always ask what lies behind the authority's pronouncements—why does the authority say what it says? The mere fact that an authority says thus-and-so is never the last word.

It is easy to overlook this point when ethics and religion are involved. Some people argue:

(2) Leviticus says homosexuality is an abomination.

(3) Therefore, homosexuality is an abomination.

But what lies behind this judgment? Why does Leviticus say that homosexuality is an abomination? We need to focus on the reasons behind the pronouncement, rather than on the pronouncement itself. If the authority is reliable, then there must be good reasons for what it says. But merely citing the authority does not indicate what those reasons are. Thus, if homosexuality is an abomination, there must be some other argument that proves it. If there is none, then the authority's pronouncement is unfounded. This is not just a point about religious authority but about authority in general.

Ad Hominem. This is the reverse of the appeal to authority. "Ad hominem" is Latin for "against the man"; it is the fallacy of trying to discredit an opinion by discrediting those who hold it. Consider:

(1) Charles Darwin was an atheist.

(2) Therefore, his godless theory should be ignored.

(1) In the 1980s Cal Thomas worked for Jerry Falwell's Moral Majority.

(2) Therefore, he is a right-wing nut and his views are stupid.

But the personal remarks are irrelevant. Darwin and Thomas both have reasons for what they say, and if we are trying to assess their views, it is the strength of their arguments, not their personal histories or characters, that matters.

Begging the Question. An argument "begs the question" if the conclusion is smuggled in among the premises. Here, for example, is a fallacious argument in defense of free will:

(1) People control their own destinies—they can choose how they will behave and what sorts of individuals they will be.

(2) If people can do that, then they have free will.

(3) Therefore, people have free will.

In this argument the very thing we are trying to prove—that people have free will—is asserted (in different words) in the first premise. So the argument does not prove that people have free will; instead, the argument simply assumes it. Here is another example:

(1) Capital punishment is murder.

(2) Murder is wrong.

(3) Therefore, capital punishment is wrong.

This argument begs the question because "murder" is, by definition, wrongful killing. (If you think a type of killing is permissible, such as self-defense, then you don't call it murder.) Thus, the first premise is saying "Capital punishment is wrongful killing," which is the very thing the argument is trying to prove.

Begging the question is related to another fallacy known as *circular reasoning.* The simplest example of circular reasoning is when you give A as your evidence for B and then turn around and give B as your evidence for A—for example, "I know that God exists because the Bible says so. How do I know the Bible can be trusted? Because it is the word of God."

False Dilemma. An argument presents a false dilemma if it says we must choose between a limited number of options, when really there are more options available. Here is a version of an argument that we discussed in chapter 2:

    (1) Either the wonders of nature came about by chance, or they are the product of intelligent design.

    (2) They could not have come about by chance.

    (3) Therefore, they are the product of intelligent design.

The problem is that there are at least three ways of accounting for the amazing intricacies of nature: chance, intelligent design, and natural selection. So the first premise of the argument is false.

5. Don't Reject an Idea Merely Because You've Heard a Bad Argument for It.

One final word of caution: We should not reject a thesis merely because a particular argument for it is unsound. People sometimes make this mistake when they are passionately committed to their opinions and don't want to see them challenged. But we should not be in such a hurry. The failure of an argument only means that this particular argument does not prove anything. Better arguments might be found, even for views we don't like, and if we are interested in discovering the truth, we should want to find them.

Notes on Sources

Chapter 1: The Legacy of Socrates

"pushing them on the streets of Athens" Gregory Vlastos, *Socrates: Ironist and Moral Philosopher* (Cambridge University Press, 1991), p. 294.

"Suppose that while we were preparing to run away . . ." Plato, *Crito,* tr. Hugh Tredennick, in *The Last Days of Socrates* (Harmondsworth, Middlesex: Penguin, 1969), p. 89.

"Then since you have been born . . ." Plato, *Crito,* pp. 90–91.

"'[A]ny Athenian, on attaining to manhood . . ." Plato, *Crito,* p. 92.

"He is absolutely unique . . ." Plato, *Symposium,* tr. Michael Joyce, in *The Collected Dialogues of Plato,* ed. Edith Hamilton and Huntington Cairns (Princeton University Press, 1961), p. 572.

Chapter 2: God and the Origin of the Universe

The "recent Gallup Poll" was conducted in May 2007.

The Pew Center surveys are from the Pew Global Attitudes Project, "Among Wealthy Nations . . . U.S. Stands Alone in its Embrace of Religion" (released December 19, 2002), and from the Pew Global Attitudes Project: Spring 2005 Survey.

The Gallup International Millennium Survey: http://www.gallup-international.com/ContentFiles/millennium15.asp

"They are made upon the same principles . . ." William Paley, *Natural Theology: or, Evidences of the Existence and Attributes of the Deity* (London: Faulder, 1802); repr. in *A Modern Introduction to Philosophy,* 3rd ed., ed. Paul Edwards and Arthur Pap (New York: Free Press, 1973), p. 425.

"[I]ts several parts are framed and put together for a purpose . . ." Paley, *Natural Theology,* repr. in *The Cosmological Arguments,* ed. Donald R. Burrill (Garden City, NY: Anchor, 1967), p. 166.

"I was charmed and convinced . . ." *The Autobiography of Charles Darwin,* ed. Nora Barlow (New York: Norton, 1958), p. 59. The next quotation is from p. 87.

"To suppose that the eye . . ." Charles Darwin, *On the Origin of Species* (London: John Murray, 1859), p. 186.

"In living bodies, variation will cause . . ." Darwin, *On the Origin of Species,* p. 189.

"I can remember having a picture of the cosmos . . ." Peter van Inwagen, *The Possibility of Resurrection and Other Essays in Christian Apologetics* (Boulder, CO: Westview Press, 1998), p. 5.

"I can still call the image to mind . . ." van Inwagen, *Possibility of Resurrection*, p. 5.

Anselm, Gaunilo, and Kant on the Ontological Argument: The relevant writings are in *The Cosmological Arguments*, ed. Donald R. Burrill (Garden City, NY: Anchor, 1967).

Chapter 3: The Problem of Evil

All quotations from the Book of Job are from chs. 8 and 11 of *The Holy Bible, Revised Standard Version* (New York: Thomas Nelson, 1952).

Plantinga's view: Alvin Plantinga, *God, Freedom, and Evil* (Grand Rapids, MI: Eerdmans, 1978).

"Every human being has an eternal future . . ." Peter van Inwagen, *God, Knowledge, and Mystery: Essays in Philosophical Theology* (Ithaca, NY: Cornell University Press, 1995), pp. 101–102.

"a man who drove a cement mixer truck . . ." Alvin Plantinga, "Self-Profile," in *Alvin Plantinga*, ed. Peter van Inwagen and James E. Tomberlin (Dordrecht: Reidel, 1985), p. 34; quoted in Daniel Howard-Snyder, "God, Evil, and Suffering," in *Reason for the Hope Within*, ed. Michael J. Murray (Grand Rapids, MI: Eerdmans, 1999), p. 77.

"That there is much suffering in the world . . ." Darwin, *Autobiography*, p. 90.

A Note about the Book of Job. Chapter 3 begins with the story of Job, but readers familiar with the Bible might have noticed that I did not mention the beginning or end of the story. The reason is that modern scholarship tells us that the Book of Job as we have it today consists of two parts, an original core and a "frame"—an introduction and conclusion—added later by unknown editors. In the original story we meet Job, we learn of his suffering, and we hear the accusations of his friends. But we are assured that Job is blameless. That is why his sufferings are a mystery. The mystery is deepened when Job observes that other, less virtuous men suffer no such misfortunes. The original story ends there, as a mystery that has no answer.

The frame eliminates the mystery and changes a profound parable into an exasperating story about a capricious God. In the introduction that was added, an explanation is given of why God permitted Job's suffering. One day, we are told, when God's angels had gathered around, God singled out Job for special praise. But Satan scoffed and said that Job was God's loyal servant only because God had rewarded him with riches and a loving family. To prove Satan wrong, God allowed him to take away all that Job had. Thus, God permitted Satan to torment Job simply to make a point: He wanted to demonstrate that Job would remain faithful to him no matter what.

In this version of the story, God is not the just ruler that Job's friends believed him to be. Instead, he is no better than a human father who would allow his children to be tormented to prove to a skeptic that they would still love him. The tacked-on conclusion makes things even worse. In an apparent attempt to vindicate God, he is shown restoring Job's prosperity. This does not really help, though, for the terrible, unmerited suffering that Job has already endured cannot be wiped out. It remains forever a part of his history.

The original story of Job touches deep feelings we have about the relation between virtue and faring well in life. Virtue, we think, should be rewarded—good people deserve to have good lives—and we think that we should try, as far as we can, to make this happen. But why doesn't God do his part? The author of the original story of Job, unlike the later editors, had no answer.

Chapter 4: Do We Survive Death?

"By death do we not mean . . ." Plato, *Phaedo,* tr. R. Hackforth (Indianapolis: Bobbs-Merrill, 1955), p. 44.

"Your view about the soul . . ." Plato, *Phaedo,* p. 58.

Raymond A. Moody, Jr., *Life after Life: The Investigation of a Phenomenon—Survival of Bodily Death,* 25th Anniversary Edition (New York: HarperSanFrancisco, 2001; originally published in 1975). The quotations are from pp. 169 and xxv–xxvi.

What to Do When You Are Dead: Living Better in the Afterlife by Craig Hamilton-Parker (New York: Sterling, 2001).

"Of male survivors of cardiac arrest . . ." Quoted by Paul Edwards in *Reincarnation: A Critical Examination* (Amherst, NY: Prometheus Books, 1996), p. 150.

Ronald K. Siegel, "Life after Death," in George O. Abell and Barry Singer, eds., *Science and the Paranormal* (New York: Scribner, 1981), pp. 159–184.

The quotations from A. J. Ayer are from his *The Meaning of Life* (New York: Scribner, 1990), pp. 200, 201, 204.

"It is little less than scandalous . . ." Paul Edwards, *Reincarnation: A Critical Examination* (Amherst, NY: Prometheus Books, 1996), pp. 223–224.

The calculation of historical populations is the work of Arthur H. Westing; it is quoted in Edwards, *Reincarnation,* pp. 226–227.

"an Ireland that never was . . ." Quoted by Martin Gardner in *Fads and Fallacies in the Name of Science* (New York: Dover, 1957), p. 316.

Champe Ransom's critique of the Stevenson studies is quoted in Edwards, *Reincarnation,* pp. 276–277.

"I should be willing now to stake . . ." William James, *Proceedings of the Society for Psychical Research,* vol. 6 (1889–1890), p. 654; quoted in Martin Gardner, *On the Wild Side* (Buffalo, NY: Prometheus Books, 1992), p. 217.

For information about cold reading, I am indebted to Joe Nickell, "John Edward: Hustling the Bereaved," *Skeptical Inquirer,* November/December 2001, pp. 19–22.

"More than 6,000 people were asked . . ." Richard Wiseman and Ciaran O'Keefe, "A Critique of Schwartz et al.'s After-Death Communication Studies," *Skeptical Inquirer,* November/December 2001, p. 28.

"They're telling me to acknowledge Anthony." Nickell, "John Edward: Hustling the Bereaved," p. 19.

"When anyone tells me that he saw a dead man restored to life . . ." David Hume, *An Enquiry Concerning Human Understanding,* ed. Charles W. Hendel (New York: Liberal Arts Press, 1955; originally published in 1748), pp. 123–124.

"We frequently hesitate concerning the reports of others." Hume, *Enquiry,* p. 120.

"an everlasting check . . ." Hume, *Enquiry,* p. 118.

Chapter 5: The Problem of Personal Identity

The quotations from David Hume about the Bundle Theory are all from Hume's *A Treatise of Human Nature* (1739), I, IV, 6.

"a conscious system in its own right . . ." Roger Sperry, quoted by Norman H. Horowitz in *Roger Wolcott Sperry,* published by the Nobel Foundation, Stockholm, 1999.

Derek Parfit's argument about the split-brain cases and the Bundle Theory is from his essay "Divided Minds and the Nature of Persons," in Colin Blakemore and Susan Greenfield, eds., *Mindwaves* (London: Blackwell, 1987). Parfit points out that the Bundle Theory was the Buddha's view and that Buddhist recommendations about what attitudes to adopt toward oneself go along with this theory.

Plutarch discusses the Ship of Theseus in *Vita Thesei* (The Life of Theseus), pp. 22–23.

The information about cell turnover was gleaned mostly from Nicholas Wade, "Your Body Is Younger Than You Think," *The New York Times,* August 2, 2005.

"Every one sees he would be the same person . . ." John Locke, *An Essay Concerning Human Understanding* (1690), II, xxvii, 15. I have embellished Locke's example without changing its point.

"Consciousness alone unites actions . . ." Locke, *Essay*, II, xxvii, 16.

"Suppose a brave officer . . ." Thomas Reid, *Essays on the Intellectual Powers of Man* (1785), III, 6.

The study of people's memories of the *Challenger* disaster is Ulric Neisser and Nicole Harsch, "Phantom Flashbulbs: False Recollections of Hearing the News about *Challenger*," in E. Winograd and U. Neisser, eds., *Affect and Accuracy in Recall: Studies of "Flashbulb Memories"* (New York: Cambridge University Press, 1992), pp. 9–31.

"[O]ne should really think it self-evident . . ." Joseph Butler, *The Analogy of Religion* (1736), Dissertation I: Of Personal Identity.

Derek Parfit discusses how a belief in the Bundle Theory can be liberating in *Reasons and Persons* (Oxford University Press, 1984), pp. 281–282.

Chapter 6: Body and Mind

"I beg of you to tell me how the human soul . . ." Princess Elizabeth, Letter to Descartes, May 6–16, 1643; in René Descartes, *Philosophical Writings,* tr. Elizabeth Anscombe and Peter Geach (Indianapolis: Bobbs-Merrill, 1971), pp. 274–275.

"I cannot see why this should convince us . . ." Princess Elizabeth, Letter to Descartes, June 10–20, 1643; in Descartes, *Philosophical Writings,* p. 278.

"[T]he immaterial . . ." Princess Elizabeth, Letter to Descartes, June 10–20, 1643; in Descartes, *Philosophical Writings,* p. 278.

"the dogma of the Ghost in the Machine" Gilbert Ryle, *The Concept of Mind* (London: Hutchinson, 1949), pp. 15–16.

Wilder Penfield's work is described in his book *The Excitable Cortex in Conscious Man* (Springfield, IL: Charles C Thomas, 1958).

Place, Smart, Armstrong, and Lewis: U. T. Place, "Is Consciousness a Brain Process?" *The British Journal of Psychology* 47 (1956), pp. 44–50; J. J. C. Smart, "Sensations and Brain Processes," *The Philosophical Review* 68 (1959), pp. 141–156; D. M. Armstrong, *A Materialist Theory of the Mind* (London: Routledge, 1968); David Lewis, "An Argument for the Identity Theory," *The Journal of Philosophy* 63 (1966), pp. 17–25.

"Behaviourism is certainly wrong . . ." D. M. Armstrong, "The Nature of Mind," in C. V. Borst, ed., *The Mind/Brain Identity Theory* (London: Macmillan, 1970), pp. 72–73.

The example about beer cans is from John R. Searle, "The Myth of the Computer," *New York Review,* April 29, 1982, pp. 3–5.

"what it is like" Thomas Nagel, "What Is It Like to Be a Bat?" *The Philosophical Review* 83 (1974), pp. 435–450. Nagel introduced this phrase into the discussion of the mind–body problem as a way of marking the subjective dimension of consciousness.

Chapter 7: Could a Machine Think?

"It is indeed conceivable . . ." René Descartes, *Discourse on Method,* tr. Laurence J. Lafleur (Indianapolis: Bobbs-Merrill, 1960; originally published in 1637), pp. 41–42.

Alan Turing, "On Computable Numbers, with an Application to the *Entscheidungsproblem,*" *Proceedings of the London Mathematical Society,* series 2, 42 (1936–1937), pp. 230–265.

"I won't say that what Turing did made us win the war . . ." Quoted in Jack Copeland, *Artificial Intelligence: A Philosophical Introduction* (Oxford: Blackwell, 1993), p. 10.

Alan Turing, "Computing Machinery and Intelligence," *Mind* 59 (1950), pp. 433–460.

"If trees could converse with us . . ." Copeland, *Artificial Intelligence,* p. 38.

Daniel Bobrow, "A Turing Test Passed," *ACM SIGART Newsletter,* December 1968, pp. 14–15; quoted in Copeland, *Artificial Intelligence,* p. 39.

The Chinese Room Argument was first presented in John R. Searle, "Minds, Brains, and Programs," *The Behavioral and Brain Sciences* 3 (1980), pp. 417–424.

Chapter 8: The Case against Free Will

All quotations from Clarence Darrow are from *Attorney for the Damned: Clarence Darrow in the Courtroom,* ed. Arthur Weinberg (University of Chicago Press, 1957): "I really do not in the least believe in crime" is from p. 3. The headline from the *Chicago Evening Standard* is from p. 19. "Intelligent people now know" is from p. 56. "I do not know what it was" is from p. 37. "Is Dickie Loeb to blame" is from p. 55. "Nature is strong and she is pitiless" is from pp. 64–65.

Laplace's *Philosophical Essay on Probability* was published in 1819. The relevant portions are translated by John Cottingham in *Western Philosophy: An Anthology,* ed. John Cottingham (Oxford: Blackwell, 1996).

Wilder Penfield, *The Excitable Cortex in Conscious Man* (Springfield, IL: Charles C Thomas, 1958).

The story of the patient who heard Guns n' Roses when his brain was stimulated is told by Daniel Dennett in *Consciousness Explained* (Boston: Little, Brown, 1991), pp. 58–59.

"head turning and slow displacement . . ." Jose M. R. Delgado, *Physical Control of the Mind* (New York: Harper, 1969), p. 115.

For information about the Kornhuber experiment, see Benjamin Libet, "Unconscious Cerebral Initiative and the Role of Conscious Will in Voluntary Action," *The Behavioral and Brain Sciences* 8 (1985), pp. 529–566.

Differences in what we name our children: Steven D. Levitt and Stephen J. Dubner, *Freakonomics: A Rogue Economist Explores the Hidden Side of Everything* (New York: HarperCollins, 2005), pp. 184–185, 192, 202. The authors rely on Roland G. Fryer Jr. and Steven D. Levitt, "The Causes and Consequences of Distinctively Black Names," *Quarterly Journal of Economics*, vol. 119, no. 3 (August 2004), pp. 767–805.

The information about imprisonment is from the U.S. Department of Justice website.

Social factors predictive of criminal behavior: Levitt and Dubner, *Freakonomics*, pp. 138–139. The authors give sources for their claims on pp. 222–223.

Information about Eric Rudolph: *Newsweek*, July 27, 1998, pp. 16ff.

"If we are to use the methods of science . . ." B. F. Skinner, *Science and Human Behavior* (New York: Free Press, 1953), p. 6.

"We select a relatively simple bit . . ." Skinner, *Science and Human Behavior*, pp. 63–64.

"Give me a dozen healthy infants . . ." John B. Watson, *Behaviorism* (New York: Norton, 1924), p. 104.

The guards-and-prisoners experiment: Philip Zimbardo, "The Pathology of Imprisonment," *Society* 9 (1972), pp. 4–8.

The Milgram experiment: Stanley Milgram, *Obedience to Authority* (New York: Harper and Row, 1974).

"And who is my neighbor? . . ." Luke 10:29–37, *The Holy Bible, Revised Standard Version* (New York: Thomas Nelson, 1952).

The Good Samaritan experiment: J. M. Darley and C. D. Batson, "'From Jerusalem to Jericho': A Study of Situational and Dispositional Variables in Helping Behavior," *Journal of Personality and Social Psychology* 27 (1973), pp. 100–108.

"a consequence of random events . . ." Richard Lewontin, *The Triple Helix: Gene, Organism, and Environment* (Cambridge, MA: Harvard University Press, 2000), p. 36.

Information about twins is from Lawrence Wright, *Twins: And What They Tell Us about Who We Are* (New York: John Wiley, 1997).

Information about biology and violence is from William Wright, *Born That Way: Genes, Behavior, Personality* (New York: Routledge, 1999).

"Though we no longer say . . ." Judith Rich Harris, *The Nurture Assumption* (New York: Free Press, 1998), pp. 295–296.

"Many misinterpret biosocial explanations . . ." John Townsend, *What Women Want—What Men Want: Why the Sexes Still See Love and Commitment So Differently* (New York: Oxford University Press, 1998), p. 2.

Chapter 9: The Debate over Free Will

I have given Isaac Bashevis Singer's dates as 1904–1991. However, some respectable sources say he was born in 1902; others say 1908.

The quotations from Dr. Johnson are from Boswell's *The Life of Samuel Johnson, LL.D.* (1791), section 273.

"If Determinism is true . . ." Peter van Inwagen, *An Essay on Free Will* (Oxford University Press, 1983), p. 16.

"No man treats a motorcar . . ." Bertrand Russell, *Why I Am Not a Christian* (New York: Simon and Schuster, 1957), p. 40.

Chapter 10: Our Knowledge of the World around Us

"I will therefore suppose that . . ." René Descartes, *Meditations Concerning First Philosophy*, tr. Laurence J. Lafleur, in Descartes, *Philosophical Essays* (Indianapolis: Bobbs-Merrill, 1964), p. 80.

"I suspect that [the man in Ireland] . . ." Leibniz, quoted by Colin Turbayne in his introduction to George Berkeley, *A Treatise Concerning the Principles of Human Knowledge* (Indianapolis: Bobbs-Merrill, 1957; originally published in 1710), pp. vii–viii.

"But, though it were possible . . ." Berkeley, *A Treatise Concerning the Principles of Human Knowledge* (Indianapolis: Bobbs-Merrill, 1957; originally published in 1710), pp. 31–32 (paragraphs 18 and 20).

Bertrand Russell's phrase "the advantages of theft over honest toil" is from his *Introduction to Mathematical Philosophy* (London: Allen and Unwin, 1919), p. 71.

"When [organisms] apprehend the world . . ." Steven Pinker, *How the Mind Works* (New York: Norton, 1997), p. 212. My summary of how vision works is based largely on Pinker's discussion.

"Objects have regular, compact silhouettes . . ." Pinker, *How the Mind Works*, p. 217.

Irving Biederman introduced his theory of geons in "Recognition-by-Components: A Theory of Human Image Understanding," *Psychological Review* 94 (1987), pp. 115–147.

On Jonathan I., see Oliver Sacks, *An Anthropologist on Mars: Seven Paradoxical Tales* (New York: Knopf, 1995), pp. 3–41 (quotation on

p. 7; also see p. 15). At first, Jonathan I. thought his experience was like watching a black-and-white television (p. 3), but later he retracted that description (p. 10). He also denied that the word "grey" accurately described what he saw—rather, he said, ordinary language had no words for his experiences (p. 11). Eventually, Jonathan I. grew accustomed to his world, relishing its aesthetic properties as well as his extraordinary night vision (pp. 37–39). When given a chance to try to regain his color vision, he found the suggestion to be unintelligible and repugnant (p. 39).

Chapter 11: Ethics and Objectivity

"While we had been talking . . ." Plato, *The Republic*, tr. H. D. P. Lee (Harmondsworth, Middlesex: Penguin, 1955), p. 63.

"The life of a man . . ." David Hume, *Essays: Moral, Political, and Literary* (Oxford University Press, 1963; originally published in 1741–1742), p. 590.

The example of the Pakistani girl is from *Newsweek*, July 15, 2002, p. 18.

The example of the Nigerian woman is from *The New York Times*, August 20, 2002, p. A12.

"Take any action allow'd to be vicious . . ." David Hume, *A Treatise of Human Nature* (Oxford University Press, 1888; originally published in 1739), p. 468.

"There are no moral phenomena . . ." Friedrich Nietzsche, *Beyond Good and Evil*, tr. Walter Kaufmann (New York: Vintage Books, 1966; first published in 1886), p. 108.

Chapter 12: Why Should We Be Moral?

Glaucon's account of how Gyges became king is in Book I of Plato's *Republic*. Herodotus's story is in the opening chapter of his *Histories*. Both books are available in many translations.

Homosexuality is condemned in Leviticus 18:22. Washing your clothes after touching a menstruating woman's chair is required in Leviticus 15:22. Bearing false witness is condemned in Exodus 20:16.

"In all determinations of morality . . ." David Hume, *An Inquiry Concerning the Principles of Morals* (Indianapolis: Bobbs-Merrill, 1957; originally published in 1752), pp. 12–13.

"[T]he question depends . . ." John Stuart Mill, *Utilitarianism* (Indianapolis: Bobbs-Merrill, 1967; originally published in 1861), p. 28.

"I feel that I am bound . . ." Mill, *Utilitarianism*, p. 34.

"The firm foundation . . ." Mill, *Utilitarianism*, p. 40.

Seven million children under the age of 5 die each year of preventable diseases: UNICEF Annual Report 2006, p. 4.

"[M]orals, if they are to be rational . . ." Jan Narveson, *Moral Matters* (Peterborough, Ontario: Broadview Press, 1993), pp. 130–131.

"What about parting with the means . . ." Narveson, *Moral Matters*, p. 145.

"Reason makes it possible . . ." Peter Singer, *How Are We to Live?* (Amherst, NY: Prometheus Books, 1995), p. 229.

Chapter 13: The Meaning of Life

"I had what might truly be called an object in life . . ." John Stuart Mill, *Autobiography* (1873), in *Essential Works of John Stuart Mill*, ed. Max Lerner (New York: Bantam Books, 1961), p. 83.

"I was in a dull state of nerves . . ." Mill, *Autobiography*, p. 83.

"Relieved from my ever present sense . . ." Mill, *Autobiography*, pp. 87–88.

Frank J. Bruno, *Psychological Symptoms* (New York: Wiley, 1993).

The phrase "the point of view of the universe" comes from Henry Sidgwick, *The Methods of Ethics* (London: Macmillan, 1874), p. 382.

"In seeing ourselves from outside . . ." Thomas Nagel, *The View from Nowhere* (New York: Oxford University Press, 1986), p. 214.

The empirical claims made in this chapter about happiness come largely from three sources: David G. Myers, *The Pursuit of Happiness* (New York: Avon Books, 1992); Michael Wiederman, "Why It's So Hard to Be Happy," *Scientific American Mind* (February/March 2007), pp. 36–43; and Bruce Stokes, "Happiness Is Increasing in Many Countries—But Why?" at http://pewglobal.org/commentary/display.php?Analysis ID=1020.

"Ask not that events should happen as you will . . ." *The Manual of Epictetus*, tr. P. E. Matheson, in *The Stoic and Epicurean Philosophers*, ed. Whitney J. Oates (New York: Random House, 1940), p. 470.

Americans have gotten richer but not happier: from David G. Myers' analysis of data from the 2000 U.S. Census and the National Opinion Research Center, as reported by Wiederman, "Why It's So Hard to Be Happy," p. 38.

Ronald Inglehardt, *Culture Shift in Advanced Industrial Society* (Princeton University Press, 1990).

Americans are richer than Mexicans but less happy: from a survey conducted in 2007 by the Pew Global Attitudes Project. See p. 2 of Stokes, "Happiness Is Increasing in Many Countries—But Why?"

"Once beyond poverty . . ." Myers, *The Pursuit of Happiness*, p. 44.

80 percent of variations in happiness is due to genetic differences: the study by Auke Tellegen and David Lykken (1996) is mentioned on p. 40 of Wiederman's article.

"Those only are happy (I thought) . . ." Mill, *Autobiography*, p. 88.

"Death is nothing to us." Epicurus, *Letter to Menoeceus*, tr. C. Bailey, in Oates, ed., *The Stoic and Epicurean Philosophers*, p. 30.

"Where are now the warring kings . . ." W. B. Yeats, *Song of the Happy Shepherd* (1889).

Appendix: How to Evaluate Arguments

The discussion of justice between Socrates and Polemarchus is from Plato's *Republic*, tr. H. D. P. Lee (Baltimore: Penguin Books, 1955), p. 61.

*I*ndex